Assembling the Local

INTELLECTUAL HISTORY OF THE MODERN AGE

Assembling the Local

Political Economy and Agrarian Governance in British India

Upal Chakrabarti

PENN

UNIVERSITY OF PENNSYLVANIA PRESS

PHILADELPHIA

Published by
University of Pennsylvania Press
Philadelphia, Pennsylvania 19104-4112
www.upenn.edu/pennpress

Printed in the United States of America on acid-free paper
10 9 8 7 6 5 4 3 2 1

Library of Congress Cataloging-in-Publication Data
Names: Chakrabarti, Upal, author.
Title: Assembling the local : political economy and agrarian governance
in British India / Upal Chakrabarti.
Other titles: Intellectual history of the modern age.
Description: 1st edition. | Philadelphia : University of Pennsylvania Press, [2021] |
Series: Intellectual history of the modern age | Includes bibliographical references and index.
Identifiers: LCCN 2020016824 | ISBN 978-0-8122-5273-6 (hardback)
Subjects: LCSH: Agriculture—Economic aspects—India—History—19th century. |
Land tenure—Political aspects—India—History—19th century. | Agriculture and state—
India—History—19th century. | India—History—British occupation, 1765–1947. |
India—Politics and government—1765–1947.
Classification: LCC HD2072 .C39 2021 | DDC 338.1/85409034—dc23
LC record available at https://lccn.loc.gov/2020016824

CONTENTS

INTRODUCTION

Universality as Difference

Model, Limit, and Difference

This book explores the problem of models and their limits over three interrelated sites in the first half of the nineteenth century: questions of landed property in a small area on the eastern coast of British India called Cuttack, debates over the method and categories of political economy in Britain, and practices of agrarian governance across different regions of British India. The category of the "local" featured recurrently in these three sites, signifying the limit of models. The local has been also similarly fashioned across a range of histories as an analytical tool to mark the limit, of models and frames. Interrogating the analytical constructions of this category in both the archives of the nineteenth century and more recent historiographic practice, I contend that it is more productive to read this limit as the model itself, rather than its outside.

In considering the model-limit problem, the book proposes a relation between political economy and liberal governance in the imperial world of the nineteenth century, different from the prevalent understandings of this relation in the histories of empire, liberalism, and agrarian South Asia. The use of the category of the local in the nineteenth-century sites examined here enables and directs us to trace the complexities of this relation—between political economy and governance—in the light of the model-limit problem. In each of these sites the local expressed a limit of, or difference from, a model. In the interregional debates over principles of agrarian governance in British India, models of revenue settlement were constantly scrutinized and revised as they failed to address local specificities. In Cuttack, long-ranging contests took place between different kinds of land controllers over the local peculiarities of proprietary rights in the area. In Britain the public sphere witnessed raging contentions on the method and categories of political economy, where the dominant model of Ricardian political economy was questioned for being inapplicable to the different local conditions of the world.

Generally, therefore, the local connoted difference from the universalizing claims of models. Specifically, it expressed differences in relations between forms of property and modes of sovereignty. In Cuttack, the local was mobilized by various kinds of native land controllers and colonial officials to highlight the differences in the proprietary forms of that place from other adjoining territories. At the same time, the category was repeatedly used across various levels of the imperial bureaucracy to argue that different regions in British India exhibited great differences in land tenures. In Britain over the same period, the debates that I refer to suggested that differences in property forms all over the world question the universal applicability of the method and categories of the prevalent and dominant framing of political economy. Differences in forms of property, in all these sites, were explained as effects of varying modes of sovereignty or political power existing in different places.

The book engages with both general and specific articulations of the local, weaving out of them, simultaneously, reflections on the problem of difference and a critical commentary on connections between political economy, agrarian property, and governance. It is evident that over the three sites examined in the book, through the expression of the local, the problem of political economy and governance became the same, namely, that of understanding and managing difference, in this case, of property-sovereignty relations. I make sense of this problem by setting up a conversation between the early and late works of Michel Foucault, namely, between his reading of political economy as a discursive formation of the modern episteme and his lectures on liberal governance. I suggest that the workings of the local can provide a critical analytical mediation in understanding how, as Foucault argues, the principle of self-limitation of power emerged as the concurrent rationality of political economy and governance over the late eighteenth and early nineteenth centuries. This principle, as I demonstrate in greater detail later in this chapter, can be seen to manifest itself in the local, where difference was construed as constitutive of, and immanent to, universality.

By making the local foundational to the universality of the discourse of political economy as governance, this book attempts to release the category of its predominant analytical use—in a range of historical works on empire, liberalism, and agrarian South Asia—as something outside the universal. In most of these works the local is presented as a form of social reality, which by being located at a geographical distance from the center, seems to be necessarily capable of producing a space different from the universal.

Its geographically bounded condition is taken to imply its natural mark of difference from the boundless expanse of the universal. The book attempts to reconceptualize the local, refusing to perceive it as equivalent to a locality, or a geographical particular, typically understood as signifying radical alterity by both the historical context and the historiography I examine here. The archival sites I bring together demonstrate that the local, as a problem of difference, was absolutely central to the structuring of the universal, or the making of political economy as governance in nineteenth-century British India. Although the local was posited in these sites as something outside the universal, I argue that instead of merely existing as such an outside, it functioned as the key category in the making of the universal itself. Therefore, the inside-outside opposition was an effect of the way the local was presented in this discourse. I probe this presentation in the book, to understand how *difference* constituted universality. At the same time, I argue that a range of historical works uncritically adopted this construction of the local as an outside, using it pervasively to explain connections between imperialism, liberal abstractions, and the shaping of agrarian societies in British India.

To displace the geographical foundationalism in these historiographic uses of the local, I do not argue that the local is already and always implicated in other more expansive spaces, like the regional, the national, the metropolitan, the imperial, and the global. Such an argument cannot fundamentally unyoke analysis from its geographical foundation. Contrarily, I argue, the local can be rethought as an abstract machine, producing spatial formations, which involve, but are not constitutive of, fixed geographical locales. This machine is assembled by releasing the local from its functioning in terms of the hardened binary of inside-outside, across the archival and historiographic sites mentioned earlier.[1] I understand the machine as an immanent capacity to open up, which can also become a conceptual model for all those "rigidified territorialities that open the way for other transformational operations."[2] What this book presents through this opening is not only a movement of perpetual displacement but also a capacity to effect transformations of meanings in practices.

It is with this philosophical imperative that I construct the local, from within its multifarious deployments in a range of practices. Examined in different chapters, these practices are epistemological debates over scientific methodology and categories of political economy in nineteenth-century Britain, contentions between officials at various levels of the imperial bureaucracy over principles of agrarian governance, practices of agrarian governance in several localities of British India, along with Cuttack, and a variety of strategies by landholders of different kinds in Cuttack negotiating the rationalities of rule. The local was mobilized variously, by these practices, as difference constitutive of universality. In each of these sets of practices, therefore, it operated simultaneously as a critique and a model of universality. In the process, it became a transformative potential, opening up old universals, only to propose new closures.[3]

The practices examined in this book do not make a space where connections are simply established geographically, either as authoritarian flows from the metropole or as rebellious counter flows from the colony. This is also not a space in between, that of the empire. The book does not have the intention to argue, as Frederick Cooper and Ann Laura Stoler do, that "Europe was made by its imperial projects, as much as colonial encounters were shaped by conflicts within Europe itself."[4] Histories inspired by this methodological move, despite establishing the dynamic space of imperial circuits as the object of analysis going beyond the metropole-colony division, remain analytically tied to geographical foundations.[5] As a result, the imperial often falls back upon different kinds of movements between the clearly segregated geographical spaces of the metropole and the colony.[6] It displays none of the dynamism that might be expected of what Cooper and Stoler identify as an "imperial" space, generated by contestations at various levels of a network of practices in the unified analytical field of the metropole-colony. Most important, these histories do not unchain space from physical geographies.

Moving away from such physical-geographical spatial organizations, this book makes sense of the local differently. I show how the spatial meaning of this category—generated from within the practices studied—served as an engagement with the problem of universality, and as its critique. From this point, I build the local up as a conceptual space, which had the capacity to transform old meanings and build new ones. I further demonstrate that all of this, across the diversity of the practices considered here, developed with reference to an astounding variety of physical geographies. The local, however, had a far more complex relationship with these locales than merely being their geographical expression.[7] The geographical was an effect of this machine. But before dwelling further on the nature of this machine, let us turn to the practices themselves and to the locales they were entangled with.

Contextualizing Cuttack

I will begin by noting the reasons behind choosing Cuttack as one of these locales in relation to which these practices making the local are studied in this book. Cuttack was the nineteenth division of the Bengal Presidency, which the East India Company's government occupied in 1803, defeating its erstwhile Maratha rulers. The conquest of Cuttack was crucial to a geographic consolidation of Company rule. Cuttack occupied an area along the eastern coast of British India that began beyond the borders of the Midnapore district of the Bengal Presidency and continued up to the districts of Ganjam and Koraput, which were part of the Madras Presidency. Evidently, Cuttack was the missing link in the possibility of a continuous territorial consolidation of the Company's government. On top of that, being ruled by a strong regional force, the Marathas, from their headquarters in Nagpur, the area of Cuttack remained a potential gateway for threatening incursions of the Marathas into Company territory. This was reason enough for the governor-general, Lord Wellesley, to propose to the raja of Nagpur the establishment of a British subsidiary force in the raja's territories. Given its strategic location, it can be assumed that a total military control of this territory was necessary for the government. Predictably, therefore, as the raja of Nagpur refused to permit the posting of Company soldiers in his territory, British troops marched in and conquered the area of Cuttack. In December 1803, as the Treaty of Deogaon was being concluded with Raghuji Bhonsle—the raja of Nagpur and the Maratha chief—Cuttack came under Company rule.

The Company's government divided Cuttack into two administrative areas—the Mughalbandi and the Garhjat. Mughalbandi was governed by company regulations, while the Garhjat was marked as a princely domain. The Mughalbandi was composed of three districts: Balasore, Cuttack, and Puri. In 1804, the annual revenue of the Mughalbandi was estimated at Rs. 11,78,000. As an entire division within the Bengal Presidency, in terms of its revenue-yielding capacity, Cuttack was a tiny dot on the Company's financial map. As this book bears out, however, in the organization of its agrarian territory, Cuttack received a distinct kind of governmental attention. Right from the beginning it was perceived as an anomalous zone. In spite of being a part of the Bengal Presidency, a permanent zemindary settlement—the mode of revenue administration prevalent in the greater part of this presidency—was never introduced in Cuttack. During the initial years, settlements spanning brief periods, like one, three, or five years, were made with zemindars, or big landlords. Very soon, in the aftermath of an insurrection, known as the Paik rebellion (1817), changes were introduced in the nature of land settlement in certain parts of the division. More significant shifts took place in the agrarian life of the territory over the years 1837–45 when an extensive survey and settlement operation was launched in Cuttack, which fixed rents, classified proprietary titles to lands, and, more generally, carefully defined the agrarian social as an economy of roles, capacities, and relations. Soon after the completion of this settlement, the division witnessed a plethora of disputes over property in land, which reshaped, yet again, the sinews of agrarian power in the district.

What brings these practices of governance and self-identification of agrarian groups in a particular place, like Cuttack, within the fold of this book is their critical implications in the making of the local there, and elsewhere. This is because throughout the first half of the nineteenth century an intense debate went on at various levels of the imperial bureaucracy regarding the local specificities of agrarian conditions in different regions of British India. Cuttack, like other locales, was centrally implicated in this conversation. In fact, it is in the light of this debate that the Bengal Code, or the regulations pertaining primarily to revenue administration in the areas of Bengal Presidency acquired earlier by the Company, was perceived as inapplicable to Cuttack.[8] Accordingly, the so-called Permanent Settlement signed in 1793 was never extended to this division of the Bengal Presidency. A brief historiographic digression is in order here. The major works of South Asian agrarian history focusing on Bengal have very little to say about Cuttack. These histories have defined Bengal only in terms of its permanently settled areas, thereby excluding those vast tracts within it which were temporarily settled. Consequently, their conclusions about Bengal's agrarian development have been skewed.[9]

The aborting of the Permanent Settlement, or the Bengal model of revenue settlement in Bengal itself, was spurred by a general critical disposition within Company governance toward itself. This strategy of self-critique was, in turn, an expression of the problem—epistemological and political—that universality posed for governance. The category of the local was mobilized to make sense of and resolve this problem. The local, as I understand it in this book, did not give up on universality but refigured the way in which it had appeared as a problem. This is why, I argue, histories ignorant of the non–Permanent Settlement areas of Bengal betray not only a gap in the knowledge of agrarian conditions of a locality; they also demonstrate a blindness toward the very nature of the epistemological project that shaped governmental rationality during this period. This book suggests to the earlier historical works that nothing in Bengal or within the foundations of governance was permanently settled.

Instead, practices of governance in Cuttack were aimed at assembling the local as difference. In the process, there emerged a gamut of strategies of different kinds of agrarian groups, who tried to make sense of their location in conversation with the rationality of these practices. Inside and outside Cuttack, therefore, this book follows lines and circulations of the local that were spun around a variety of localities, about specificities of agrarian conditions in British India. I locate Cuttack as various congealed moments in this interconnected field of motion, only to point toward their continuous decomposition and recomposition. Interestingly, the idea that Cuttack was not only one of the innumerable localities in British India but stood for something much greater than itself came out in several official enunciations. Perhaps their pinnacle was reached when this obscure locale found an exclusive mention in John Stuart Mill's "Memorandum of the Improvements in the Administration of India During the Last Thirty Years" presented in 1858 to the British Parliament.

Mill argued that Cuttack represented the best system of settlement, because it combined the specific respective advantages of different models of settlement. That is why, he further noted, it should serve as the leading model for agrarian governance. He proposed its extension to other recently conquered territories of the Company.[10] Settlements, as I discuss later in detail, primarily involved making sense of the varying forms of property in land in different regions of British India and, thereby, instituting a framework for their governance. Accordingly, from the time of the earliest of such settlements, namely, the Permanent Settlement of Bengal of 1793, till the end of the first half of the nineteenth century, the greatest task faced by the East India Company's government was that of understanding and managing property in land in India. In appreciating the model of settlement adopted in Cuttack, Mill was, therefore, actually indicating that it represented the ideal form of government of the regional differences in property in India.

Mill's declaration was deeply embedded in a long and complex debate over property that animated an astounding range of levels and regions of governance in British India over this period. The question of specificity was formulated, and answered, albeit temporarily, by these discursive practices of governance. This book explores how governmental rationality engaged with the problem of universality versus difference, in comprehending specific forms of property in land in British India. Cuttack appeared as one of the seminal lines in this field of engagement, which, in turn, generated other lines traversing a great variety of categories and geographies in British India and beyond. What brought these lines together was the problem of universality-difference, fashioned as the category of the local; its operations were also visible in other analytical spaces, like the interface of science and political economy in contemporary Britain. Empirically speaking, J. S. Mill was important for both these spaces—debates over property in Cuttack and British India, and debates over categories and methods in science and political economy in Britain. For a preliminary understanding of these entanglements, let us now turn to an outline of the chapters of the book.

Transformations

The first chapter introduces the local with an examination of a range of debates over the methodology of political economy in early nineteenth-century Britain. To appreciate the significance of this material, it will be useful to briefly revisit the seminal scholarly assessments of the relations between political economy and empire in early nineteenth-century Britain. It is widely accepted that in this period the theoretical field of political economy in Britain was predominantly defined in terms of David Ricardo's system. Historians have, however, qualified the extent of the intellectual authority of Ricardian principles within political economy circles. Ricardian principles were critiqued within political economy from different perspectives.[11] Such critical qualifications are, however, absent in the histories of empire and British India. Here, since Eric Stokes's pioneering work, which compellingly demonstrated how the rising tide of utilitarian ideals in Britain played a defining role in shaping different aspects of governance in nineteenth-century British India, the singularity of the authority of Ricardo's doctrines have been almost taken for granted in the historiography, especially in making sense of the Company's land revenue policy.[12]

Ricardian political economy, Stokes argues, made its way to the agrarian affairs of British India through James Mill, Ricardo's close friend and reputed scholar-administrator. Mill made Ricardian thought, particularly its conceptualization of rent, the basis of property governance and land tax in British India.[13] Most important, since land was the biggest source of revenue for the Company, it is through agrarian governance, that the authoritarian, universalizing, reforming impulse of Western liberal principles, in its utilitarian avatar, made its most forceful mark on an indigenous society.[14]

In contrast to this interventionist liberalism, Stokes notes, there emerged a preservationist tradition, "the 'Romantic' generation in British Indian history." This tradition approached Indian/indigenous society with a sentiment "with which Wordsworth and the Romantics invested the noble peasant. . . . They brought to the Indian problem Burke's notion of history."[15] Stokes's characterization of the philosophical basis of governance—not only agrarian but in general—in nineteenth-century British India in terms of a division between the utilitarians/liberals and the romantics/conservatives has been repeated later, even in its critique.[16] Lynn Zastoupil, for example, points to the absence in Stokes's work of any consideration of John Stuart Mill's entanglement with British India. He fills this gap by providing a rich discussion of the influence the younger Mill exerted in formulating policies in various areas of governance in British India.[17] In narrating this involvement, Zastoupil understands the philosophical outlook of J. S. Mill as composed of a mixture of the course of his intellectual development as a thinker, and that of his experience at India House as an administrator. Accordingly, he interprets Mill's philosophy as a reinterpretation of the senior Mill's abstract authoritarian universalism in the light of an appreciation of historical and cultural specificities. This reworking, Zastoupil argues, emerged out of the simultaneous impact on Mill of the romantic sensibilities of his time and the ideas of the "empire of opinion" group of British Indian administrators, who espoused a Burkean sensitivity toward indigenous life.[18]

It is important to note that Zastoupil's empire of opinion group refers to exactly those administrators who, in Stokes's work, were categorized as the "Romantic generation." Although he insists that Mill's enunciations not only reflected engagements with varied strands of metropolitan thought but were also shaped by the imperial experience of administration through the ideas of the empire of opinion group, in reading these latter ideas in turn as Burkean and Whiggish articulations, Zastoupil ends up rewriting the "imperial" mind of J. S. Mill as a metropolitan one. In an attempt to explain Mill's philosophy in terms of an imperial intercourse, he ends up reproducing Stokes's analytical framework. Within this framework, formations of South Asian societies are understood as being directly caused by dominant metropolitan currents of thought. This is a diffusionist model resting on a series of binaries, like metropole-colony, Western theory–indigenous reality, abstract utilitarian universalism–concrete romantic particularism, inside-outside, and many others.

Keeping in mind these historiographical trends, this book suggests a different way of thinking about the very epistemological conditions of possibility for a relation between political economy in Britain and governmental rationality in early nineteenth-century British India. The first chapter shows that Ricardian ideas—which these diffusionist histories identify as the dominant articulation of metropolitan thought influencing governance in South Asia—were themselves questioned in Britain in debates over the method and categories of political economy. These debates revolved around the problem of universality-difference. The way this problem was posed and resolved, I argue, opened up grounds for the recasting of political economy as governance. It is these relations—universality-difference and political economy–governance—which were made in and through the category of the local. The local unified disparate sites—Cuttack, British India, and Britain—not through diffusionist hierarchies but as simultaneous and intersecting lines of force in an apparatus.

Political economy in Britain over the first half of the nineteenth century got involved with the question of methodology in relation to a broader intellectual movement aimed at rethinking the epistemological basis of scientific knowledge. This movement claimed that an inductive methodology must be followed in building up knowledge in all forms of sciences. It was spearheaded by William Whewell, a meta-commentator of science, based at Cambridge. Whewell along with John Herschel, Charles Babbage, and Richard Jones formed a group that tried to programmatically develop an inductive methodology as the epistemological ground of all branches of science. Individually, these men were scholars working in different fields of the natural sciences, other than Jones, whose interests were in political economy.[19] Whewell was a polymath who wrote on diverse fields, like mathematics, geology, architecture, political economy, and moral philosophy, among others. But above everything, he was what can be described in retrospective terms as the first "philosopher of science."[20] He attempted a systematic epistemological redefinition of the sciences, based on a championing of the inductive method. This was programmatically spelt out in his twin publications, which complemented each other, "History of the Inductive Sciences, from the Earliest to the Present Times" and "The Philosophy of the Inductive Sciences, Founded upon Their History."

Whewell's inductivism entered political economy through Richard Jones. Jones critiqued Ricardo's system, pointing out that it was not grounded in inductive reasoning. Along with Whewell, he argued that Ricardian categories were based on deductive and, hence, false generalizations. Together, they declared that the manner in which Ricardo defined the chief constituent categories of his system made them inapplicable to, even meaningless for, the vast majority of the peoples living in different nations of the world. This is when, I argue in this chapter, the local became a category internal to, and constitutive of, political-economic reason. The debate sparked by this critique of Ricardianism was then taken up in the writings of several other political economists, like Thomas Malthus, J. R. McCulloch, James Mill, and John Stuart Mill. This chapter tracks this debate as it was conducted in terms of a series of substitutable conceptual oppositions, like inductive-deductive, hypothesis-observation, theory-practice, and abstract-concrete. This epistemological battle was carried out in a string of essays published in reputable contemporary British periodicals as well as in the more well-known texts of these authors.

This epistemological conflict was most sharply articulated in a series of debates over the definition of the category of rent. In responding to Jones's charge that Ricardo's definition of rent was not able to explain the lifeworlds of the greater part of the world's populations, defenders of Ricardo's system, like McCulloch and James Mill, brought out their own detailed examinations of the conditions of collective life of populations in non-Western parts of the world. Their representations invariably took India as an empirical ground and became an analysis of the relation between political structures and property relations of the country. This analytical direction assumed a more comprehensive form when Jones published *An Essay on the Distribution of Wealth and on the Sources of Taxation.*[21] The book proposed a rewriting of political economy in the light of the indigenous conditions of different nations in the world. Jones argued that meanings of the chief categories of political economy, like rents, wages, and profits, were determined by the variety of conditions under which production and distribution take place all over the world. He emphasized that agricultural production, or the very act of laboring on land, was always and already grounded in multifarious frameworks of the distribution of produce. These conditions of distribution, in turn, were historical outcomes of complex and multilayered entanglements between property and political power. Jones elucidated his perspective by highlighting the various kinds of rents prevalent in different nations. From Western European nations to Russia to Central Asian lands to China to India, he explained these rents as reflections of relations of power, shaped by relations between varying modes of political sovereignty and forms of proprietorship, existent in different nations.[22]

This is how, I argue in this chapter, these debates effected a general reconfiguration of the epistemological object of political economy. Political economy became invested in understanding *differences* in the sovereignty-property complex of nations. The local stood for this *transformed* object of knowledge of political economy. The local was not simply nationally varying specific formation(s) of sovereignty-property relations. It was a framework for making sense of the problem of universality-difference. It acted as a tool with which the universal could be reassembled in and as difference.

Of course, this difference was organized as a hierarchy. In the debate over the meaning of political-economic categories, the form of sovereignty-property linkage existent in Europe, which provided the basis for Ricardo's definition of rent, was considered ideal in many cases. Accordingly, the form of such linkages visible in other nations was perceived as an inferior one. But across a range of positions, self-identifying as Ricardian and anti-Ricardian, this hierarchization was put under suspension. In this moment of an epistemological shift, difference was more important than hierarchy. The local emerged, therefore, as the conceptual possibility of making difference the new epistemological object for political economy.

The chapter also argues that difference was fundamental to the Whewellian program of inductivism. Whewell's induction, I suggest, was not simply about replacing "theory" with "facts" or putting "observation" ahead of "hypothesis" in building knowledge. Taking a close look at how Whewell uses these terms, and more technical ones like "colligation" and "superinducement," in his writings, I contend that his proposed method had grand ambitions of universalization. The method's emphasis on observed particulars, or "facts," was already and always embedded in a scheme of classified, successive, and hierarchized concepts. Pivotal to this scheme was the methodological possibility of observing, understanding, managing, and interpreting *difference* in observed particulars. The shift in the epistemological object of political economy, thus, gathered conceptual force from this immanent centrality of difference in Whewellian inductivism. The program of induction had a totalizing imperative. It wanted to develop a super-synoptic eye, which, in one compact look, would be able to introduce an integrated meaning into the bewildering heterogeneity of the world.

This is what the local was supposed to perform for political economy. It was meant to become a framework for the achievement of a greater universality, superseding the epistemological limits of the Ricardian system. The inductivist critique of Ricardianism, therefore, did not entail a rejection of universals in favor of empirical particulars. Rather, it offered a new method of universalizing, in and through difference, which articulated itself also as a redefinition of political-economic categories. Political economy was no longer understood as a set of fixed law-like relations operating between the natural, pregiven, and universal domains of production and distribution. Rather, these domains were considered to be conditioned by globally varying constellations of sovereignty and property. Accordingly, all the categorial constituents of these domains, namely, rent, wage, profit, and, most important, labor itself, were posited as contingent on power differentials.

Agrarian South Asia

This remapping of political economy in the first chapter sets up tracks for forays into agrarian governance in British India in the subsequent chapters. It also establishes one of the important directions of historiographic critique informing this book. It destabilizes the series of interchangeable binary oppositions that have constituted the analytic of most works on South Asia's agrarian past. The conceptual separation between (abstract) political economy and (concrete) indigenous reality is invalidated as I show how the indigenous became *internal* to the discourse of political economy in early nineteenth-century Britain. The emphasis on historical specificity that Stokes and others associate with the preservationist, romantic-conservative sensibilities, as opposed to the interventionist utilitarian liberalism, is also questioned by this interpretive move. I argue that history, indigeneity, specificity, and preservation were not opposed to the universality of political-economic categories. On the contrary, they were constitutive of its universality. In making this argument I also point out that a large number of richly textured histories of the making of agrarian societies in British India have used the category of the local to signify an indigenous essence of these agrarian orders. In doing so they have reproduced a series of oppositions, like inside-outside, abstract-concrete, theory-practice, deductive-inductive, and others, that structured governmental rationality in the nineteenth century. Having introduced readers to the chapters of the book, I note how we can reassess meanings of the local in agrarian histories of South Asia.

Over Chapters 2, 3, 4, and 5, the book examines practices of agrarian governance and the production of proprietary subjects in British India over the first half of the nineteenth century, all along reflecting on the interrelationship between political economy and governance. Chapter 2 traces the production of the category of rent through practices of governance in various localities, including Cuttack. It shows how specificities, as local conditions, were construed in these practices as a hierarchized gradation of property rights existing in different parts of British India. Rent was used as a historical clue to determine, and assemble, these proprietary conditions. This, I argue, inaugurated the search for an authentic, indigenous, "Indian" sovereignty-property complex in British Indian agrarian governance. Moving away from the Ricardian definition of rent, as the measure of differences in soil fertility, rent was staged as a transaction, which brought out differences in the entanglements of property and political power in the different agrarian territories of British India.

Chapter 2 tracks the career of rent, in the aftermath of the permanent settlement of Bengal, over several sites of governance. It shows how within Bengal Presidency itself administrators reinterpreted the proprietary provisions of the Permanent Settlement, in the light of this understanding that rent was the chief vehicle of power in agrarian societies. The chapter notes that there were attempts to fix rent in Ricardian terms in the North-Western Provinces in the early decades of the nineteenth century, which were, however, quickly abandoned. By the time the Company's government started a detailed settlement of Cuttack, that is, between 1836 and 1845, rent became generally perceived as a regulator of political power. This led to the granting of proprietary privileges to village leaders and hereditary cultivators. Their right to share the rent with the state was reconstructed out of the historical remnants of sovereignty-property relations in India. In this chapter, therefore, I demonstrate how rent operated for governance as a *trace* of the sovereignty-property ensemble that determined conditions of production in India.

Chapter 3 engages directly with the ways in which governmental rationality constructed this distributed field of proprietary power as the authentic political (sovereignty-property complex) of India. It begins with the earliest and most systematic deliberations in the nineteenth century, on sovereignty and property in India presented to the British Parliament. Examining these representations, the chapter shows how the category of the local was assembled to make sense of the sovereignty-property problem. Administrators from different parts of British India suggested that there existed a direct proprietary relation between the state and the peasant cultivator in an ancient Hindu polity that was distorted, obfuscated, or lost over time. With time, other landholders emerged in between these two primary constituents of the sovereignty-property matrix, displacing their unmediated intercourse. Accordingly, localities were understood as embodying this scarred past in their proprietary landscape, exhibiting varying dispersals of power between the state, the big landlords, the village leaders, the peasant cultivators, and the village itself.

The chapter shows how governmental mobilizations of the local—the universality-difference problem, posited in terms of the new political-economic object of sovereignty-property relations—*re-cognized* different kinds of landholders in different parts of British India in terms of their connections with the original form of the proprietary cultivator. They were considered as absent presences, as transformed representatives of a lost origin. In the settling of revenues of regions like Cuttack, the claims to proprietary privileges of these different kinds of landholders were accordingly adjudged on the basis of the authenticity of the marks of the past they exhibited in the present. One kind of landholder was fixed as the authentic proprietary figure in each locality. Others were not completely displaced. They were granted positions depending on the degree of authenticity they could evince. The selection took place over circulating practices of governance, which continuously drew upon other localities in order to justify a specific selection in a specific locality. The chapter documents such circulations and selections over a variety of territories, debates, and practices in the first half of the nineteenth century.

Determining the prospects of production, or agricultural "improvement," the chapter argues, was also one of the major aims of these practices. Governance was invested in the identification of a prospective improver, from within the specific sovereignty-property relations that conditioned the possibilities of production in India. In positing "despotism" in India as inherently fractured, leading to a dispersal of power, governmental reason in the nineteenth century destabilized the earlier official investments in the big landlords, or zemindars. Operations of the local enabled other kinds of landholders, especially the substantial peasantry, influential at the level of the village, to gain proprietary entitlements out of this shift. A preference of peasant proprietors over big landlords, as ideal agricultural improvers, also expressed an important stand of political economy in Britain during this period. Some historians have tried to explain this shift in agrarian policy toward an appreciation of such dominant peasant groups in British India as reflective of this political-economic argument.[23]

This chapter, in tune with the general argument of the book, disagrees with such understanding of the relationship between political economy and governance. Unlike the dominant historiographic portrayal of this relationship in terms of "influences" of the "outside," the book shows how political economy was immanently connected to governance.[24] Political economy here functioned as a governmental rationality that aimed at totalizing the proprietary field through production and management of difference. Consequently, it argues that the move away from big landlords in practices of agrarian governance in British India did not signify a straightforward translation of a political-economic preference of the peasant proprietor. As this chapter shows, none of the figures who were selected as the chief proprietors of a locality, or its potential improver—the "village zemindars," or the proprietary ryots grounded in the putteedaree tenure, or the mukaddams and surburakars of Cuttack—reproduced the figure of the farmer-like peasant proprietor of the discourse of political economy. The figure of the improving peasant farmer of the Continent was mediated by the discourse of the local. It was recast in terms of the construction of the authentic indigenous "political," as a despotism fractured from within. Accordingly, a huge variety of land controllers, with varying degrees of proprietary rights, were upheld by the government in different regions.

The chapter ends with John Stuart Mill. It argues that even the younger Mill's political economy moved away from the classical Ricardian frame. Here too the epistemological object of political economy was refashioned, but in a manner different from that of Jones. Once again, most historians analyze the relationship between Mill's political economy and property governance in British India as an "influence" of Mill's exaltation of the peasant proprietor on the revenue policy of the Company's government. In some works, this argument is further grounded in an imperial context of Mill's engagement with the Irish land question along similar lines.[25] But these works, as I have argued about Zastoupil earlier, thrive on the imperial-local binary.[26] I analyze Mill's entanglements with agrarian property in India by contextualizing Mill's political economy within its own discursive field in Britain, and pursuing its further transformations in the practices of the local in British India. Therefore, what become important in this analysis are the transformations within the apparatus, not the direction of flows between analytically separable points.[27]

Chapter 4 argues that the category of the village played a crucial role in territorializing the object of political economy/governance, that is, differences in property-sovereignty relations, in British India. This chapter demonstrates how the village was produced by the practices of agrarian governance as a distinct territorial *economy* of property, power, and production. The village as an archetype, and the countless individual villages of British India, was fixed, by political economists and administrators alike, as the customary domain that organized production by protecting the proprietary status of the peasant cultivator from the encroaching tendencies of the big landholders. Custom, here, was a category internal to the discourse of political economy, not construed as opposed, and external, to it.[28] The authenticity of the village was once again traced back to an ancient Hindu India. It was seen as the smallest territorial unit of power, formed by interrelations between different kinds of cultivators, occupational groups, and officers of the state engaged in the supervision of production and collection of revenue. Practices of agrarian governance privileged village-based proprietary titles, enacted surveys, and granted rent-free lands to occupational groups and officers of the state, thereby organizing the village as the quintessential domain of power and production in India, and the primary unit of agrarian governance. As in other chapters, here too I move in and out of Cuttack to demonstrate how interregional, imperial, metropolitan, and local practices spoke to each other in territorializing the local.

Chapter 5 focuses entirely on Cuttack. It documents a variety of moments when the governmental framework of agrarian power collapsed, only in order to be reinforced again. Here I examine situations where the government found it difficult to identify proprietors according to its own classificatory categories. I take a close look at governmental strategies of abstraction that tried to recast different kinds of payments around land as rent. In the process, these practices redefined other relations of power into those which fit into the frames of the local. This chapter also carefully examines the myriad ways in which dominant landholders of Cuttack articulated their identities in terms of governmental categories, in order to overturn older equations of power and create new relations of hierarchy. I show how all actors—the state, the big landholders, the village proprietors, and smaller cultivators—forged different kinds of alliances and enmities, to extract proprietary gains. Once the revenue settlement was over, Cuttack turned into a legal battlefield between various kinds of land controllers. This showed that governmental property classifications, in fixing certain equations of power, set free the possibilities of developing others.

It is important to note that this chapter does not use the familiar theoretical strategy of a gap between the "theory" and the "practice" of governance in analyzing its material. Rather it argues that the rationality of the practices of governance immanently produced a dynamic field, which perpetually deferred the closure of the apparatus. In this chapter, the book suggests, one can discern the mechanism by which a series of linked transformations in science, political economy, and governance were rearticulated as ceaseless battles over the control of landed property in localities. The meaning of production by the end of the first half of the nineteenth century became, therefore, conflict over agrarian power in the locality. The book ends with a brief chapter reflecting on the career of "production" in British India in the years to follow.

This highly differentiated regime of agrarian proprietary relations, I contend, was not produced out of contingencies of governance or failure of metropolitan imperatives to transform traditional indigenous social forms. The local has been deployed as an influential analytic by agrarian histories of nineteenth-century British India to make these kinds of arguments. In this scholarship it represents one side of a series of conceptually isomorphic binary oppositions. For some works, it stands for empirical realities of the ground, which could not be correctly perceived by distant metropolitan abstractions.[29] In a related vein, others find in it the resilience of the traditional, which can block the penetrating zeal of the modern.[30] In empirical terms, this body of work identifies the rise of the village-level land controllers as evidence of the power of the local. The suggestion is that the village, as the remote interior, away from the centers of power, is the local, which is also an embodiment of tradition, indigeneity, and the absence of colonialism/modernity; it is this interior that escapes the abstractions of the metropole and forces governance to accommodate concrete contingencies of the ground.[31]

There are works that offer a more nuanced explanation of the making of agrarian societies in British India during this period. Some argue that agrarian proprietary relations were formed out of contradictory movements of colonial law that in a particular phase of its operation introduced modern forms of property, only to reinforce traditional ones in another phase.[32] Some suggest that agrarian relations were formed out of dialectical encounters between state and society.[33] Others argue that they were outcomes of interactions between European and indigenous ideas and practices.[34] But each of them continues to work within the master binary of inside-outside, where the local remains the key explanatory category, posited either as the pure inside or as a fusion of the two parts of the binary.

The binary reappears in a different guise in even one of the more recent and theoretically sophisticated studies of early colonial governance in Bengal. This work argues that conditioned by the anxieties and insecurities of colonial officials, and their search for certainty in a world perceived as strange and alien, governance remained uncertain, unstable, and restless in the face of an intractable reality that kept on escaping its categorizing clutches. This, however, is where we find a return of the binaries of abstract-concrete, representation-reality, and ultimately, inside-outside. Like the older histories of agrarian South Asia, even this work insists, in its analysis of agrarian governance, that colonial codes failed to capture the reality of agrarian interiors. As the author notes, "Hidden away in their offices, collectors rarely physically encountered rural social relations."[35] He seems to suggest that the very act of physical confinement also signified an imprisonment in the false structures of representation, from where one could break free by tasting the free air of the countryside, the organic reality outside.[36]

Practices of governance in British India had since the turn of the nineteenth century used the local to mean differences in proprietary relations, which, over the next fifty years, led to the assembling of a national indigenous complex of sovereignty-property relations. Agrarian histories of South Asia, so far, have mostly reproduced this governmental understanding of the local as difference, embodied in indigenous forms of proprietary power relations.

My book argues that the local can be more productively understood as the category in terms of which political economy became governmental rationality in the nineteenth century. Probing the category in this manner can help us displace the indigenist essentialism it is currently invested with. All the chapters of the book meticulously demonstrate how an entire conceptual infrastructure of indigeneity acted as constitutive of governmental/political-economic reason across linked sites of philosophy of science, practices of governance, and proprietary conflicts in Britain, British India, and many more locales in the period under consideration. What the East India Company's government and dominant forms of South Asian historiography present as indigenous insides of the agrarian, like proprietary power in villages and a non-absolute field of rights, can be rethought as effects of a modern liberal governmental rationality.

Property, Sovereignty, Governance

In this concluding section, I reflect on the discursive function of the category of the local in the interconnected lives of political economy, imperial governance, and South Asian agrarian societies in the first half of the nineteenth century. This is a conceptual elucidation of the specific form of universality achieved by the local, in and through difference. Here, the book turns to an engagement with the works of Foucault, in order to construct a theoretical relation between political economy and governance. I propose a conversation between his characterization of political economy as a formation of knowledge in the modern episteme and his genealogy of liberal governance.

Foucault argues that the shift in the structure of discourse from the classical to the modern episteme was marked by a change from representation to its limits. As he demonstrates, by the end of the eighteenth century a new discursive constellation had emerged, of producing knowledge about life, labor, and language, congealing around the disciplines of biology, philology, and political economy, respectively. This epistemic shift generated labor, or production, as the epistemological object of political economy. The manner in which the category of labor as production was formulated in political economy, especially with Ricardo, Foucault notes, revealed changes at a deeper level of thought.[37] The mode of being of things was no longer considered as representable. They could not be horizontally distributed over a table of equivalence in terms of identities and differences. Rather "they turn in upon themselves, posit their own volumes, and define for themselves an internal space which, to our representation, is on the exterior. . . . The very being of that which is represented is now going to fall outside representation itself."[38]

Particularly speaking, in terms of the birth of political economy, this entailed a move away from exchange as the basis of analysis of wealth to labor as the condition of possibility for exchange. In the classical episteme value was defined as representation of the equivalence of all objects established through exchange. In the modern episteme, value was seen as rooted in a deep, primordial, organic force, beyond and beneath representation—in the activity of labor. Accordingly, production displaced circulation, in becoming the foundational principle of political economy. All constituents of the process of production were perceived as ultimately reducible to units of labor, applied at different moments.[39] In Ricardo's system, production was invested with a historicity, which was the continuous historical time of the application of successive units of labor.[40]

Let us now look at Foucault's presentation of political economy in the light of the local. The primacy of production was not rejected in the debate over the legitimacy of the method and categories of Ricardian political economy. Concurring with Foucault, I argue that production, as the organizing principle of political economy, was discursively constituted at an autonomous level of reality. Right at a time when Ricardian ideas were gaining public attention in Britain, however, the local reconstituted the universality of production as difference, using the same epistemic logic. Historicity, marking production's depth, was mobilized to rewrite the category as determined by sovereignty-property differences. This meant that on the one hand the universality of production got reconfigured as difference, while on the other its autonomy got displaced by power, in the form of sovereignty-property ensembles. This is why political economists like James Mill, McCulloch, Richard Jones, and John Stuart Mill, in the debate over the universality of Ricardian political economy, ultimately moved toward examinations of the different forms of political power existent in different nations of the world. In arguing over the definition of rent, they ended up emphasizing how forms of sovereignty, giving rise to different kinds of property relations, functioned as conditions of production. Production, therefore, became a derivative of power and difference at the very moment of the inception of political economy as a particular epistemic formation of modernity.

This reconditioning of political economy by the category of the local, I argue, can be considered a necessary analytical bridge to step into Foucault's understanding of governance. In his lectures at the Collège de France, Foucault notes that he has tried to "grasp the level of reflection in the practice of government and on the practice of government."[41] He calls his object of study the "art of government," distinguishing it from real governmental practice. Instead of taking governance as a given category, by equating it with the established universals of sociology, history, or political philosophy, he attempts to examine it immanently, in terms of its self-reflection. This reflection, he argues, changed in its character from the eighteenth century in Europe. The change was about "establishing a principle of limitation that will no longer be extrinsic to the art of government, as was law in the seventeenth century, [but] intrinsic to it: *an internal regulation of governmental rationality*."[42] This transformation gave birth to "modern governmental reason." Foucault then specifies that this principle of internal limitation came into governance from political economy. Political economy, other than being an analysis of the production and distribution of wealth, generally meant a mode of reflecting on the economy of power in society. Therefore, Foucault remarks, "I think that fundamentally it was political economy that made it possible to ensure the self-limitation of governmental reason."[43]

Before digging deeper into this connection between political economy and governmental reason, let me clarify the location of the local in it. Following Foucault, it is evident that political economy was lodged into governmental reason as a self-reflexive principle of limitation of power. By reconstituting the universality of political-economic categories in terms of difference, the local was performing the same function in early nineteenth-century Britain. In making political economy reflective not only of its method and categories but also of variations in the form and distribution of power all over the world, the local prefigured the problem of governance.[44] This is why both the debates in political economy in Britain and the practices of agrarian governance in British India extensively engaged with the question of modes of distribution of power in society, as manifested in varying arrangements of property. Political economy became governmental reason, as the meanings of the categories of the former could be only accessed as reflections on the distribution of power, from within the practices of the latter.

Agrarian governance in British India from the turn of the nineteenth century exemplified this connection. The Company's government almost obsessively started reflecting on its past, on its own principles of governance, debating carefully about its "successes" and "failures." Most important, interregional debates and local practices of the Company's government became all about considerations on the principle of internal limitation of power in understanding and managing property in land. Property was understood as an effect of the form of sovereignty. Thus, governance was all about producing an economy of power by limiting itself to indigenous forms of sovereignty-property differences. This self-limitation was practiced in terms of the category of the local, by assembling a complex field of sovereignty-property differences in different localities, one of which was Cuttack. Agrarian groups acted within these conditions to produce their own proprietary capacities. Different kinds of landholders devised an array of strategies, mostly by reconfiguring the governmental economy of power, to suit their respective proprietary conditions. In this way, the governmental framing of links between property, sovereignty, and production was mobilized at the level of the most obscure and tiny villages of British India to create a variegated and complex regime of rights and interests in land.

Over the first half of the nineteenth century, as the Company kept acquiring newer territories, there emerged a governmental framing of the relation between property and sovereignty in India, which defined the strategy of managing proprietary conditions of specific locales. Conversations between administrators executing revenue settlements in different parts of the country assembled an understanding of the authentic "indigenous" form of sovereignty-property relations in India. Officials noted that anciently property in land in India involved a sharing of interests between particular kinds of peasants, who were proprietors of villages, and the state. This also meant that the state in India was not considered the absolute owner of property. Government officials noted, out of their "experience" of working in villages, that the state's absolutism was always arrested by customary rights of a category of peasants/village proprietors on the use and alienation of land. The state had a share of the rent, as a co-owner, and could not oust these peasants from their lands. This was an arrangement of shared proprietary capacities, which also reflected a dispersed sovereignty.[45]

In this understanding the property-sovereignty condition was also explained in religious terms. The Company's government noted that this authentic indigenous condition of a shared economy of power and property existed in an ancient Hindu India, which grew corrupt over the long period of Islamic rule. Accordingly, different localities were perceived as bearing differing traces of this authentic proprietary condition, depending on the extent of the influence of Islamic rule over them. This classification of agrarian territories, in terms of local differences in sovereignty-property relations, reflected the working of political economy as governmental reason in British India. Again, the local, as difference, was deployed as the principle of limitation of governmental sovereignty from within. As and through this limitation, governance became a strategy of devising and managing property in the form of an economy of power. The Company's government distributed this power, over the productive resources of the population, between the state and different kinds of landholders in the varied territories of British India.[46]

One can find conceptual resonances of the local in Foucault's discussion of the different traditions that informed this new governmental rationality, of self-limitation of sovereignty, in Europe since the end of the eighteenth century. Foucault notes that historically there emerged two approaches to this problem, of "how to set juridical limits to the exercise of power by a public authority."[47] He terms them the French revolutionary approach and the English utilitarian approach. The former began with law and ended with government. It considered the question of juridical limits from the perspective of the original/natural rights of man against sovereignty, thereby determining how these rights can be modified and redefined. The latter moved in the reverse direction, analyzing government itself to arrive at the problem of legal limitation. Here the logic of limitation was derived from history or tradition, but in a way that matched the ends of useful and desirable government. Modern governmental reason was formed out of complex interactions between these two traditions. Interestingly, Foucault comes to this conclusion by referring to the history of property: "Between these two heterogeneous systems—that of the revolutionary axiomatic, of public law and the rights of man, and that of the empirical and utilitarian approach which defines the sphere of independence of the governed on the basis of the necessary limitation of government—there is, of course, a ceaseless connection and a whole series of bridges, transits and joints. *Consider the history of property rights, for example.*"[48]

It can be justifiably argued that governance in British India too arrived at the problem of self-limitation of sovereignty, in making sense of property, in terms of these two traditions. My book, however, claims that over the first half of the nineteenth century, history, indigeneity, and tradition served as the basis of the self-limitation of sovereignty in the field of landed property. This is because difference, as the local, played a constitutive role in determining the imperatives of a governmentalized political economy. It not only enabled the configuration of specific strategies of governance for the particular proprietary conditions of localities. It also assembled a general economy of power, by defining the indigenous sovereignty-property condition as non-absolute and dispersed. These possibilities, going back to the debate over scientific method in Britain, emerged out of an inductivist reformulation of political economy, which had structural implications for governance.

Here it is important to note that the use of tradition in determining governmental goals was not incompatible with liberalism/utilitarianism. As the discussion in this section shows, the local made liberal governance limit itself through tradition/history/indigeneity. The work of the local was not opposed to the imperatives of utilitarian liberalism. On the contrary, this problem of limitation, as Foucault's argues, was also that of utility, "defined on the basis of what it would or would not be useful for government to do or not do."[49] This helps us rethink another set of oppositions established by the dominant historiographic understanding of the influence of liberal thought on governance in British India. A great range of historical works argue that in the first half of the nineteenth century universal ideals of liberalism determined imperatives of governance in British India, while in the second half of the century there was a turn away from these ideals in governance, to more particularistic visions of the social.[50]

This book contends that governmental investments in assembling indigenous arrangements of sovereignty and property as the foundational social fabric of the agrarian can be read as consistent with, and not contradictory to, liberalism's universal ideals. Some recent works have also pointed out in a similar vein that custom, indigeneity, and difference can be internal to the conceptual articulations of liberal universalism. Karuna Mantena powerfully demonstrates how late nineteenth-century governmental strategies of upholding the "native" social in British India drew its intellectual inspirations from the universal frames of Henry Maine's ideas and were not "pragmatic" accommodations to local realities.[51] Likewise, questioning the separation between metropolitan thought (abstract) and colonial practice (concrete), Andrew Sartori deftly explains the development of property relations and peasant identity in late nineteenth- and early twentieth-century Bengal as a historical reproduction of the abstractions intrinsic to the discourse of liberalism. He makes sense of the specific "vernacular" articulations of property amid the peasantry of this rural hinterland of British India, in the form of a Lockeanism, transformed and retold as a critique of property. In doing so, he notes that the "the role of colonial contexts in shaping colonial liberalism was not only one of interrupting liberal universalisms and of demarcating spaces of exclusion and exception."[52]

This is also how I locate the argument of this book within histories of entanglements between empire and political theory. The book shows how staple problems of political theory, like connections between sovereignty and property, constituted rationalities of imperial governance, but only in and through a network of connections between transformations in the epistemological object of political economy, methodological debates in the philosophy of science, and strategies of subjectification by agrarian actors. In these connections, the local did not function as a category of colonial exception. On the contrary, it was absolutely central to the liberal governmental imperative of self-limitation. The local was not the margin of the empire—it was at the heart of its logic of rule. In recent times an impressive body of scholarship has brought out striking connections between the canons of Western political theory and imperial practices across the world. But these connections are still grounded only in readings of canons.[53] My book suggests that such connections can be, and need to be, made over a much wider and heterogeneous field of practices. Further, in positing the local as the constitutive logic of this field, the book argues for a recentering of the category, against its construal as the contingent margin of encounter and difference in some influential histories of empire.[54] This can help us deromanticize the local while rewriting its centrality in the making of complex connections between science, political economy, imperial governance, and agrarian power in colonial locales.

CHAPTER 1

Science, Method, and Indigeneity

Political Economy

> The universal, in fact, explains nothing: it is the universal which needs to be explained.
>
> —Gilles Deleuze

This chapter documents a key transformation of the epistemological anchors of political economy in early nineteenth-century Britain. I understand this transformation by positing a conceptual relation between two apparently disparate debates—over political economic categories and scientific method—in Britain during this period. Both debates were over the appropriate method of acquiring knowledge of the world, of its physical and social forms. I argue that the question of method was framed in them in terms of a series of *substitutable* binary oppositions, like deductive-inductive, abstract-concrete, universal-particular, a priori–observational, and theory-practice. Different positions in these debates championed one side of these oppositions, rejecting the other. The chapter demonstrates that despite these visible oppositions, there was an invisible analytical space of consensus in these debates. Although they were couched in a language of conflict between "theoretical" and "empirical" modes of knowing, both sides were still rooted in universal forms of reasoning. As they inflected each other, however, their respective foundational assumptions got disturbed. This process produced, as I see it, new universalities, and discursive linkages with other apparently unrelated fields of practice, like imperial governance, and agrarian social formations in British India.

In political economy the debate over method took place between self-styled deductivists and inductivists, who were also identified by contemporary intellectual circles as Ricardians and their opponents, respectively. The claim for inductivism in political economy was entangled with a wider engagement with epistemological foundations of science, spearheaded by one of the most important meta-commentators of science during this period, William Whewell. This chapter slips in and out of both Whewell's scholarly endeavor and the churnings within political economy. It unpacks the fundamental postulates of both, from within their own terms, and spells out the conceptual implications of this exercise for the relation between the two. The projection of inductivism as the best method of scientific inquiry, as we will see, turned the empirical attention of political economy to different nations of the world, and their particular social forms. I read these related moves, of inductivism in science and empiricism in political economy, as generating a new universal, constitutive of governmental rationality during this period. The chapter investigates the logic of this universal, as it was produced out of the self-assessment of science, and conflicts over meanings of political-economic categories. I argue that difference was posited as the constitutive principle of this new universal. The universalizability of political economy became predicated, through this epistemological reconfiguration, on its ability to generate, organize, and explain difference. This theoretical ability, to universalize by differentiation, was also evident, in a transformed fashion, within the practices of governance in British India during this period. There, as I show in subsequent chapters, this capacity was built in and practiced as the category of the local.

Interestingly, rent featured as the most important site over which these epistemological conversations conducted themselves. It was also where the whole discussion got linked, most directly, to imperial governance and agrarian societies in British India. The inductivists argued that the deductivist/Ricardian construction of rent did not have an empirical basis, thereby bringing different kinds of rents in different parts of the world into the fold of analysis. In this foregrounding of empiricism, there was also the suggestion that the Ricardian definition of rent was embedded in certain fundamental assumptions about structural features of human societies, which were arrived at by faulty methods of inquiry. Adopting a different method did not, however, imply a rejection of fundamentals. It led to the positing of a different set of structural features as the building blocks of human society. This was because the "empirical" method in question was itself constituted by an universalized framework, which predetermined the scope of its operation. I make this case by reading the political-economic in the light of the epistemological in Whewell's philosophy of science.

Rethinking rent, therefore, produced a new epistemological object of political economy. It redefined the chief categorial constituents of political economy, production and distribution, as contingent outcomes of the different interrelations between property and political power in different nations of the world. This reconfiguration did not emerge only out of the critique of Ricardo's opponents. Even in the writings of self-declared Ricardians there was a clear indication of this refashioning of political economy, irrespective of their explicit acknowledgment of it. By this epistemological move, I argue, particularity, indigeneity, and local power became key conceptual constituents of political economy. They were no longer considered as opposed to or outside the universality of political-economic categories. On the contrary, they became the defining markers of a new kind of universality, of a new program of totalization. The category of rent functioned as one of the key discursive resources that made local power immanent to political economy and the governmental rationality constituted by it.[1] This chapter, therefore, also indicates the process that prepared the conceptual ground for connections between political economy and governance. In separate, yet related sites, there were these simultaneous occurrences. Difference became the foundational principle of the new universal of political economy, and governance in British India entered the density of agrarian life through the category of the local, which was in turn a grammar of producing and managing difference.

Inductivism and Facts

In reviewing Richard Jones's book *An Essay on the Distribution of Wealth and the Sources of Taxation*, Whewell noted: "Political economy . . . must be concerned with the laws of the production and distribution of wealth as they actually operate in different countries and different forms of society. It must be a science concerned with actual facts and daily observations."[2] Whewell was an old friend of Jones's. Their friendship developed at Cambridge, where they met as students. At Cambridge, along with Charles Babbage and John Herschel, they had formed a group that thought similarly, in their respective areas of study, about methodological questions involved in the formation of scientific knowledge. Other than Jones, the rest were all students of, and subsequently famous scholars in, the natural sciences. Whewell was the intellectual nerve center of this group, who articulated, in an organized fashion, those interests that had built strong intellectual and personal ties between these men since their student days.[3] Over successive and systematic treatises,

Whewell developed the philosophy of inductivism, which, he argued, was the only proper method of gaining true knowledge in any branch of science—natural, moral, or political.

Whewell wrote on diverse subjects, including mechanics, astronomy, geology, mineralogy, political economy, education, architecture, and moral philosophy. The nature of his scholarly practice, which aimed at generating a metascientific discourse, was part of, as Richard Yeo notes, the contemporary efforts of legitimizing science as a cultural activity. In making the case for inductivism, Whewell was attempting to formulate a philosophy of knowledge itself—"as critic, adjudicator and legislator of science without being a major practitioner or discoverer."[4] In his review of Jones's book, Whewell performed the same role. That book, he believed, was a fine example of the adoption of an inductivist approach to political economy. Moreover, he argued that it was particularly important to rebuild political economy as an inductive science, because most of its leading doctrines, claiming to explain complex issues affecting the lives and livelihoods of the masses, were nothing but a bunch of false conclusions; yet at the same time they were influential enough to become part of popular common sense. He spelt out these worries clearly in the review. "Political economy . . . must be a science of *induction* and not of *deduction.* It must *obtain* its principles by reasoning upwards from facts, before it can *apply* them by reasoning downwards from axioms . . . these maxims . . . have been strangely lost sight of, and indeed have of late been absolutely denied. In recent times, and especially since the publication of Mr. Ricardo's treatise, the science has been put altogether in a deductive form."[5]

Jones shared Whewell's critique. In his book, as well as in other scattered pieces of writing, he made Ricardian political economy the central object of his criticism. Almost echoing Whewell's words, Jones wrote in his book: "Mr. Ricardo was a man of talent, and he produced a system very ingeniously combined, of purely hypothetical truths; which, however, a single comprehensive glance at the world as it actually exists, is sufficient to show to be utterly inconsistent with the past and present condition of mankind."[6] On the face of it, facts seemed to be the epistemological basis of the kind of political economy Jones attempted to develop. In the same vigor, Whewell noted that a deductivist approach to knowledge explained each and every element of the field under study by reasoning logically from a very small number of fundamental axioms. Ricardian political economy was a classic example of such a methodology. It explained everything related to production and distribution by the application of various combinations of three fundamental principles—the theory of population, the doctrine of rent, and the measure of exchange value. None of these principles was obtained on the basis of a systematic collection of facts. As a result, when the principles were made occasion for sweeping generalizations, they naturally produced nothing but absolutely false conclusions.

This is where we need to look more closely at Whewellian inductivism, especially the way it understood facts. It has been argued by several studies that Whewell never explained knowledge as generated simply by observation and factual compilation. On the contrary, his method argued for, in a complex way, the centrality of mind in the production of knowledge. As Laura Snyder notes, for Whewell, induction involved, most importantly, a mental act called "colligation," which brought together a number of observed particulars, or facts, into a class by "superinducing" on them a conception that allowed them to be expressed by a law.[7] These conceptions, which organized facts, did not arise from experience. They were accounted for by a theological explanation of the ontology of the external world. In the Whewellian scheme, God made the world as the expression of certain ideas. Human beings, divinely capacitated, possessed these ideas, which, accordingly, corresponded to the external world. There were, therefore, certain ideas appropriate to certain kinds of facts. The latter could be made sense of as facts only in light of the ideas.

Within this epistemological fold, therefore, facts were already potentially idealized, and truths were always necessary ones. This broke the separation between "fact" and "idea." Snyder notes that "the line we draw between them, like that between fact and theory, is a relative one . . . which change as our Ideas become more distinct. As we explicate our Ideas, we recognize empirical truths to be necessary consequences of these Ideas; and the truths are thus transferred from the empirical to the necessary side of the antithesis."[8] Such synoptic mental operations defined induction for Whewell. Analytical operations like association, unification, and affinity were crucial to this method. Observed particulars, or facts, could be re-cognized only in and through them. In praising Herschel's seminal *Discourse*, Whewell noted that in it induction was presented as "'the process of considering a class, or two associated classes of phenomena, as represented by . . . a single conception of the mind.'"[9] From another perspective, Robert Butts notes the constitutive role of the principles of affinity and unification in Whewell's ideas. Whewell explained the force of gravitation, Butts notes, as a capacity to establish an "affinity between the otherwise observed-to-be different paths of motion," which, being the cause of all laws of planetary motions, was presented as a "unifying generic form for all such motions." This was what Whewell called "consilience of inductions," or the successful ability of induction as a method to bring together those observed (and yet-to-be-observed) particulars that appear as different kinds of data but are actually of the same kind.[10]

A deductive approach was not inherently flawed. Whewell argued that there were parts of physical science where it could be successfully exercised. But they were those rare areas of science where idealization of facts was complete, and one could proceed from well-established advanced levels of generalizations. Not more than two or three branches of physics, namely, physical astronomy and mechanics, and partially optics, could claim such a status. But these were ancient disciplines, which had taken the time and labor of generations to attain this state. They were outcomes of a systematic process of the "dramatic inductive leap by great discoverers and the more routine scientific work of the sequel that followed each inductive epoch." Almost echoing a metaphor of colonization, Whewell described this process in his *History of the Inductive Sciences* as "a work of time and labour, often of difficulty and conflict." Compared to them, he noted, "it will . . . be a most strange and singular circumstance in the history of sciences, if political economy, the youngest of them, the most complex, mixed and vast in its subjects, depending on the most subtle, obscure and unmeasurable elements, should have sprung at once to this ultimate condition, this goal and limit of its possible intellectual progress."[11] Thus, political economy was considered in its infancy from this perspective, of inductive reasoning. It was seen as a field of inquiry that had not yet reached the necessary stage of forming deductive generalizations.

Evidently, the theory-fact opposition in Whewellian inductivism was far more complex than the commonsensical view of empiricism dominant in the public life of Britain during that period.[12] I argue that Whewell's framework was as much "theoretical," that is, tied to universal reasoning, as that of Whewell's presumed opponents. Further, the former's emphasis on facts, in terms of their mediation/organization through key cognitive operations like association, classification, and unification, allowed its universality to be more capacious than the latter. Let us now turn to an examination of the latter form of universality, which produced itself through the opposition between theory and practice. This opposition featured in the writings of all leading political economists of this period, irrespective of their allegiances to a deductive or an inductive method. In the next section, I argue that despite their diatribe against a priori generalizations in political economy, all of them operated with such generalities, which organized their field of study. In this sense, therefore, nothing in political economy was beyond what was identified in this methodological debate as the domain of theory.

Theory Versus Practice?

J. R. McCulloch used the opposition to answer the criticism aimed at Ricardian political economy. As a committed Ricardian, he came up with a harsh and dismissive review of Jones's book in the *Edinburgh Review*. Referring to the theory-practice divide, McCulloch exclaimed that Jones had confused elements as different as weight and color in his work. Accepting the critique that was directed at Ricardo from the perspective of a "practical"/"factual" political economy, McCulloch declared: "Mr. Ricardo's book is one of principle only, and that it is not to be judged by a merely practical standard."[13] McCulloch's support for theory is worth probing in greater detail, keeping in mind the way the category had been defined by Whewell and Jones. After claiming Ricardo for theory, McCulloch immediately pointed out that Ricardo restricted his research and conclusions to rents that were paid by farmers cultivating for profit under a system of free competition. In other words, McCulloch noted, Ricardo's work referred to "rents as they actually exist in England, Holland, the United States, and a few other countries."[14] Ricardo did not intend, McCulloch continued, to define "taxes on the land imposed by the sovereign, and the sums wrung by taskmasters from the reluctant labour of slaves, [as] rent,"[15] just as he did not wish to call allowances to slaves in the West Indies "wages."

These statements clearly bring out the conceptual investments in McCulloch's use of the category of theory. I will sort out what seems to be a contradiction in this use. McCulloch initially seemed to argue that theory is a mode of explanation that does not represent actual conditions of life. But later he noted that in Ricardo's work theory does represent actual conditions of life, but not all of them. So the argument for theory did not necessarily exclude the condition of representability. McCulloch did not drive an absolute wedge between theory and actual life. Rather, he segregated certain kinds of practical conditions that according to him legitimately belonged to the domain of representability from others that did not. Political-economic principles, and, by extension, the practical field they adequately resembled, his vivisection suggested, were only for populations that lived and produced under free markets. The rest, like slave labor in West Indies and the labor of Asian cultivators, were banished from both the theoretical and the practical in political economy. This is how the contradiction in McCulloch's statements got resolved. McCulloch did retain both arguments: (a) theory and practice were in opposition, and Ricardo's work did not cover practical situations; here theory stood for free markets and practice for slavery; (b) theory and practice were unified, one neatly representing the other, in this case Ricardo's work explaining rents in England, Holland, and the United States. Thus, theory in political economy did not exclude the practical. On the contrary, it was rooted in practical conditions only. Despite this, for McCulloch, there were some forms of the practical that did not feature in this debate. Among them were the slaves and the ryots. They were pre-epistemological, unworthy of being considered part of the principles of a philosophy of knowledge—in this case, the theoretical and the practical of political economy.

The participants in the theory-practice debate soon suggested, as they explicated the conflictual terrain in greater detail, that the opposition was actually between good and bad theories. Ultimately, all of them defined theory as a form of explanation in which was included all practical phenomena. Apparently, Whewell and Jones, from a supposedly practical perspective, argued that in Ricardo's work theory did not represent factual conditions of life. But by the same token, they also implied that, it was not a theory at all. I have already noted that Whewellian inductivism emphasized the importance of facts, but only insofar as they expressed ideas or existed as appropriate materials for theory. In the same light, for Whewell, Jones's exposition of political economy, since it successfully explained all practical conditions of life, was theory in the true sense of the category. The debate, therefore, I argue, was not between theory and practice; rather, it was a conflict over different forms of the theoretical. Everyone agreed that true theory should be able to explain practice, or facts. The disagreement was over the conditions of production of these facts, or the principles that would determine what can be legitimate facts for political economy. There were different sets of a priori generalities with which all contestants in the field began their respective journeys toward the writing of political economy.

For example, in Ricardian political economy the definition of rent was based on the assumption of an economy where production was carried out by capitalist farmers and agricultural laborers on land leased from landlords. It is these practical conditions that the theory of rent sought to represent. Wherever production was carried out differently, those practical conditions remained out of its theoretical scope. In other words, it was a particular conceptualization of production (and distribution) that determined what theory, unified with practice, would look like. Whewell and Jones thought such a theory was useless, because it failed to explain the greater part of the world, where production (and distribution) prevailed in other forms.

Their attack was double-edged. On the one hand, Whewell argued that even if he accepted McCulloch's retort that Ricardo's definition of rent did not intend to cover all those payments that are commonly called rent, "the reader might be left to decide for himself which subject of inquiry may be the better worth his notice,—the rents that are actually paid in *every* country, or the Ricardian rents, which are *not* those actually paid in *any* country."[16] On the other hand, Whewell also emphasized that, contrary to what McCulloch represented, Ricardo did not confine his research to a small section of the world. His conclusions did have a claim of universality. Even Jones, in one of his letters to Whewell, maintained this position.[17] Keeping in mind this claim, Ricardo's theory seemed all the more baseless. Jones was amused by such universal claims that did not even remotely correspond to the facts of life. He asked his readers to imagine a situation where different kinds of landholders were being taught the fundamental doctrines of Ricardian political economy. The teacher was telling these landholders that their interest was opposed to the rest of the society, that rent depended on the fertility of soil only, that no improvements of their income might emerge from an increase of rents, or an increased fertility of the soil, and many more such Ricardian precepts. Jones remarked that the audience "would be apt to believe, that the philosopher they were listening to must have fallen from some other planet: that the scene of his experience must have differed widely from the scenes of theirs."[18]

For Jones and Whewell, all along it was a battle to prove greater universality. Thus, incorporating the practical, or, as I will document later, the "local/indigenous," into their explanatory framework, was an analytical move toward that end. I will show how Jones's political economy can be read as proposing a conceptual cast for the constitutive categories of political economy that was very different from the Ricardian one. This was indeed a more capacious political economy, not because it was more consistent with facts of the world and, therefore, could explain the world more truthfully. Its superiority inhered in the ability to produce, explain, and manage difference, which made it consonant with the imperatives of governance, imperial and otherwise. The epistemological constitution of this political economy was produced by a reworking of what I have previously identified as the key strategies of Whewellian inductivism, namely, association, classification, and unification. For Jones and Whewell, theory was about power in the form of governance—of ideas, facts, and the world, woven into each other. In this sense, Ricardo was powerless, as his theory was fragile. Whewell was pretty candid about this will to power. In a letter to Jones, he wrote: "You know as well as I do that those who theorize rightly are in the end the lords of the earth."[19] The program of induction, in its political-economic articulation, had the ambition of a super-synoptic gaze, which wished to wrap, at a single glance, the infinite diversity of lives and livelihoods in the world into a single frame of explanation.[20]

A New Land for Theory: James Mill and a Reinterpreted Ricardian Universalism

McCulloch was not the only interpreter of the problematic of representability in Ricardian political economy. Another Ricardian, James Mill, had a very different take on the matter. Like Whewell and Jones, he believed that a true theory should be able to account for all practical conditions of the world; unlike McCulloch, he did not think that Ricardian categories explained only the practical conditions of countries where production and distribution of wealth took place under conditions of a large population, a free market, and a capitalist economy. I am tempted to call him a truer follower of Ricardo. His systematic demonstration of the universality of Ricardo's system evinced his unwavering faith in it. Although Mill was perceived as an opponent of Whewellian inductivism, in his defense of theory there were critical underlying similarities with the kind of reorientation of political economy that Jones proposed. Like Jones's, Mill's political economy too tried to account for difference. Ultimately, however, it limited this possibility by making sense of difference in strictly Ricardian-universalist terms. In the process, it opened up a ground for the reconfiguration of the building blocks of political economy, only to close it hastily with a Ricardian consensus.

James Mill did not think, like McCulloch, that what Ricardo defined as rent was categorically different from other kinds of payments, like "taxes on the land imposed by the sovereign" in an Eastern country.[21] It is important here to highlight the presuppositions of this notion of difference. McCulloch argued, "From the remotest era down to the present moment, the land of almost every Eastern country has been regarded as the exclusive property of the sovereign, who was thus enabled to fix the terms on which it should be occupied."[22] In England, land belonged to individuals, and cultivators were not enslaved. For McCulloch, a difference in the structures of property ownership between England and the "Eastern countries" made the Ricardian category of rent inapplicable to the latter. Evidently, this was a view based on the perception of a fundamental linkage between property and political power. It is this linkage that defined despotism as an absolute and arbitrary form of power rooted in the total ownership of property by the sovereign. In

McCulloch's scheme, such was the basis of the polity of all "Eastern countries," different from the free and individual forms of property ownership in England, which laid the foundation of its polity. In this conceptual constellation, property ownership was imagined to be constitutive of political power, and a property-power complex was supposed to demarcate the epistemological field of political economy. Based on these assumptions, McCulloch reasoned that "despotic" polities cannot be legitimate domains of political-economic inquiry. For him, they harbored those practical conditions that the theory of political economy did not need to address.

James Mill, however, did not envision these despotic polities as lying beyond the scope of Ricardian political economy. While admitting that political-economic analysis is embedded in the relation between property and political power, he defined this relation differently. He argued that not only the form of property ownership but also the category of property itself in India was different from its European counterpart. He noted, "In a state of society resembling our own, in which property is secure, and involves very extensive rights or privileges . . . in minds of little range . . . the particulars combined together under the idea of property appear to be connected by nature."[23] It would be presumptuous, Mill emphasized, to infer from this perception of property that the category expressed the same kinds of rights at all times and in all places. On the contrary, by the gradual association of different kinds of rights, the category of property came into shape differently in different places. It is only with a considerable civilizational progress, Mill suggested, that property can be found to convey all those rights that characterized its European form.

But in India, Mill argued, although the sovereign was the lord of the soil, there were important restrictions to his right of property. The ryot, or peasant cultivator, who held land, could not be removed from possession by the sovereign if he continued to pay the amount of assessment demanded from him. His right of possession was saleable during his life and inheritable after his death. Describing the proprietary status of the ryot, Mill remarked: "I should think it might be more properly expressed by saying that he has a property in the land, than that he has the property of the land. There is no doubt that he has a property in it, because he has a right of perpetual occupancy, and the right of cultivation, subject to the demands of government."[24]

Although Mill admitted that landed property in India was different from that in Europe by including the right of the ryot within the semantic fold of "property," he did not take this redefinition too far. His explanation ultimately took a Ricardian turn, when he chose to make two connected analytical moves. First, he marked the right to receive rent as the defining feature of property, thereby acknowledging the (rent-receiving) sovereign's right in the land as superior to the (rent-paying) ryot's.[25] Therefore, he also contended that the ryot's right, instead of being "proprietary," was, effectively, merely a right to cultivate the same field.[26] Second, he categorized the government demand on the ryot as rent, in the Ricardian sense of the term, by describing it as "the surplus, after the capital and labour bestowed upon the produce has been replaced and paid."[27] He argued that "according to the practice and law of India, the full rent is due of Government."[28] This practice, he emphasized, "has no inconsiderable recommendation from science itself. Previous to allotment, the productive powers of the soil are the joint property of the community; and hence are a fund peculiarly adapted to the joint or common purposes and demands."[29] By representing the state in India as the sovereign proprietor of land, or the universal landlord, he established the contemporary political-economic category of rent as something consistent with age-old "Indian" practice.

As an administrative prescription, therefore, which had already been established by him as a practice continuous with the past, Mill noted that the legitimate limit of the government demand was the full rent. He admitted that this limit had not been always followed in the past, when arbitrary exactions took over the political-economic or "scientific" principle of taxation. But even then he did not believe "that such is a necessary consequence of the system by any means."[30] Not only did Mill graft the Ricardian category of rent onto the government dues from land in India, he also used Ricardo's critical attitude toward the rent receivers, or landlords, in a significantly reinterpreted manner. By defining the government dues as rent, and not as a tax on either capital or revenue, he exorcized what Ricardian political economy had called "the great evil of taxation."[31] Rent, as an income of private landlords in Europe, had already been identified in political economy as devoid of productive value. Mill's construal of the state in India as the paramount landlord was, therefore, fundamentally, a critique of the institution of private property arising from the reception of rent. Mill suggested that it was only a particular form of property ownership, where the state was the universal landlord, that allowed the full rent to be the basis of the fund derived from taxation, as this was to be spent by the state toward the improvement of the community. At this point his analysis took a turnaround, as Mill hierarchized difference in the reverse direction. The kind of linkage between property and political power he favored was present in India and absent in Europe.

This difference was becoming crucial to the field of inquiry of political economy itself. The question of universalizability, or the "theory-practice" conversation, was predicated on varying constructions of difference. More important, in the process the linkage between property and political power was being perceived as the (new) constitutive ground of political economy. For McCulloch, this perception was brought out in his review of Jones's work. In Mill, it was clearly recognized and discussed in detail but ultimately analyzed in a Ricardian light. Other than in his administrative works, Mill also highlighted it in his book *The Elements of Political Economy*. After defining rent in the same manner as Ricardo, Mill argued that "it is sufficiently obvious, that the share of the rent of land, which may be taken to defray the expenses of the government, does not affect the industry of the country."[32] He further noted that while in the major polities of Asia "almost the whole expenses of the state have in all ages been defrayed from the rent of land," in Europe such defrayal took place only in the remote past when the sovereign was the proprietor of land and the greater part of the expenses of the country was defrayed from the rent of the land. Interestingly, this equivalence between the European past and the Asian present was not cast into the mold of a progressivist hierarchy. Europe's present did not feature as the final teleological destination in James Mill's analysis of the linkage between property and political power. Rather, Mill seemed to lament over Europe's present. His anguish was blurted out in *The History of British India*:

> The benefits of the soil have . . . over the greater part of the globe, been employed, first, to supply in whole, or for the greater part, the necessities of government, next to enrich the individual occupant. The most remarkable exception to this rule is in modern Europe. After the conquests of the Gothic nations, the land was thrown in great portions into the hands of the leading men; and they had power to make the taxes fall where they chose; they took care accordingly that they should fall any where rather than upon the land; that is, upon any body rather than themselves . . . they not only threw the burden off their own shoulders, but taxed, as they have continued to do, and sometimes on a progressive ration, to the present hour, the rest of the community for their benefit.[33]

This is how James Mill established the relation between property and political power as the structuring principle of the field of political-economic knowledge. His elaboration of differences between the modes of property ownership, and their attendant forms of political power, in India and Europe was a necessary epistemological building block for his subsequent political-economic analysis, which was unambiguously Ricardian. But his vision expanded the theoretical scope of Ricardian political economy, by using it to explain conditions that were based on a linkage between property and political power radically different from that of England. This reinterpretation suggested that the Ricardian framework was suited equally well to the relationship of property and power that it claimed to be based upon, and to conditions that were radically different. Thus, for Mill, Ricardian theory seemed to be valid for both "free" and "despotic" forms of property ownership and the polities based on them.

It is here that my reading of James Mill deviates from that of Stokes. Stokes argued that Ricardian ideas were radicalized by Mill when he used the Ricardian definition of rent to put forward an absolute critique of private property. As he noted about Mill's program: "To advocate state ownership or nationalization of the soil was to strike at the whole Liberal tradition for which the institution of private property was the tap-root of progress and individual liberty."[34] But this was not a simple radicalization of Ricardian categories. Mill's reinterpretation of Ricardo needs to be located within the epistemological turn in contemporary political economy. As I have demonstrated, Mill's political-economic articulations were constituted by careful examinations of indigenous forms of interrelations between property and political power. In other words, Mill's political economy was suggestive of a new vocabulary but was limited in not being entirely able to exorcize its Ricardian commitments. That is why, for Mill, the argument about state ownership of land did not signify a particularity of "Eastern/despotic" polities. On the contrary, it stood for the past condition of all nations of the world, and the ideal route for progress. In this scheme, it was England's polity that was exceptional, since at its foundation was a regressive form of linkage between property and political power.

Thus, the practical conditions identified by McCulloch as external to political-economic theory were explained by Mill in the light of a redefined Ricardianism. His construal of rent, property, and taxation in the context of British India, I argue, were linked to, and consistent with, his methodological position on the theory-practice debate. Unlike McCulloch, Mill believed that true theory should be consonant with all practical conditions of the world. A return to the theory-practice opposition at this point is imperative, as James Mill was a seminal contributor to this methodological debate. In an imaginary dialogue entitled "Theory and Practice," written for the *London and Westminster Review*, Mill analyzed the problem. The essay presented a conversation between two men, marked X and Y, in which the former began by positing a total inconsistency between theory and practice, while the latter gradually and successfully persuaded the former about the necessary unity between the two. Interestingly, at the end of the conversation Y declared: "When a man says that he follows practice, he says by the same words that he follows theory. All men, therefore, in every rational action of their lives are followers of theory; and they may be divided . . . into the two following classes—those who follow good and those who follow bad theory; the first sort acting always right."[35]

Almost echoing the convictions of Jones and Whewell, Mill seemed to argue that the difference between theory and practice is actually that between good and bad theories. This was because his work showed that (good) theory is based on an ability to account for difference within its universality. Accordingly, Mill believed that a philosopher, whose task is to make theory as expansive as possible, was also the best practitioner, an idea suiting the rationality of governance.[36] The emphasis Mill places on observation in this essay, his call to make all practice consistent with theory, and also his argument that ultimately all practice is reducible to a small number of fundamental philosophical principles—all these commonalities, in my opinion, question the methodological distance Whewell and Jones posited between themselves and the Ricardians.[37] These opposed positions did merge into each other in many important ways. They created the necessary ground for an epistemological shift in political economy, rewritten by difference as the constitutive ground for its new universality. Let us now turn to Richard Jones to explore the clearest articulations of this shift.

Redefining Political Economy

Jones wrote *An Essay on the Distribution of Wealth and on the Sources of Taxation* in 1831, following which, in 1833, he was appointed as professor of political economy at King's College, London.[38] The *Essay* was a treatise on rent, and also the first part of a projected work on other major categories of political economy. Jones, however, was not a prolific writer. The other parts never got written. Jones became significant, to his contemporaries, primarily as a critic of Ricardo, which obviously reflects the enormous influence Ricardo's theory of rent—with which Jones directly engaged—had in intellectual circles in Britain at that time.[39] In 1835, Jones was appointed by the Court of Directors of the East India Company to the chair of political economy and history at the East India College at Haileybury.[40] This appointment indicated that his political economy had acquired a different kind of significance in contemporary Britain. Jones called his work a political economy of *nations*, which, I believe, made him important for an institution like the East India College. As is well known, the East India College was that pedagogical site where future administrators of British India were educated in all those branches of knowledge that were considered the intellectual backbone of governance. Political economy, as is evident, was one of the most important subjects in this curriculum of governance. Interestingly, this subject was taught at the East India College, as "political economy and history," which shows that within the scheme of imperial governance these two branches of knowledge were considered necessarily interdependent. Also, such a mode of classification was almost naturally suited to Jones's work, where "history" had a constitutive role to play in reconceptualizing political economy. For Jones, such intimate connections between his work, the East India College, and the college's way of classifying knowledge, remained lifelong. He died in the college on 20 January 1855 and was buried in the neighboring churchyard of Amwell.

When he was appointed professor of political economy at King's College, London, Jones gave a public lecture on what he considered to be the fundamental problem of this domain of knowledge. He argued, not surprisingly, that the main task of political economy was the analysis of "*differences* in the productive power and operations of different nations."[41] Political economy, as was commonly understood, produced knowledge of the laws governing production and distribution of wealth. Jones emphasized that although, temporally speaking, production preceded distribution, analytically considered the latter should be the core area of inquiry in political economy. The mode of distribution—of the surplus produce of the soil—was embedded in the different forms of property ownership in different nations. These proprietary relations, in turn, expressed the organizing principle of political power in every society. Jones declared these linkages in unequivocal terms. The distribution of produce, in the form of property, he noted, "has served, in the great majority of instances, to establish the first rude framework of political society. We see wealth, and the mode of its distribution, assuming an active influence, in creating the ties which bind the body politic together, and determine, by their form and complication, its character, and often its resources."[42]

This exposition, I argue, signaled the first coherent reinterpretation of political economy in nineteenth-century Britain. It brought out the linkage between property and political power as the epistemological object of political-economic analysis. We have already seen that its universality was a hidden assumption among Ricardians of various kinds. The analytical significance of the interrelationship between property and political power was teased out in the debates over theory and practice, which took place between political economists who *claimed* to be methodological enemies of each other. Further, the problem of difference became central to the determination of the nature of the universality of this new foundation of political economy. McCulloch circumscribed its universalizability by denying Eastern/despotic nations a place in its fold. It was reinvested with a greater explanatory potential, however, with James Mill's rewriting of Ricardianism in the light of the relationship between landed property and political power in British India. All of this reflected the constitutive role of difference in the making of political-economic universals.

Richard Jones's work, I argue, represented a logical culmination of these related—even if posited as opposed—conversations. Jones foregrounded difference as the key to the reconfigured object of political economy by drawing attention to the varying forms of property-power linkages in different nations of the world. These relations between modes of property ownership and the frameworks of political power that sustained them, argued Jones, structured the sphere of "distribution" in political economy. He insisted that that it should be considered as analytically prior to the sphere of "production." Here was his crucial critique of contemporary political-economic frameworks, especially the dominant Ricardian one. Ricardo understood the sphere of distribution as consisting of a tripartite division of the produce into "rent," "wage," and "profit," between landlords, capitalist farmers, and agricultural laborers, respectively. The temporal assumption here was that distribution of the produce could take place only *after* its production. The universality of this temporal sequence was, however, dependent upon a crucial analytical excision of distribution from the temporality of a narrative where production was located as an absolute, pristine point of beginning. The problem with the narrative's internal logic of temporality is that its imagined autonomy of production as a transcendental point of origin sat awkwardly with its general characterization of the relation between production and distribution.

It was assumed in Ricardo's work that this *relation* between production and distribution is universal. The variation is only that "in different stages of society, the proportions of the whole produce of the earth which will be allotted to each of these classes, under the name of rent, profit and wages, will be essentially different."[43] But at the same time, Ricardo's theory of rent stated that rent as a proportion of the produce distinct from profits and wages can arise only at an advanced state of cultivation, with the gradual extension of cultivation beyond the most fertile lands. It is only when cultivation is pushed to inferior soils that rent as a measure of differential natural fertility of soil emerges as a separately identifiable proportion of the produce. At an early stage of cultivation, when fertile land is abundant, Ricardo noted, "there will be no rent; for no one would pay for the use of land, when there was an abundant quantity not yet appropriated, and, therefore, at the disposal of whosoever might choose to cultivate it."[44] If the division of the sphere of distribution into rent, profit, and wage was an universal one, as argued by Ricardo, then what did the sphere of distribution consist of when there was no rent? The framework of property itself—within which distribution took place as rent, profit, and wage—disappeared at this point in Ricardo's analysis. Ricardo seemed to suggest that this was a temporality of pure production, uncontained by the shackles of distribution, which his general framework, where production and distribution were necessarily interrelated, did not allow.[45]

For Jones, however, the temporality of production and distribution remained unified, at all times and in all places. Production, Jones argued, was already-always imbricated in distribution. In fact, in the Jonesian scheme of things, it was the mode of distribution that organized production and, therefore, made the category of production itself contingent—differently shaped according to different modes of distribution. As I argued earlier, the sphere of distribution, according to Jones, was the framing of property forms by political power. This ensemble in Jones was also the container of the "social." In his King's College lecture, he traced its operations."Labour, continuously bestowed upon the soil," Jones noted, "supposes property in the soil to be established."[46] Further, he pointed out that "property in the soil almost universally rests, at one time of a people's career, either in the general government, or in persons deriving their interest from it."[47] It is this primary relation of property—between owners and cultivators of the soil—that, Jones noted, "practically bind[s] together different ranks in all the regions of the world."[48] From this point, Jones started outlining the emergence of different relations over time in different nations, out of these primary ones. As he had pointed out earlier, they determined the conditions and capacities of production in these nations.

This was certainly a hierarchical scheme, although Jones remained cautious about extolling the virtues of advancement.[49] He began with "Asiatic nations," where the primary division of the surplus was between the sovereign, his officers, and the cultivators. The nonagricultural populations in these nations, he argued, were paid by the sovereign from this surplus. Coming to Eastern European nations, he noted that similar relations persisted between the bondsmen, the nobility, and the nonagricultural classes.

As he came to countries of Western Europe, particularly England, he argued that there was a notable difference in the structure of these relations. This change in assemblage of proprietary relations and political power strikingly affected and improved the conditions under which production took place, or, in Jones's words, "the management and productiveness of labour."[50]

The change was primarily signified by the arrival of the capitalists, as an intermediate class between proprietors and laborers, both agricultural and nonagricultural. Capitalists brought in their wake "capital," which Jones defined as "accumulated wealth with a view to profit."[51] This distinct portion of wealth constituted the fund from which laborers of all kinds received their wages. This is how Jones explained the emergence of the specifically Ricardian sphere of distribution, marked by its tripartite division of wealth as rent, wages, and profits. In Jones's political economy, therefore, the distribution of wealth among landlords, capitalists, and laborers in one form of society did not exclude its distribution in other forms. Rather, Jones regarded these different distributions as conditional upon different articulations of the national property-power enmeshment. Thus, he explained rent, profits, and wages in all those countries where the capitalists had not yet appeared in a different way, as produced by the particular relations between proprietors, laborers, and nonagricultural classes. This structuring logic, however, as he emphasized, remained strong even after the significant change introduced by capital, as old forms gave way to new ones. He noted that "the ties which formerly bound the community together are worn out and fall to pieces; other bonds, other principles of cohesion connect its different classes."[52]

Jones's inductive political economy, along with its hierarchy of nations, was undoubtedly rooted in historical determinism. But Jones was less interested in its grand teleological implications. Political economy's task, he believed, did not consist in predicting the future on the basis of a common temporality of progress for all nations. He clearly pointed out that "the future of all other people will, however, at some time, be like our present. Be it so . . . but still the interest we have in the future, however great, can but be a subordinate interest after all."[53] Contemporary political economists, Jones believed, suffered from the assumption of a single future for the entire world. This prevented them from looking at the world around them in its own terms, in the light of different histories and different presents. By focusing solely on their own conditions, political economists believed that "if we do not get a knowledge of the phenomena which the rest of the people of the earth present to the philosopher as his materials, we shall at least get a knowledge of a state of things, which will one day be theirs and is destined to be universal."[54] Such blinkered futurism, Jones argued, doomed political economy to false generalizations based on gross ignorance. The world, he said, was not going to erase its differences and become one in any conceivable future. Change would be slow and extremely imperceptible. This approach, therefore, would provide political economy with no analytical means to look at the world as it was and explain the various conditions of livelihood existing in it.

Method, Rent, and Governance

History primarily inspired Jones as an organizing principle of political economy. It explained the present of all nations. Political economy, Jones argued, could establish general principles only on the basis of a rigorous observation of facts. For this, he noted, "there are open to us two sources of knowledge,—history and statistics, the story of the past, and a detail of the present condition of the nations of the earth."[55] These two modes of knowledge constituted the analytical "eye" of inductivism in political economy. While "history," during Jones's time, had become accepted as a legitimate mode of knowledge, "statistics" had not. Jones remained emphatic about its use in political economy. He argued for its systematization and urged the formation of statistical societies in England.[56] In one of his letters to Whewell, he also mentioned his plan of proposing the formation of a statistical society to the British Association for the Advancement of Science. The society, he noted, should deal with various kinds of statistics. He enlisted them as: "Economical statistics . . . Political Statistics . . . Legal Statistics . . . Finance . . . Medical Statistics . . . Moral & Intellectual statistics . . . Ecclesiastical statistics."[57]

Such was Jones's political-economic vision. He effected a major rewriting of the contemporary articulations of this field of knowledge. This political economy was historical, statistical, and even ethnographic. In its epistemological and methodological constitution, it was unselfconsciously Whewellian. Jones's political economy assembled itself with the main tools of inductivism, namely, association, classification, and unification. Although it claimed to be based on facts alone, in selecting and organizing a great variety of such facts, or observed particulars, according to a certain principle, it was aimed at producing universals, predicated on difference. By looking closely into the indigenous conditions of power and property in different nations of the world, this political economy produced the local as immanent to and constitutive of the universal. Jones made political economy look more like a comparative political sociology of nations. Thus, what Jones and Whewell posited in this rewriting as inductivism, or the championing of facts over abstract theory, I argue, can be more productively interpreted as a theoretical reconfiguration and a methodological diversification of political economy. As I intend to demonstrate gradually, such changes in the object and texture of knowledge in this area merged seamlessly with the imperatives of imperial governance.

This focus on the indigenous conditions of property and political power, as they emerged historically and functioned at present to define social relations, can be understood better if we look at rent, one of the central categories of Jones's political economy. Jones himself argued that the main object of his political economy was rent. He emphasized that "we may be prepared . . . to see without surprise, the different systems of rents which . . . have arisen out of the peculiar circumstances of different people, forming the main ties which hold society together, determining the nature of the connection between the governing part of the community and the governed, and stamping on a very large portion of the population of the whole globe their most striking features, social, political, and moral."[58] In a certain sense, therefore, for Jones, rent determined all aspects of a society, or the character of a nation.

Ultimately, Jones argued that it is the conditions within which human labor operated that determined the precise nature of rents, wages, and profits and, thereby, the laws of production and distribution of wealth.[59] These conditions, he argued, were structured by an assemblage of property and political power, and were different throughout the world. He argued that the different forms of distribution of wealth equate with different shares of incomes generated from land. Thus, he noted, "If that soil belongs to others, this circumstance alone makes the peasants at once tributary to the proprietors, and a portion of the produce is distributed as *Rent*. If besides the soil other things are needful to facilitate their exertions, to the owner of these things another part of the produce must be resigned, and hence the origin of *Profits*. The share of the labourer, the reward of mere personal exertion, in whatever shape, or manner, or time, it may be received, constitute the *Wages* of labour."[60]

Jones went on to document a variety of rents existing in different parts of the world. He described them as labor, metayer, cottier, ryot, and farmer's rents. He traced the origin of each of these to the different histories of the nations in which they existed. Jones argued that not only rents but also wages and profits were expressions of relations of power around land. These relations conditioned the efficiency of labor, thereby dictating production of wealth, in general. In the case of labor rents, for example, Jones stated that landed proprietors allotted a portion of their estate to cultivators, from which the latter were supposed to draw their subsistence. In exchange, as rent for that land, they were to provide their labor to the proprietors. Jones argued that such a relationship between the proprietor and cultivator of land had ruinous consequences on the conditions of labor: "The industry of serfs, then, is found to be neither continuous, skilful, nor powerfully aided. . . . The peasant who depends for his food upon his labour in his own allotment of ground, and is yet liable to be called away at the discretion and convenience of another person to work upon other lands, in the produce of which he is not to share, is naturally a reluctant labourer."[61] In this way, Jones explained rent, in each case, as an articulation of a particular calculus of power between proprietors and cultivators of land. As he developed his explanation of rent, he candidly dismissed Ricardo's. He remarked: "The necessity then, which compels them to pay a rent, it need hardly be observed, is wholly independent of any difference in the quality of the ground they occupy, and would not be removed were the soils all equalized."[62]

Ryot rents, Jones argued, were peculiar to Asia. He described ryots as "hereditary occupiers," having attributes of both tenants and proprietors. He pointed out that "they are proprietors, inasmuch as they are unquestionably and incontestably entitled to possess, and to transmit to their children, the soil which they cultivate. They are tenants, inasmuch as they have rarely a beneficial interest in the soil; or inasmuch as they have to pay rent."[63] Jones traced the origin of these rents to an Asiatic mode of governance, and their present condition to administrative arrangements of the British government. Like James Mill, he also argued that Asiatic sovereigns used to be supreme landlords. But he drew a different sketch of India's property-power structure. Unlike Mill, he did not view the ancient Asiatic state as the unambiguous embodiment of the particular complex of proprietary relations and political power that the ryot rents were embedded in. In Jones's understanding, India's property-power matrix was less centralized than what Mill thought it to be. Jones depicted it as a much more diffused and dispersed arena of sovereignty. In his scheme, it looked like a mélange of various kinds of landholders and landholding bodies. Rent was a transaction that defined this complex and determined the overlapping yet separate jurisdictions of power.

It is in such inductive operations of dealing with the facts of India's property-power complex that Jones's political economy found its conceptual resonance with governance in British India during that period. As will be evident in the upcoming chapters, the ways in which practices of governance understood, classified, defined, and governed interrelations of property and sovereignty in British India had remarkable similarities with Jones's foregrounding and examination of indigenous property-power relations in different nations of the world. Such simultaneities will be explored later within a more contextualized discussion of agrarian governance. This is how Whewellian inductivism as a method, Jonesian formulation of rent as a category of political economy, and the rationality of practices of governance in British India established constitutive connections between each other.

Conclusion

In this way a critical epistemological reorientation took place in the world of political economy in early nineteenth-century Britain. As I argued in the Introduction, this opened up a novel horizon for the meaning of labor, as production, which, as Foucault argues, emerged as the constitutive category of the discourse of political economy during this period.[64] It is here, at the very moment of the foundation of this political economy, that production (conditions of laboring), was redefined as local/indigenous forms of power, understood in terms of nationally varying interrelations between sovereignty and property. This was a profound transformation at the level of the object of knowledge of political economy. This chapter has argued that this change came about through a conceptual struggle over the appropriate ground for the universality of political economy. The struggle went on within the Ricardian framework, ending with the foregrounding of difference as the foundation for the new universal of political economy. Here, I track the making of this theoretical capacity in political economy—to universalize, in and as difference. It shows how inductivism, beyond its self-styling as a "factual" enterprise, provided crucial theoretical tools toward this end.

To grasp the significance of this reconfiguration at another, connected level, I argue, it will be necessary to see how similar processes were at work in the governance of quotidian agrarian affairs in British India during this period. The ensuing chapters bring out the rationalities immanent in a range of governmental practices across a variety of localities in British India. They argue that the new political-economic universal, namely, varying assemblages of property and political power, also underpinned agrarian governance in British India, but in a transformed manner. This transformation was effected through an analytical framework that classified localities on the basis of complex spatio-temporal interconstitutivities, rallying around the idea of an original, indigenous form of a sovereignty-property matrix. The next chapter begins where this one ends. It takes a plunge into the agrarian affairs of early nineteenth-century British India by tracking the career of rent—one of its chief governmental categories, which was also, as we have seen in Jones, the gateway to the changed political economy.

CHAPTER 2

The Trace of the Local

Rent

In 1837, the East India Company's government began the first survey and settlement of the lands of Cuttack. Since 1803, when the Company established its government in Cuttack, its lands had been settled several times for varying short durations. But things were markedly different this time. The government seemed to be occupying every nook and corner of the agrarian landscape of Cuttack. In every village, on every plot of land, there were government men. They came with questions. They also came with machines. They measured land, decided disputes between villagers over field boundaries and proprietary titles, asked about the rates of different types of land, the crops, the cows, looked for deeds of ownership, and held assemblies with the headmen of villages, zemindars, and cultivators of various kinds. The proceedings of the collectorates in Cuttack, of the Bengal government, and of the India Office records suggest unequivocally that there was quite a crowd in the villages of Cuttack in these years. This chapter marks the beginning of a search in the by-lanes of these crowded places. In the upcoming chapters, the search continues, as the book attempts to understand what governance was looking for in the agrarian territory of Cuttack during this period. Instead of examining quotidian practices of governance as an infinite range of contingent and pragmatic negotiations with on-the-spot matters, the book posits an epistemological matrix as the structuring logic of governance.[1] In delineating this matrix, I follow the trail set up in the previous chapter by reorientations in political economy in early nineteenth-century Britain. I read agrarian governance in British India during this period as a particular articulation of political economy—one that established as its object of inquiry the interrelationship between property and political power. In the process, I also reflectively demonstrate the nature of this formation, that is, governance—its rhythms, connections, disjunctions, and transformations. Here, the exercise begins with the category of rent.

The chapter argues that practices of governance construed rent as the entry point, or opening, into the different property-power relationships in British India in the first half of the nineteenth century. By examining myriad articulations of rent across a range of administrative sites, it claims that the category of rent, instead of being perceived as a sign of the differential productive capacity of soil, was debated and developed as the most important historical trace of different kinds of proprietary power. Rent was used to understand the particular forms of interrelations between property and political power operative in different localities. It was defined as that crucial transaction that organized these relationships in and through constant contestations. Thus, governmental strategies produced rent as a trace of power.[2] Rent was supposed to reveal the indigenous nature of sovereignty and, thereby, the form of property in India. That is why even its Ricardian articulations got recast, or unpacked, as I will explain later, in terms of questions of power. Accordingly, over the first half of nineteenth century, the regulation of rent was set up as one of the major tasks of agrarian governance, as that was supposed to put proprietary relations in a certain order. This chapter shows how this formulation was assembled by networks of governance, along with various strategies to map, supervise, and control rent.

In following this political-economic/governmental career of rent, I travel in and out of Cuttack, through times before and after the settlement. I indicate that this small territory in British India was a complex site where governmental practices of other regions jostled as overlapping, contradictory, and interconstitutive forces. Its history has to be envisioned as necessarily intertwined, connected and, therefore, written simultaneously with histories of other regions. The nature of these entanglements are studied in greater detail in the next chapter. For the time being, it will be sufficient to note that from the moment Cuttack was presented as an anomalous zone in the world of British Indian agrarian governance, it was also made regular. Its isolation as an exception could be made possible only through its integration with the ordinary. This play in governance, which I understand as the sign of a failure to divide neatly into oppositions of inclusion and exclusion, sameness and difference, comparisons and contrasts, generality and specificity, was critically activated by the hunt for rent. I deal in this chapter both with the play and its elusive object.

Rent as Trace

In 1812, a comprehensive discussion on revenue administration in British India was presented to the British Parliament in the *Fifth Report from the Select Committee of East India Affairs*. In outlining revenue matters, the report foregrounded a general critique of the Bengal Code, namely, the Cornwallis-inspired model of administration, which was established in Bengal in 1793. It was argued in the report that the Bengal Code was ill suited to several "local" conditions. Accordingly, the report discussed a number of alternative administrative arrangements that were considered to be more sensitive to local characteristics. Such local differences mainly referred to the variety in proprietary relations, or forms of tenures, in the different territories of the Company. The report used rent as a tool to make sense of these differences in proprietary forms and the forms of political power they were embedded in. In the process, the relations—between property and sovereignty—it ended up excavating are taken up in the next chapter. Here, I focus on this particular governmental use and understanding of rent.

Generally, the report suggested that in India, the ryots, or peasant cultivators, held the most authentic form of proprietary right in land. This property right existed in the most ancient times, when the country was under Hindu rule. Since then, during the oppressive period of Muslim rule, a successively corrupt gradation of property rights had emerged in India. The report noted that traces of this authentic proprietary form were particularly evident in the lands of Jaghire, which were occupied by "the ryots, who are immediately connected to the soil" and "may be reduced to two denominations, *Meerassadars*, and *Pyacarries* or *Paracoodies*."[3] It further observed: "Though the Meerassadars appear for some years to have been regarded in the light of fixed cultivators only, with an hereditary right of occupancy, so long as they paid the dues of the government; more particular enquiry seems to have established the fact, that they possess a real property in the land, having the right of mortgaging, selling, and otherwise disposing of it; and that this right they have always, and do still exercise."[4] Wherever this tenure existed in its most "perfect," that is, ancient form, the report argued, the Meerassadars enjoyed a "landlord's rent" from the lands as cultivators or a "quit rent," if the lands were given to someone else for cultivation.

It is in these lands, which "were last invaded by the northern conquerors, and in which therefore primitive institutions and rights have undergone less change," that the government, "supposing their rights in the soil as proprietors to be indisputable," never tripped over the line between "fair assessment" and "exaction."[5] The discursive move here was that of establishing the possibility of conceptually separating "dues of government" from "rent," in order to validate the existence of property as an ancient and indigenous form in India. It was the right to rent, and not other characteristics, like transferability and heritability, that was posited as the decisive index of property. Thus, the report noted, where government assessment was so high as to disallow a rent, the "land, naturally ceased to be, either a mortgageable, or a saleable commodity."[6] In other words, where rent disappeared, so did property.

It is evident that the question of property here was also that of power. The entire attempt to prove the *presence* of an indigenous form of private property was also one of disproving the old and influential idea that in India there was an *absence* of the former, as the state was the absolute and exclusive proprietor.[7] The analytical isolation of rent in the *Fifth Report* performed as the setting up of a threshold where the absolutism of power got arrested, qualified, and divided. Like all thresholds, this too was precarious, as this rendition of history suggested. Thus, rent was staged as a trace of that threshold, which signified the presence of property. Once again, like all traces, this was also haunted by its other, its absence—the totalizing state. Henceforth, governmental practices deployed rent as a trace and, thereby, understood its regulation as the necessary ritual of exorcising it of its threatening other. Such rituals consecrated the proprietary order in British India during this period, which I examine in the next chapter. Consequently, in the representations of the *Fifth Report*, we see, rent was comprehended less as a measure of differential fertility and more as a trace of power differential.

The Unfulfilled Promise of the Permanent Settlement

John Herbert Harington came to British India as a writer in 1780, during the governor-generalship of Warren Hastings. His official career lasted for nearly half a century. Over this period Harington occupied several important judicial positions in the Company's government. He served variously as the magistrate of Dinagepore, as the register of Sudder Dewanny and Nizamat Adawlut, as a member of the Board of Revenue, and as the judge of Sudder Dewanny and Nizamat Adawlut.[8] His influential two-volume analysis of the Bengal Regulations used to function as a manual for all district officers in Bengal. Just before retirement, in 1827, Harington wrote a treatise on the question of tenures in Bengal, entitled "Minute and Draft of Regulation, of the Rights of Ryots in Bengal." It must be remembered that Harington's text was produced in an administrative milieu that was critical of the way landed property had been treated during the Permanent Settlement of Bengal. This critique was on the rise right from the first decade of the nineteenth century.[9] It was primarily invested in redefining the field of landed property, not only in Bengal, but also in other parts of British India, which were gradually coming under the Company's government.

At various levels of governance, it was being argued that the Permanent Settlement of Bengal had mistakenly established the zemindars, or big landlords, as the exclusive proprietors of the soil. In doing this it had swept away a great variety of proprietary rights possessed by different kinds of landholders.[10] Harington's essay is important as it is symptomatic of the significance of this shift in the discourse of governance. It suggested an interpretation of the Permanent Settlement focusing on the question of rent. Harrington argued that there were provisions *within* the act that, if properly implemented, would have prevented its greatest errors. He claimed that the regulations of the Permanent Settlement contained the possibilities of preserving the various proprietary rights of groups other than the zemindars—primarily the ryots, but also others, like the dependent talookdars—in Bengal. Unfortunately, such possibilities were never clearly defined and enforced by the government.

This variegated proprietary regime could have been maintained, Harington argued, only by a careful regulation of rent.[11] He noted that the systematic administration of rent had been one of the major concerns of the Permanent Settlement. By presenting extracts from the results of John Shore's investigation into the tenures of Bengal, which were supposed to be the basis of the Permanent Settlement, Harington suggested that rent, as the primary marker of property, was present at the heart of this measure of governance.[12] He viewed Shore as insisting that the Permanent Settlement should be based on a precise and transparent regulation of rent payable by the ryots and other undertenants to the zemindars. Shore wrote, "The Rents to be paid by the Ryots, by whatever rule or custom they may be demanded, shall be specific as to their amount. If by a Pottah, containing the Assul and Abwab, the amount of both shall be inserted in it. . . . In every Mofussil Cutcherry, the Nirkbundy, or rates of land, shall be publicly recorded, and the Zemindar is answerable for enforcing this Regulation, under a penalty or fine for neglect, at the discretion of Government."[13] In this manner, emphasized Harrington, Shore recommended an entire infrastructure of regulation, distributed over the village, the Pergunnah and the headquarters of the collectorate, which was supposed to record fixed rates of rents and justly govern transactions between landholders. Harington regretted that this regulatory mechanism was not instituted as part of the Permanent Settlement. He pointed out, however, quoting the famous scholar-administrator Henry Colebrooke this time, that the act reserved the right for the government to introduce measures to protect these subordinate tenures, like ryots, talookdars, and others.[14] After concluding his "Minute," Harington put forward the various clauses of the regulation he proposed for the protection of the rights of ryots. The regulation put together, in a summarized form, his central focus, namely, the ascertainment of legitimate rents and modes of governing their fair operation. This was considered the essential mechanism for protecting and maintaining all proprietary rights in land.

Both the *Fifth Report* and Harrington's "Minute" were centrally concerned with the governance of property in land. Equally important, for our purposes, is that they served as seminal instances of a style of governmental practice that is self-critical. Both presented themselves as reviews of past mistakes and proposals for future corrections. Informing each other, therefore, both urged for a self-limiting of governance, which, interestingly, could only be achieved by a greater extension of governance than before—in the form of detailed inquiries into tenures.[15] Rent was fashioned as the pivotal instrument for this grand review of property, which continued well into the latter half of the nineteenth century. Parts of southern India got connected with Bengal, and governmental imperatives in new territories were brought back to older ones, as it was admitted, for all these sites, albeit differently, that government had to re-cognize various kinds of proprietary rights on land, the definitive marker of which was a right to shares of rent enjoyed by different groups on land. Unlike the *Fifth Report*, Harington's "Minute" did not spell out these rights for specific groups in Bengal. But in arguing that a careful definition and recording of rent could have prevented the Permanent Settlement from destroying proprietary rights vested in groups other than the zemindars, Harington effectively implied that property could only be secured for these tenures by assuring them their shares of the rent. For this the zemindars and the government, as an interrelated practice, had to limit their proprietary claims, or control over rent. Repeating the future in the past, by linking the aims of an influential contemporary legislation, Regulation VII of 1822, to the failed potential of the Permanent Settlement, Harington noted: "It appears to be the duty of the Government, in relinquishing their interest in, and control over, the rents of the Ryots . . . to adopt every practicable means of guarding the established tenures against infringement by the landholders and farmers, to whom the rents are now payable."[16]

Harington's perception of rent was not completely severed from the Ricardian explanation of the category. Harington did argue that even the "pergunnah rates" or other "local rates" had some basis in the varying fertility of soil. In the complete constitution of the payment called "rent," however, the relations of property and political power in which rent was embedded were of far greater analytical significance than the differential fertility of soil, which was merely a marginal empirical aspect of the category. In the "Minute," rent did function as a political-economic category, but differently, as an index of the power relations between different proprietors of land. Regulation VII of 1822, in which Harrington vindicated his concerns, envisioned the governance of property in the same way. This regulation, which I discuss shortly, was a crucial document of governmental reason in early nineteenth-century British India. Harington quoted in detail from the ninth section of the regulation, which upheld this project—of governing property by governing rent. The section noted that government officials, in settling the land revenue, "shall embrace the formation of as accurate a record as possible, of . . . all persons enjoying the possession and property of the soil, or vested with any heritable or transferable interest in the land, or the rents of it."[17]

Legislative Determinations of Rent

Regulation VII of 1822 contained a new plan for the land-revenue settlement of the Ceded and Conquered Provinces and the temporarily settled areas of the Bengal Presidency, including Cuttack. Harington had indicated that the principles of this regulation shared his formulation of the relation between rent and proprietary rights. Ascertainment of proprietary rights was, undoubtedly, the central focus of this regulation.[18] In the achievement of this objective, however, rent remained a crucial analytical tool. It continued to function as the principal determinant of the sovereignty-property relations.

Eric Stokes has noted that Holt Mackenzie, the chief architect of this regulation, adhered to the Ricardian definition of rent, and its rearticulation in Mill's interpretation of the state being the general landlord in India and entitled to the full rent. Mackenzie can be seen expressing such views in a letter to the Select Committee of the House of Commons, where he argued that in India "the existence of private rights, limiting the right of government, so as to leave to the owners of the fields a portion of the rent, that is, a share of the surplus which remains, after paying wages and replacing stock, seems to have been rarely established. . . . The Government, in short, was the great rent-owner."[19] But unlike Mill, Mackenzie did not believe that this government did, or should, assume the same principle in fixing the assessment.

He emphasized that "it was not indeed the intention of our Government to enforce its full rights. It was generally allowed that the interest of the country must suffer if it were attempted to draw the entire rent into the exchequer . . . with reference to the risk of taxing, and restricting production by an excessive assessment on the part of Government, as the general landlord, it was expedient to leave to individuals a valuable property in this land, whether permanent rights of property were admitted or not."[20]

It needs to be noted that, for Mackenzie, maintaining the right of groups, other than the government and the zemindars, to a share of the rent, meant the creation of a "valuable property," which, however, he distinguished from "permanent rights of property." Here also rent was being understood as the marker of property. But this property, in turn, was seen as incomplete or restricted. Rent, therefore, worked as the common index to mark different kinds of relations to land as "property," but by the same operation, it also specified the difference of these relations (as those of political power, which the next chapter discusses). The discourse of governance construed the structural logic of this category in such a way that its capacity of achieving closure also became that of producing openings. Mackenzie spoke in terms of this complex relationship between rent and property—where one marks the other in a way that creates the possibility of probing the frontiers of that marking itself—as a witness to the Select Committee. He was asked how legitimate proprietary rights could be recovered in Bengal, the land of the ruinous policy of the Permanent Settlement. In reply, Mackenzie argued, like Harington, that the regulation of rent was absent in Bengal, which resulted in a destruction of proprietary rights in land. This allowed the superior landholders, or zemindars, to usurp that restricted proprietary right—by extracting full rent.[21] The government, however, had intended that the inferior landholders, or cultivators, should retain this restricted property right.[22]

Mackenzie summed up the tasks of governance, I argue, when he pointed out that a settlement "embraced two great branches of inquiry; first, *the relation of the people to each other and to the government*; and, secondly the extent of productiveness of the land. . . . The first branch of inquiry has been almost wholly neglected. . . . It was yet the branch of inquiry that most demanded attention . . . in it, inaccuracy is fatal to utility."[23] It can be clearly seen that although Mackenzie, like Ricardo, described rent as the surplus over profits of cultivation and wages of labor, he understood its political-economic function as an exercise in exploring, disaggregating, and governing a web of relations between the state and various kinds of landholders—relations constituting a complex of property and political power. Like Harington, once again, he did not neglect the link between rent and productiveness of soil. But he insisted that the task of assessing differences in power, rather than those in fertility, was of greater importance yet, unfortunately, most neglected. For the same reason, Mackenzie, unlike Mill, did not abhor all property arising from rent. He believed that the maintenance of property in land, albeit of a limited kind, was consistent to the principles of utility, as this kept power equations in place. This property did not merely consist of a right to occupy and cultivate the same land for a long period. It came into being only when the ryot owned a certain portion of the rent.

Now, let us see whether Stokes's reading of Mackenzie can be vindicated. Stokes argues that Mackenzie's proposals for the assessment of the land revenue demand of the Ceded and Conquered Provinces were rooted in the net-produce (Ricardian) criterion declared by James Mill. But Stokes notes that *in practice* Mackenzie applied this principle very cautiously, as he knew that it would be impossible to extract information on soil fertility from the multiplicity of local practices that determined payments between cultivators and revenue payers. [24] I argue that Mackenzie's move away from Mill's Ricardianism can be better understood as a position grounded in a different political economy. Mackenzie's dig into the thickness of local tenurial forms was not inspired by contingencies of practice, which the theory could not address. Rather, his primary aim, as this section shows, was to excavate and govern rent in and as a complex field of proprietary power.

As the settlement was conducted on the basis of the principles of Regulation VII of 1822 in the Ceded and Conquered Provinces, officials observed that it progressed very slowly.[25] Such circumstances necessitated a modification of this regulation. William Bentinck, then governor-general, organized a conference of revenue officers on this matter at Allahabad on 21 January 1833. Recommendations from this discussion led to a new plan of settlement, which was legislated as Regulation IX of 1833.[26] The settlement in Cuttack, which began in 1836, was executed according to the principles of this regulation. As expected, a particular relationship between rent and property framed this regulation, which was discussed in detail in a minute written by Bentinck. The entire governmental investment in an examination of the productive capacities of land, by separating the constituent elements of agricultural production, like cost of production, soil quality, and wages of labor, was dismissed in framing the agenda of settlement. Bentinck stated unequivocally: "As far as the rights of the Government are concerned . . . a minute inquisition into the capacity of each field or each village of the country is unnecessary."[27] He went on to outline the rights and figures of property, which he considered authentic and legitimate indigenous forms of India. His prescription of the retention of a portion of rent by these proprietary figureswas part of this strategy of authentication. This is why Bentinck noted that the assessment for every village could be fixed by following the "actual produce and collections of former years."[28] This did not mean that he decided to simply endorse existing local practice, limiting governance. Instead it showed that the government demand no longer needed to be based on the assessment of the productivity of soil, even if it was perceived as rent. In distributing this demand in varying portions between different groups on land, it was established that rent, as property, as sovereignty, was solely a marker of indigenous relations of property and sovereignty , the dispersals of which had by this time been categorically mapped by the networks of governance. Bentinck's minute formed a part of the guidelines of the settlement in Cuttack. The function of rent in vindicating proprietary claims, especially of subordinate groups different from zemindars, made rent a ground of contest in localities. As district officials grappled with these churnings in the locality, rent performed to define new networks of power relations.

The Crowd in Cuttack

Fixing rates of rent was an immensely complex affair in the settlement of Cuttack. Rent unearthed various relations of power embedded in contending proprietary claims; it could never be linked to an assessment of variations in soil fertility. In Talooka Bishnupur, Pergunnah Bakrabad, Mr. Hunter, the collector, tried to derive rent solely from the productive potential of lands of various kinds. F. J. Halliday, secretary to the Board of Revenue, noted the terrible incomprehension resulting from such a method. Halliday pointed out that "these sorts he [Hunter] found to amount to three hundred! And he reduced them by a process not explained to the less alarming but still unintelligible number of twenty nine."[29] Such a method faced immediate rejection. The commissioner, Mr. Mills, called such estimates "conjectural." As we will now see, instead of being based in varying soil fertility, rent was used to debate and define the specific proprietary status of different kinds of landholders. The *thanee* ryot in Cuttack, for example, was one such figure who was critically marked by such uses of rent. Typically understood as hereditary cultivators in the classifications of agrarian governance, the thanees acquired new capacities from these operations of rent.

Officials in Cuttack debated over the portion of the produce to be reserved for the thanees in fixing the assessment. In settling Talooka Koorkoora,

Pergunnah Kowakund, Mr. Taylor stated: "I have based all my calculations on the principle of leaving to the cultivators after payment of the tax on his land, & defraying the necessary expenses of culture half at least of the produce."[30] Halliday, deputed as a supervisor of settlement, objected to such a decision, noting that Taylor had underassessed the lands in reserving such a big share of the produce for the cultivators.[31]Halliday did not consider the thanee ryots of Cuttack to be proprietors. He described them as "resident farmers" and contended that by fixing their rents low, the government was making proprietors out of farmers:

> In the case of the Thanees . . . they are not said to be proprietors but farmers who have we are told a right to a fixed money rent and to permanent occupation of their tenures as long as they pay that rent. To the latter portion of their supposed rights, I have no objection, but the former appears to me to involve a contradiction in terms. For in order to avoid trenching upon profits and wages which we are of course utterly unable to define and which after all may often be infringed we are obliged to exceed the other way and trench upon rent. But a farmer who receives in addition to wages and profits, a share of the rent is pro tanto a proprietor, which the Thanees do not claim to be.[32]

This debate, I argue, is an interesting example of the governmental articulations of political economy in British India during this period, which laid the foundations of a complex regime of proprietary power. It might seem that the debate was being articulated in the vocabulary of Ricardian political economy, where "rent" signified that share of the income from the produce, which was in addition to profits and wages, while these different, and distinct, shares of the produce were understood to be possessed by landlords, farmers, and laborers, respectively. It is in correspondence with this classificatory scheme that Halliday described thanee ryots as "farmers," arguing that granting them "rent" would make them landlords/proprietors. He believed "that the true protection of the ryot is to be found not in violating for his sake the laws of political economy."[33] He was in favor of fixing rents at "market rates," thereby reserving proprietary profits only for the zemindars, who were, according to him, the true "landlords."

But a closer look reveals that these categories were used in a different sense, not to accurately measure shares of incomes, but to mark property relations, of a different order. That is why Halliday, despite using these categories, exclaimed that the government could not define any of them, and, in other cases, all attempts of the officials to calculate rent by examining soil quality were dismissed. Rent, however, remained the most important site of contention. This is because it continued to be perceived as the most authentic marker of proprietary status, and, therefore, relations of agrarian power. Its Ricardian framing worked in a residual fashion for practices of governance that recast it as the key to unlock a heterogeneous matrix of property and power. So, Halliday's assertions were in vain. The rent of thanee ryots was fixed in Cuttack. Officially, these ryots were not registered as "proprietors," receiving proprietary allowances. But fixing their rents and that too at a low rate implied that provisions were being made for them to possess, *as a part of the rent*, the portion of their produce that was in addition to what they paid as their dues to the government. So, although the government was the "proprietor," as it received "rent" from the thanees, by fixing this rent low, it was *in effect* sharing it with the thanees, thereby admitting their proprietary capacities, even if these were restricted.

In Pergunnah Saibeer tobacco was cultivated extensively. It was one of those rare estates in Cuttack that produced in abundance a commercially valuable crop. Owing to the vulnerability of the tobacco lands to encroachment of the river, rent on those lands used to be settled by the zemindar at the close of the rains every year. But during the settlement, the commissioner noted, "the Thanee ryots insisted on their tobacco lands being secured to them . . . at a particular rate, and in order to indulge them. . . . . the rates were lowered some forty five per cent, and to those holding lands the situation of which is very precarious a small portion of waste of a good quality has been given."[34] The commissioner thought that the earlier arrangement was more suited to the conditions of agriculture and situation of ryots. He pointed out, "Every order which tends to the division of the profits of cultivation amongst greater numbers is injurious to every interest connected with the land, these 'independent' ryots themselves not excepted for notwithstanding the reductions made they will be ruined the first year in which the deposit necessary for the growth of the plant shall be wanting, the zemindar will afford them no assistance, and exercise no forbearance, he will be the person ultimately to benefit by the sacrifice."[35] But, in spite of the commissioner's judgment, which reflected a typically Malthusian belief in the potential of the landlord to act as an "improver," settlement was made by fixing rates of each of the ryots and providing a culturable plot of land to all those ryots exposed to risks of flood. It is to be noted that while the zemindar was still reckoned to be the proprietor, in being the recipient of rent, at the same time, the thanee ryots were awarded a low rent and lands for protection from damage to agricultural activities. This implied that both zemindars and thanees were invested with qualified and partial proprietary capacities, through provisions to own rent in different ways.

It was not only the zemindars, as superior landowners, with whom thanees were enabled to share rent by virtue of these mechanisms of protection. In Cuttack, as we will see in detail in the next chapter, there were other prominent landowners. These groups were dominant at the level of the village, variously named as surburakars, mukaddams, and pudhans. They were also officially recognized as proprietors, along with the zemindars, in Cuttack. The proprietary claims of even these groups, however, were critically examined by practices of governance, especially with reference to their effects on the conditions of the thanee ryots. For example, in Talooka Patamoondee, when the measuring *aumeens* prepared the *jummabundee*, the collector argued that the returns were full of exaggerated and erroneous estimates. This was because, he noted, "no confidence could be placed on the surburakars records." Finally, "the only means left were to take the zemindars papers as the guide and to assess the lands according to their quality and advantages of situation."[36]

But the official understanding of rent, by this time, had fashioned this category as the most authentic reflector of the density of power relations in agrarian societies. Therefore, such records of past payments of rents produced by superior landholders like zemindars and village proprietors were perceived more as instruments of power and less as mere information. So, in several places, their accounts were made to pass through assemblies in the villages. In Patamoondee too, the zemindar's papers were accepted only through such an assembly. As the collector noted in his report: "I also visited every village in the Pergunnah, reviewed the mouzawarree estimates prepared by the Deputy Collector on the spot and heard the objection of the people to the demand which it was proposed to fix on the village, so that I can with confidence state that no little pains has been taken to make an equitable and fair settlement. . . . The surburakars are satisfied, the Thanee ryots have willingly engaged . . . and the demand is on the whole moderate."[37] Reflecting the same spirit, in settling Talook Rughoonathpore, the collector noted: "After checking the measurement and classification and making notes where it was necessary, I took up the case of each Thanee Ryot separately[,] examined the papers of the zemindar and canoongoe [district accountant] as to the quantity and quality of his land[,] enquired into his condition viz., whether he had risen or fallen in the world and why, heard any thing he had to say for himself and then fixed his Jummah."[38]

Settlement reports in Cuttack went on representing such regular and unmediated intercourse of officials with the supposedly organic constituents of agrarian societies. This is how governmental reason delineated the matrix of power in the locality: by laying down its boundaries, drawing up criteria of authenticity in order to differentiate between its members, and finally, establishing an entire calculus of relationships as the object of agrarian governance in British India. I do not suggest that the measures taken to fix rent in Cuttack reflected a governmental intention to remove inequalities of power by granting protection to cultivators against landlords. Rather, I argue that the critique of big landlords during this period was simultaneously a celebration of new wielders of power in agrarian localities. This foregrounding of new bodies of power, like the surburakars, the thanee ryots, or even the "village," was based on further exclusions and other hierarchies. It will be shown in subsequent chapters that despite being presented as ryots, or peasant cultivators, these figures were far removed from the tillers of the soil. Moreover, the same governmental strategies that awarded greater privileges to them than they had enjoyed earlier also denounced and devalued the rights of other cultivators. Rent played a critical role in determining the contours of this landscape of agrarian power. Its governmental deployment, embedded in the constructions of a different political economy, was assembled over a variety of sites. As this chapter shows, these sites were simultaneously particular localities and governmental articulations of the local.

A Theory of Practice

The previous chapter showed how this difference in the conceptualization of political economy, which emerged out of a critique of Ricardianism in contemporary Britain, was refused recognition, in being explained as one between theoretical and practical forms of the body of knowledge, by its dominant practitioners. The same discursive move can be identified in the domain of governance in British India. This different political-economic reason was often staged as a practical form of governmental operation, more effective than ones informed by theoretical abstraction, by administrators working in localities. The local was represented, and used, in this strategy of governance as that quintessential space of the concrete and practical, which was able to mirror empirical reality, thereby exposing the falsity of theory. Interestingly, as in Britain, in British India these conversations and strategies were effected in terms of the category of rent. The work of rent was understood through the construction of substitutable oppositions like theory-practice, political economy–governance, abstract-concrete, and metropolitan-local. These oppositional forms get unpacked, however, if we read into governmental practices a different order of political economy. Here I make this argument by rearranging certain threads of governance that were woven around these oppositions across a variety of locales, including Cuttack.

In the 1860s Henry Ricketts wrote a series of four essays from London on the question of rent in Bengal. Ricketts was an experienced administrator who had climbed the ladders of the British Indian bureaucracy between the 1820s and 1840s. Beginning as a collector, he ended his administrative career as an influential and respected member of the Board of Revenue. For my purposes, Ricketts is particularly relevant, as a large part of his lower-level administrative career was spent in the Cuttack Division. He began as the magistrate and collector of Cuttack in 1827 and eventually left the division in the 1840s as its commissioner. Other than Cuttack, he served in Chittagong and parts of the Central Provinces. Later, as a member of the Board of Revenue, to which he was appointed in 1849, he regularly expressed strong opinions on various matters of agrarian policy. He took an active role in the debates preceding the formulation of the Rent Act, or Act X of 1859.[39] Ricketts's essays referred mostly to disputes between Indigo planters and ryots over the issue of enhancement of rent. As such cases flooded the district courts accompanied by a number of incidents of violent conflicts between ryots and planters, a range of opinions were generated at different levels of the administration on more general questions regarding the category of rent. Administrators started critically reviewing the history of agrarian governance in Bengal since the establishment of the Permanent Settlement. Even in this context rent was framed as that critical transaction that expressed and shaped all proprietary relations of power in the agrarian economy of Bengal.[40]

Ricketts pointed out confidently in his essays that the foundational problems of agrarian governance in Bengal were the handiwork of the policy of Permanent Settlement, which left undefined a vast gamut of relationships between landlords and cultivators in the countryside. Once the problems were interpreted in this way, Ricketts was also quick to suggest that their only solution resided in a detailed settlement of agrarian relations in the discontented areas of Bengal. Such a settlement, he further noted, should take its inspiration from the model of land survey and settlement that was carried out in the Cuttack Division between 1836 and 1843. Thus, he was suggesting that the whole of Bengal should draw its model for an efficient, productive, and peaceful resolution of the problems experienced in the domain of land relations from one of its marginal territories, namely, Cuttack. At the heart of this proposal, the category of rent loomed large. Like other administrators of Bengal, Ricketts shared the assumption that rent was the constitutive thread of the relations of power between landholders. So it was necessary to devise means to formulate it correctly.

Commenting on the Indigo disputes in the first of these four essays, entitled "The Real Difficulties in Bengal and How to Settle Them," Ricketts noted: "The real struggle is, which party is entitled to the advantages accruing to the different classes engaged in agriculture, from the increased value of all agricultural produce."[41] The problem, in his opinion, originated from the range of administrative mistakes committed during the policy of Permanent Settlement. Ricketts lamented, "We have ever since continued to write and speak of the rights of the ryots, but they were never ascertained; of the Pergunnah rates, which were never adjusted; of the settlement, at which nothing was settled, but the revenue to be paid by each superior holder to the state."[42] All this litigation, Ricketts observed, displayed that rent was the battleground of interests between superior and inferior landholders. While the superior landholders tried to enhance the rent, the peasant cultivators tried hard to resist such an increase. Thus, Ricketts noted that in resolving these disputes, "There is but one complete remedy, and that is to do now what ought to have been done in 1793, to make forthwith a field survey, and a complete registry of all rights and interests in the lands."[43]

With this confident declaration, Ricketts brought Cuttack into the discussion. He pointed out that there should not be any apprehension on the part of the state in proceeding with such a plan of settlement. On the contrary, he suggested that there were examples within Bengal only that displayed excellent results in the administration of land relations, produced out of such a settlement. "Previously to the settlement of Cuttack, the province deteriorated each year, the people were discontented, and embarrassments and difficulties increased. Since the settlement, the province has flourished, the inhabitants have been among the most peaceful and well-disposed of our subjects, there has been less litigation than in any other part of the empire. . . . Let Bengal be treated precisely in the same manner, and there is no reason why there should not be the same result."[44]

Ricketts followed this essay with one entitled "The Rent Difficulties in Bengal and How to Remedy Them; The Rent Facilities in Cuttack and How to Preserve Them." Here Ricketts developed his critique of the official interpretation of the disturbed agrarian conditions in Bengal. He raised the example of the Great Rent Case, between Hills and Ishwur Ghose, and began systematically recording his points of difference with the opinion of the judge. The chief justice, in his judgment, had proclaimed that a "fair and equitable" rate of rent could be reached only by applying the Malthusian definition of rent. In laying a guideline for the special commissioner deputed in the Indigo districts to settle the rent disputes, the judge said: "We cannot lay down any better rule for his guidance than that we have quoted from Mr. Malthus in his *Principles of Political Economy.*"[45] The judgment further observed, "He there defines rent to be 'that portion of the value of the whole produce which remains to the owner of the land after all the outgoings belonging to its cultivation, of whatever kind, have been paid, including the profits of the capital employed, estimated according to the usual and ordinary rate of agricultural capital at the time being.'"[46]

In arguing against the official opinion, Ricketts pointed out that such political-economic prescriptions cannot be followed in fixing rent. He had his own propositions to offer, which were spelt out in another essay, entitled "A Few Last Words on the Rent Difficulties in Bengal." In both these essays, one of the primary objections he raised against the implementation of the Malthusian definition was the impossibility of calculation of the "outgoings of cultivation." Indicating the infinite variety of costs related to cultivation, he pointed out that it was *practically* impossible to make an accurate calculation of all of them. He noted that the plan of basing the assessment on a comparison between costs of production and value of produce was proposed through Regulation VII of 1822 but later rescinded in Regulation XI of 1833. Ricketts had his own explanation of how a settlement could overcome such practical difficulties. Throughout the three essays, he maintained that questions of practice can only be sensitively tackled in the field, but not by adhering to rigid political-economic guidelines.

Moreover, Ricketts argued that the true relations of power that the category of rent was rooted in were always distorted, and turned into falsities in the practice of law. Almost metaphorically, he represented the law and its performative arena, the courtroom, as prisons of errors and opacities, contrasting them with the space of the open field, symbolizing truth and transparency. "The same point would be ruled in many different ways by the different courts. Good lands would be assessed at a low rate, and bad land at a high rate, the courts having been misled by clever representations, which they were unable to test by the only efficient test, investigation conducted over a considerable tract of country."[47] The field was also represented as that authentic, embodied, organic space of those relations of power that determined rent. Ricketts went on to say that the same people who, in the courtroom, stood as agents of corruption and deceit became the torchbearers of truth and objectivity in the open country. "He who might for a very small douceur be brought into the court to substantiate any story, however improbable, when taken into the field with all his neighbours among whom he has lived from his youth, and among whom he must live till his dying day, will, in a few hours, class a thousand acres of land, varying in every imaginable way, without making a mistake or causing a single remonstrance or murmur from all the eager listeners around him."[48]

For Ricketts, political economy and law were incapable of being correct measures of governance: in different ways, both were understood as forms of representations, or (theoretical) codes, far removed from the true practice. As a representation (of reality) political economy was simply false, while the law was structurally open to manipulation. In Ricketts's statements the field was posited as beyond, and opposed to, all such representations: it was reality itself. But, I argue, Ricketts's perception of rent, as an articulation of the true nature of relations of power, nevertheless remained tied to a political economy, which had a different conceptual structure. Ricketts's notion of the practical, therefore, was already-always inscribed by a theoretical framing of the category of rent, just like the notions of most of the political economists of his time.

It is easy to see how Ricketts garnered faith in this conception of the practical. As a settlement officer in Cuttack, he was bewildered by the inexplicable variety of rates of the lands in Talook Noanud. He noted that "land of the same description and in every respect equal advantages not only pays at various rates in different villages, but in the same village and on the same Chuck. In one village, I found as many as 34 rates for rice lands alone."[49] Guided by a Ricardian common sense, I will argue, he made an attempt to correspond rent to the productive capacity of the land. He tried to introduce a consistent scale of classification for different soils. The effort was futile, as he remarked: "In the hope of establishing something approaching uniformity for future guidance I appointed a Punchayet consisting of 5 Zemindars 9 Serberakars and 18 Ryots who met for several days and endeavoured to adjust 3 or 4 rates for each sort of land but they completely failed."[50] So he left the variety in the way it existed, in a form that was incomprehensible to him. The rates reached in this way were, however, satisfactory to the different landholders in the Pergunnah. So, the Ricardian framing of rent, as an index of varying fertility, when deployed in this practice of governance proved to be dysfunctional. Interestingly, even in order to introduce this standard of measuring rent, Ricketts had to reconfigure the category, as a consensus on rates could be attempted only in terms of a mediation by recognized equations of local power. It seemed that rent could be defined only when it was approved by a "village assembly" of surburakars, zemindars, and ryots. Moreover, this was possible because, as I argue in the following chapter, these approvers themselves had been approved as legitimate ones by complex discursive networks of governance by this time in British India.

But even this was not effective. This implies that there were greater complexities or a different set of equations at work in the relations of proprietary power in this locality, which refused to accept Ricketts's "people." In any case, Ricketts was already debating, defining, and governing rent as a category that reflected certain identified arrangements of proprietary power in localities. Contrary to what he had argued in his essays, the "field" did not necessarily yield organic truths of rent. At least in this instance Ricketts could not cultivate its truth, despite remaining committed to it. But this shows that his governmental strategies were already implicated in a different political economy that framed rent as an index of power. Time and again, Ricketts understood the truth of rent in the field from this perspective, without recognizing its theoretical bearings. In another case, for example, he noted how the village zemindar extracted rent from a Lakhirajdar, despite the latter's governmental sanction to own rent-free lands: "In a small village 100 Beegahs is held Lakhiraj, and not included in the Jummabundee, but . . . a considerable revenue is derived by the village zemindar from such lands. The Lakhirajdar's land is capable of growing a second crop but not without irrigation. The village proprietor has command of the water, and he allows the Lakhirajdars so much water as will bring the second crop . . . receiving half the rent realized from the land."[51]

In other words, what for Ricketts expressed the reality of the field, or the truth of practice, was the construction of rent as a marker of different kinds of proprietary power, not as one of differences in soil fertility. The kinds of tenures rent would mark as proprietary were being simultaneously determined by the discursive practices of governance across British India during this period. Ricketts's call for practical governance was shaped very much by this code of governance, despite styling itself as opposed to all codes. This chapter shows how village-level proprietors and ryots of certain kinds were being empowered by these practices of governance against big landlords. There was a different political-economic rationality immanent in this process of governance. As we have seen in the case of the debates over political economy in contemporary Britain, in British India too the question of production was being understood as constitutive of specific indigenous arrangements of proprietary power. Thus, the close engagement of governance with property needs to be understood also as a method of addressing the problem of production, evidently in a way very different from classical (Ricardian) political economy. Such linkages between proprietary power and conditions of production, forged in terms of the category of rent, were sometimes explicitly posited in texts of governance. The final section of the chapter briefly considers one such case.

Rent and Production

James Alexander wrote an essay on the relation between rent and land tenures in the *Journal of the Asiatic Society of Bengal* in 1845. In this section, I show how Alexander developed a political-economic explanation of rent, grounded in an interconstitutive linkage between property and political power. Reflecting an evident epistemological kinship with Richard Jones's political economy, Alexander's essay forged crucial analytical relations between rent, property, political power, and production. Right at the beginning, Alexander declared that rent was an expression of proprietary relations, which together produced a field of political power. He argued that the different kinds of *nerikh*, or rates of rent, reveal the specific contours of a relation of property and power between the zemindar and the ryot. That is why, he noted, "in the ryuttee as in the zemindaree tenure, *the rent* which it will yield *is the distinguishing mark of each sort of tenure*."[52] He went on to argue that since different kinds of rent articulate different kinds of relationships between landlords and tenants, they also shape the conditions of production differently. Like Jones, Alexander suggested that the context and therefore the nature of production get determined by these relations of power. Thus, he noted, "the landlord must constantly observe his tenant to ensure his honesty, and the tenant is discouraged by the reflection that one-half of his labour must be bestowed for the benefit of another."[53] It must be remembered that Jones had made the same connection between rent and the productive efficiency of labor, demonstrating how different kinds of rents led to varying productivity of labor.[54] For Jones, productivity was rooted in these relations of property and political power. As he noted, "It will be found that the motives to industry, which operate in different communities, depend upon the relations which connect the classes of those communities."[55]

Rent, Alexander argued in a manner similar to Harington, marked the contours of the field of power existing between the zemindar and the ryot. In this field, he observed, "there is a constant struggle between himself and his tenantry regarding the share which they are respectively to enjoy of the surplus profits of cultivation."[56] Various factors determined the scope of this proprietary relation. Alexander argued that customary laws of different kinds restricted the landlord's capacity of extraction. In a certain sense, as Andrew

Sartori has shown in a recent article, custom here acted as a political-economic category.[57] It was not viewed as necessarily antithetical to political-economic formulations. The political-economic underpinnings of custom here were not, however, entirely similar to those identified by Sartori in his examination of the category in the context of debates on rent laws in Bengal. There were crucial differences as well, which did not allow the political economy of custom in this case to be interpreted, as by Sartori, in terms of either Lockean or Ricardian/Malthusian frameworks. Custom here was a political-economic category only insofar as it was determined by a political economy that opposed and reconfigured the Ricardian framework.

Alexander enlisted a number of rents paid in Bengal. In describing each of them, he elaborated upon the nature of the matrix of proprietary power in which they were located. He noted that the *Nerick Mocurreree* was a fixed rate of payment granted to cultivators validated by a written document. Its basis was that the cultivator had held the land at fixed rates for twelve years prior to the Decennial Settlement, during which period he paid his dues regularly. Nerick Mowrossee, on the other hand was a rate established by inheritance. A prescriptive right to hold certain lands at fixed rates was allowed to cultivators because they were considered the first to cultivate those lands. These rents were called *Nerick-i-kudeem*. Alexander noted that the village, as a customary body, was also invested with the power to grant prescriptive proprietary rights. Such rights came with fixed rates of rent, "established for each peculiar class of soil" in the village.[58] "The *Nerick-i-Mukuddum*," Alexander continued, "is a rate established in favor of particular individuals, who claim to hold land at rates below those of the village, as a privilege of caste or office; where there is sufficient evidence to prove that this title has been previously recognized, it acquires a force from prescription which is not easily set aside."[59] Once again, similar to the way rent was settled in Cuttack, Alexander's presentation of rent shows that even when rates were related to classes of soil their determination depended upon the specific kind of proprietary capacities the occupiers of these soils were invested with, by the local matrix of tenures. The *Jungle-booree Nerick* was another class of rents, which were rates at which cultivators entered into engagements to bring forested lands under cultivation. They depended upon various factors—the density of the jungle, the markets, rivers, and roads nearby, the quality of the soil, the means of irrigation, the demand for land in the neighborhood, and also the climate.

All these factors taken together, in Alexander's analysis, accounted for the nature of proprietary power and, consequently, the category of rent. In Alexander's description of the relation between custom and rent, there was a vision of the ryot as the capitalist farmer, similar to the one Sartori identifies in George Campbell's invocation of custom in the course of debates over rent in Bengal in the 1850s. Like Campbell, Alexander argued that custom guaranteed this political-economic capacity to the ryot—of being more like a farmer and less like an agricultural labourer. He stated, "If confidence in the stability of the rates is not so strong, and tenures held under *prescriptive titles have not the same value as marketable commodities*, neither will the cultivator himself incur the risk of any extensive outlay in the formation of gardens, the excavation of tanks, and the building of houses."[60] But Campbell and others in that context had argued that "customary" rents were low because they assumed the ryot to have a right to the soil. The ryot was imagined as the original improver, thereby possessing a right to a portion of the rent fund. There was a Lockeanism at work here, Sartori argues, through the reworking of the category of custom.

In my opinion, however, Alexander's argument for a political economy of custom was rooted in a different perspective. Here, custom referred to an assemblage of property and political power, which conditioned production. The strength of custom to condition the productive efficiency of labor, in turn, derived from uninterrupted residence, inheritance, prescriptive rights of holding on to a land by virtue of being its original cultivator, making prescriptive titles equivalent in value to, and thereby the basis of, marketable commodities and, very importantly, the capacities of the village to regulate proprietary power. All these elements together defined what can be called in political-economic terms the tightly woven relation between property and political power. Alexander's political-economy of custom, therefore, did not emerge from any variety of the Ricardian, Malthusian, or Lockean analytical frames. On the contrary, it was steeped in one of their most powerful critiques—an internal one, a different kind of political economy.

Conclusion

This chapter argues that in the practices of agrarian governance rent served as a point of entry into the complex architecture of the political in British India. In the Ricardian definition of rent as a measure of differential soil fertility, the conceptual problem of property was invisibilized, as it was assumed that the form of property was naturally and necessarily the same everywhere. Richard Jones's critique of Ricardian political economy pointed out, however, that forms of property, and the natures of sovereignty in which they were embedded, varied across the world. Therefore, political economy had to understand these interrelationships in order to frame its categories correctly. For Jones, rent was the most important pointer of these interrelationships. Similarly, in British India, we see that rent, instead of being understood *from* an assumed premise of the universality of the form of property, was turned *toward* the examination of the variety in forms of interrelations between property and sovereignty/political power. Accordingly, administrators perceived rent as the defining transaction of power in the agrarian societies of British India. The critique of the Permanent Settlement showed that there was a change in the way the nature of this power got recognized in the discourse of governance. The linkages between property and political power were seen as dispersed over multiple bodies of landholders. Consequently, rent, which was construed as an indicator of this field, was used to stabilize several conflicting equations of power. These strategies of governance, as the upcoming chapters show in greater detail, were also about redefining the political-economic framing of production. The move away from Ricardianism did not mean an abandonment of its one of its organizing categories, production. Rather, it signified the recasting of production in the light of varying agrarian power relations in different localities. Rent was a gateway to this domain. Its management, thus, meant governing production in and as local power. This was a process that changed the meaning of production; settling the rent question was one of its vital aspects.

It is evident that the chapter, in the process of tracking this particular political-economic deployment of rent, opens up a lot of questions about property in land. At all those sites, where rent got administered, an array of proprietary relations sprang up. These relations are examined carefully in the next chapter. There I show how a range of proprietary figures, taken together in their varying relations to each other, constituted the domain of power on land. This property-power complex was instituted as the object of agrarian governance in British India during the first half of the nineteenth century. The next chapter argues that specific arrangements of this complex, differing across regions, were organized and distributed by practices of governance in terms of the category of local. The local, I argue, was a complex spatial and temporal concatenation, which, through dynamic reconfigurations in the hydra-headed networks of agrarian governance, produced a new political economy.

CHAPTER 3

Temporal Geographies of Power

Property

This chapter is about temporal geographies generated by complex interconnections between political economy and agrarian governance. It argues that specificities of agrarian power in the different localities of British India took shape out of changing articulations of the "local." I show how the local emerged as a classificatory framework that explained these specificities as varying degrees of resemblances with, or differences from, a general spatiotemporal imagination of an authentic, ancient, "Hindu/Indian" relation between property and political power. The formulation of this authentic relation between property and political power was continuously reinterpreted over multifarious sites of governance. The chapter, however, also reclaims the local for political economy, in and as governance. I argue that the structuring principle of the local—a search for the authentic national property-power complex—was resonant with the reconfigured epistemological object of contemporary political economy in Britain. As I have shown, Richard Jones made the political economic category of production contingent upon different interrelations between property and political power existing in different nations of the world. This chapter explores in detail the manner in which Jones analyzed the specificities of the property-power complex in India, relating these specificities to the universality of categories like rent, wage, profit, and production. From Jones, I move on to introduce another articulation of the local in John Stuart Mill's political economy. Mill, in a way different from Jones, forged constitutive conceptual linkages between property, power, and production. It is in this light that Mill interpreted agrarian conditions in Britain, India, Ireland, and other nations of the world. This is how the chapter brings together political economy and governance as part of the same analytical field.

In the years after the permanent zemindary settlement of Bengal, it was argued at different sites of governance that the original proprietary relation to land was between the state and the peasant cultivator, which existed in an erstwhile, Hindu India. This chapter contends that this vision was marked by a discursive elasticity that enabled administrators to reinterpret this relation differently in different localities, without moving away from its founding principle. That is, the proprietary peasant of the ryotwar (the mode of settlement where the proprietary subject was the peasant cultivator) was refashioned variously, as a hereditary cultivator, or khoodkasht ryot, as a village proprietor, or putteedar/mokuddum, or even as particular kinds of zamindars and talukdars, whose roots were in the "village community." The indigenous (Indian) form of property was thus understood as inherently qualified. Although the landlord state was considered an absolute/despotic source of power, its despotism was seen as limited and arrested by a range of landholders and landholding bodies. These figures and bodies, along with the state, therefore, were perceived as forming a distributed matrix of agrarian power. Further, property was seen as a conjunction of rights vested in both the soil and the offices of revenue collection. The local was construed as a diffused field, constituted by zamindars, talukdars, village proprietors, like mokuddams, serberakars, and pudhans, and cultivators, like the thanee and khoodkasht ryots, each having their share of rights, along with the state.

This diffusion was, however, persistently reorganized by the governmental strategy of positing one landholding figure in each locality as its dominant one, based on arguments about its greater proximity to the original proprietary ryot than others. The choice of this figure also emerged out of a preference for the productive potential of peasant proprietors over big landlords. This preference was evident in John Stuart Mill's political economy as well. But the productivist emphasis marking this choice, both in Mill and in the practices of British Indian agrarian governance, was articulated in and through a complex interpretation of the interrelationship between property and political power in nations. In other words, it was the play of the local in the discourse of political economy that made the question of production *internal* to that of local power.

In conversation with earlier chapters, this chapter traces the work of the local in the field of governance. In doing that, it accounts for the formations of agrarian relations in different localities of British India. Various sites are taken up here, like the *Fifth Report*, an insurrection in Cuttack, an authoritative text on tenures in Cuttack, debates over settlement in the North-Western Provinces, Governor-General William Bentinck's intervention in these debates, settlement practices in the different locales of Cuttack, and finally, the political-economic writings of Richard Jones and John Stuart Mill. These sites also serve as routes both of entries to and of exits from Cuttack. More generally, I suggest that both the sites themselves and the form of analysis indicate the entangled character of all localities. These entanglements were not only between forms of agrarian relations in the localities of British India, they were also across forms of the local in political economy and governance; I highlight their overlaps as well as their differences. In other words, I underscore the changes in the local from its previous articulations. Of course, in doing all of this, I argue that specific configurations of agrarian power in localities were not outcomes of contingent, on-the-spot, pragmatic administrative measures. On the contrary, specificities were implicated in, and constituted by totalizing networks of knowledge, governance, and quotidian practice.

Early Connections: A Report, a Rebellion, and the Ordering of Difference

To begin with, I take another look at the *Fifth Report*. This report, as I noted in the previous chapter, represented the first systematic attempt to put together an ensemble of property relations and political power that would remain, over shifting arrangements, the object of agrarian governance in British India throughout the first half of the nineteenth century. I documented earlier how rent operated in this report as an indicator of these relations. But the report was primarily organized around the category of the local. This chapter brings forth the importance of this category in the assembling of the proprietary matrix. It argues that the local signified a spatiotemporal frame within which an ensemble of property and power assumed a national form and was distributed over various geographical sites, or localities, as a hierarchized range of difference. In other words, the local of each locality was always interpreted by practices of governance as *specific* manifestations of a *general*, national, Hindu/Indian complex of property and political power. Moreover, this ordering of difference was framed by a hierarchy. A Hindu/Indian form of the property-power complex was construed as the authentic one, and the proprietary power relation specific to each locality was assessed in terms of its distance/difference from the former. Within this interpretive grid, time and space were the twin markers of distance/difference. The local performed this analytical function. It was both a point and a range. It acted as both specificity and generality. In the local, time and space defined each other. Every locality, as a space different from the original, was also explained by practices of governance as a time distant from the ancient. The logic of the local was all pervasive. This section argues that from the *Fifth Report* to an insurgency in Cuttack the local reigned supreme.

The *Fifth Report* criticized the Bengal Code of administration by pointing out its inapplicability in other localities. The report presented administrative experience from various regions of British India, as evidence of local differences in the forms of land tenure. This body of evidence emerged from experiences in governance in the old and new areas of the Bengal Presidency and also in the Presidency of Fort St. George. By demonstrating the unsuitability of the Bengal Code to some of both the old and the newly acquired territories of the East India Company, the report pointed out that significant alterations were made in the revenue administration of these areas. These new arrangements were considered to be more sensitive to local conditions, and consequently, highly successful in effecting improvement in the material conditions of these places.

The model of permanent settlement of revenue with zemindars established by the Bengal Code faced severe opposition from a number of localities. In all these areas, government officers pointed out, local circumstances did not warrant the settlement of revenue with zemindars. Among the old territories of the Company, such a contradiction of the revenue policy of the code was first experienced in Benares in 1795. The principal landholders of Benares seemed to differ substantially from the proprietary figure of the zemindar enshrined in the code. Proprietary rights in land in Benares were vested in groups described in the report as "village zemindars," which also seemed to be comparable with equivalent forms of proprietary bodies in other localities of British India. "The village zemindar of Benares appears to be the mokuddum found in certain parts of Bahar, and the Potail of the Carnatic, both of whom are headmen of villages, who are responsible to the government, for maintaining and promoting the cultivation of the land, and who in the first-mentioned portions of territory possessed the right of disposing of their situations by sale or gift to others."[1]

The greatest challenge to the Bengal Code came from the new presidency of Fort St. George. The report noted that in many parts of this presidency local conditions did not allow an unmodified application of the code. A number of representations from collectors in different divisions, spearheaded by Thomas Munro's vision of a new revenue arrangement, produced significant changes in the revenue policy of the Bengal Code. In some parts of Fort St. George the revenue arrangement was made with individual cultivators, or ryots, while in some other areas a "village settlement" was adopted, by which the "chief cultivators" of villages were appointed as payers of revenue.

Generally, the report argued vigorously in favor of the mode of revenue settlement with the ryots. It stated that the ryotwar system of revenue management had contributed much to the improvement of the province. "It appears . . . that . . . operation of the ryot-war principle of collection, duly conducted and superintended; having for its leading objects, the confining every man to the cultivation of his own land, and defining the specific amount to be paid by each; and thus, securing to him the need of his own industry had, in the . . . two years, during which the country continued under this system of management, effected an improvement in its internal condition."[2] The report further pointed out that the exactions of the village headmen or the superior ryots had been disallowed by this mode of revenue settlement. "Pottahs signed by the collector and his assistants, were granted to each individual cultivator, specifying the rent he was to pay; the grammatans were prohibited from collecting any thing more from the ryots, than the pottah demand; while the latter became encouraged to resist the exactions of the native servants, from a confidence in the protecting power of the government."[3]

From village headmen to chief cultivators to individual ryots, the report used the analytic of the local to make sense of difference. The local forms of land tenures were identified as corrupt versions of an originary and authentic form of proprietary relation, between the government and the cultivator, which existed in the ancient times, when India was under Hindu rule. The report pointed out that apart from the sovereign, only the ryots, or peasant cultivators, held proprietary rights in land. Other groups, like the village headmen, chief cultivators, or zemindars, emerged as usurpers of those rights during the subsequent period of tyrannical Muslim rule. The report recognized certain areas of the Presidency of Fort St. George as containing, in its form of land tenure, traces of the original proprietary relation. In this manner, it inaugurated the classificatory principle by which a particular combination of property and political power was repeatedly represented as the local of the nation and, by extension, of each and every locality. Cuttack was soon harnessed into this analytical space, whereby the initial inexplicability of an insurgent moment in this new division of the Bengal Presidency was quickly tamed by the calm assurance of the calculus of the local.

In the spirit of the *Fifth Report*, an oppositional stance to a permanent settlement was displayed with regard to revenue administration in Cuttack as well. The Company acquired Cuttack in 1803, after which a number of short-term settlements of the land revenue were carried out in the province.

As I mentioned earlier, in spite of the introduction of the Bengal Code of regulations, the policy of permanent settlement was not extended to Cuttack. In 1817, an insurrection spread rapidly over parts of Cuttack. The insurrection was led by a group of paiks, who were the landed military servants of the raja of Khoordah. After the conquest of Cuttack, in making revenue engagements with landholders of different kinds in the area, the new government introduced changes in the mode of settlement of the estate of Khoordah. Prior to the British, when the area was ruled by the Marathas, the raja of Khoordah paid only a nominal tribute to the rulers for the estate. But when the British occupied Cuttack, the raja tried to resist them. The British defeated and deposed the raja and resumed his estate. Later, when the raja was released, he was asked to take charge of the estate, but only against a regular revenue payment. The raja refused to consent to such an offer, and so the government leased out his estate to revenue farmers. The estate consisted of several rent-free lands gifted to the paiks. These lands were resumed by the government as well. One of the raja's principal servants, high in rank and commander of his paiks, was Bakshi Jagabandhu. The bakshi owned several rent-free lands, which were resumed by the Company's government.

These matters appear to be a necessary background to the acts of agitation in Khoordah, as these acts were led by Bakshi Jagabandhu and committed in the raja's name. At least, the Cuttack-based government officials were quite emphatic in claiming that the raja was centrally implicated in these acts, as soon as the rebellion broke out. Thus, the magistrate reported to authorities in Calcutta: "I have no doubt of the proceedings of the Insurgents being countenanced and secretly encouraged by the Rajah Makoond Dea, they repeatedly call upon his name in their violent acts, and the Buxee Jugbundoo issues all orders in the Raja's name, whilst their intention is declared to be, to proceed to Poory, and convey, the Raja into his own territory."[4]

Authorities in Fort William, the headquarters of the Bengal Presidency, however, perceived the event in a very different way. From the very beginning, they saw the insurrection as symptomatic of a general failure of governance in the province.[5] Due to this perception a number of investigations were carried out in different branches of the administration in Cuttack. Questions of land revenue occupied a substantial space in these inquiries. The Revenue Department at Fort William noted, "We see reason to apprehend both that the Bengal system of Revenue Law has in some respects, been ill-adapted to the District of Cuttack, and that the executive management of the Revenue affairs has been defective."[6]

I argue that the authenticity of the local was posed as the central object of contention in the aftermath of the insurrection in Cuttack in the same way it was framed in the *Fifth Report*. In fact, the structure of reasoning within which the act of insurrection was explained in Cuttack emerged entirely from the prevailing discourse of the local, articulations of which, as I showed in the previous chapter, could be found at every level of the imperial bureaucracy.[7] In order to decide upon a policy of revenue administration in Cuttack, the Court of Directors in London urged the Bengal government to gather "more complete information . . . regarding the system of Village Policy prevalent in Cuttack, particularly the nature of the rights and privileges enjoyed by the different classes of persons who have an interest in the soil from the zemindar down to the actual cultivator of the land."[8] The questions of a permanent settlement and the authentic proprietor of land with whom the settlement was to be made were considered as interrelated; they could only be decided through a minute investigation into tenures.

Following these orders, the collector and the commissioner in Cuttack reported on the forms of land tenure in Cuttack. Both men pointed out that in Cuttack before the British occupation the agents of government in revenue affairs were not zemindars. They were mostly village headmen, with different names in different parts of the district. The commissioner, Walter Ewer, pointed out in his report that "*by the ancient original institutions of the country the ryots of every Mouzah* under the immediate direction and management of their Pudhon Mundel or Moquddum *were the only class besides the sovereign who could claim a proprietary right in the soil*. . . . [T]hey once enjoyed the privilege of paying their revenue direct to the state, and . . . no middleman had anciently a right to intervene between them and the Government."[9] But the commissioner also argued that it was difficult to trace historically at what point of time the system changed. During the British occupation, it was found that in both Khoordah and other parts of the district the mokuddums were preponderantly in charge of revenue affairs. Ewer further noted that historically Cuttack was divided into two administrative units, one known as Rajwareh and the other as Mughalbundee. Khoordah was the principal unit of the rajwareh, the seat of the ancient raja of Orissa. So Ewer argued that "the Political state of Khoorda . . . previous to the conquest . . . by the British arms exhibited an *exact picture in miniature of the condition of Orissa under its ancient native sovereigns antecedent to the Mogul invasion and . . . that condition much resembled what I am informed is still observable in some of the Hindoo states of Hindostan and the Deccan.*"[10]

The collector and the commissioner inferred that because in ancient times the entire province of Cuttack was the territory of the raja of Khoordah, the forms of land tenure in Khoordah would indicate the original system of revenue management prevailing throughout the division. In this manner, they came to the conclusion that "the pudhan in Khoordah appears to be precisely what the mokuddums are in the Moghulbundee."[11] The commissioner's report finally recommended that future settlements be made with mokuddums or pudhans, as the supposedly original, ancient revenue managers of the country.

The *Fifth Report*'s preference for the ryotwar and classification of different forms of property rights were echoed in discussions at Cuttack. The ryotwar principle was reworked in establishing the pudhans or mokuddums as the legitimate revenue officers. Since the original peasant cultivator who shared a proprietary right with the state could not be recovered in Cuttack, the pudhans or mokuddums were considered nearest to, and the zemindars furthest from, the original proprietary figure. They were perceived to have a proprietary right in the office of revenue collection, unlike the ancient ryots, who had a proprietary right in the soil. But, as the chapter will demonstrate gradually, the local, as an assemblage of property and political power, was considered to include proprietary rights both in the soil and in the offices of revenue collection. Within that scheme, therefore, the pudhans or mokuddums could be incorporated as legitimate "proprietors." It is evident that the figure of the pudhan was rediscovered with a corresponding reconstruction of a putative ancient Hindu form of administration in Orissa, the present territorial remnant of which was taken as Khoordah, the seat of the raja. It is by reimagining the forms of land tenure in Khoordah as the symbols of an ancient Hindu administration and projecting this imagination onto the rest of Cuttack that the authenticity of the pudhan was consolidated. This is how the local of Cuttack was reintegrated into that of the nation. This principle of ordering difference was inaugurated in the *Fifth Report* and reenacted in Cuttack. Figures and relations existing at that time on the lands of Cuttack were visualized as living embodiments of an authentic spatio-emporal point—the Hindu/Indian local. Not only were they correlated to past forms, like the ancient proprietary ryot, they were also compared with present forms, like those lands of British India that still exhibited Hindu forms of the property-power complex. The next section shows how this spatiotemporal architecture was developed in terms of its generality as well as its specificity. I examine how "Cuttack" and "India" became related and secured their respective seats in this classificatory topography.

Property, "Cuttack," and "India"

Immediately after the Paik Rebellion, in 1821, Andrew Stirling, one of the leading administrators of Cuttack, wrote a "Minute on Tenures in Orissa." The minute was subsequently published, in 1822, in the form of a book entitled *An Account, Geographical, Statistical and Historical of Orissa Proper, or Cuttack*. I regard Stirling's work as one of those expositions that forged, for this locality, a definitive link between the local of "Cuttack" and the local of "India." Quite naturally, this work also acted as an authoritative reference for future administrators of Cuttack, as and when land tenures and governance met each other. In a sense, Stirling's propositions rearticulated the representations of the local that informed the official reaction to the rebellion. But his work, by developing the assumptions inherent in those discussions, outlined the horizon of their potential. Stirling's text described the lands of Cuttack as inhabited by an immense variety of figures, only in order to invest each one of them with the traces of the local that encapsulated lands all over India. Here, the staging of diversity was constitutive of a centralizing operation, which eventually harnessed and reintegrated all its elements into a single analytical trope.

Stirling began with a natural division of the lands. He noted that the country could be divided into three regions: "The marshy woodland tract which extends along the sea shore. . . . The plain and open country between this and the hills. . . . The hill country."[12] He immediately redescribed these three divisions as two, in terms of the landholders that populated them. "The first and third are known to the natives as the Eastern and Western Rajwara or Zemindara, that is, the country occupied by the ancient feudal Chieftains, Khandaits, Zemindars or Poligars of Orissa; and the second, as the Mogulbundi or Khaliseh, being that from which the indigenous sovereigns and the Mogul conquerors of the country, derived the chief part of their land revenue."[13] I showed in the previous section that a similar division of the lands of Cuttack was made in the report on tenures following the rebellion, and the rajwara was identified as the authentic form of the local, its tenures consisting of the remnants of the ancient Hindu form of administration. But Stirling's scheme had greater ambitions. It conjured up a gigantic spatiotemporal canvas on which the local of Cuttack was joined to not only an ancient Hindu India but also to lands and times far beyond it.

Stirling remarked, "In surveying attentively the ancient Political Institutions of Orissa as connected with the tenure of land, it is impossible not to be struck with the marked resemblance which many of their features exhibit to the system of European policy called the feudal, at certain stages of its progress."[14] In the very next line he increased the scope of this comparison: "I am strongly inclined to think that the comparison might be extended to India generally, and that a careful enquirer would not fail to discern in every quarter of the country, obvious traces of the former existence of such a system, however irregularly defined, and liable to variation in the details, from local peculiarities."[15] Thus, he established an interpretive frame that explained the local of land tenures, as variations of an original political form that existed under a Hindu form of administration and, thereby, represented the authentic Indian form of property in land. In support of his representations, he referred to similar opinions of other experienced administrators, working in different parts of British India.

Stirling argued that Sir J. Malcolm, in his report on Malwa (a region of west-central British India), noted that land administration in the Rajput principalities differed little from the feudal system that existed in Europe. He further observed that "every one knows that the Rajput, is only one branch or epithet of the great Regal and Military Caste amongst the Hindus, called the Cshetriya (Khetri), and anciently *all* principalities and kingdoms might in one sense be designated as Rajput."[16] Similar views, he argued, were held by Captain MacMurdo in a paper on the province of Cutch (a region in the western part of British India). Like the feudal form of administration in Europe, where power rested entirely on the possession of land, Stirling noted, there existed a giant kingdom in India in ancient times, "ruled by a sovereign residing at Hastinapura and Delhi," under whom the lands of the country were divided among a "vast number of great Military Chiefs and Feudatory Rajas, of the Khetri Caste, who were dependent on and owed service to the Lord Paramount."[17] Stirling described the administrative form of this kingdom, or empire as he put it, in the mirror of an archetypal European feudal system. He pointed out that the kings were subordinate to the emperor, "the great officers of state called the Gajapati, Aswapati, Chatrapati, and Narapati" were initially "dependent fiefs subject to the condition of Military service" but later established themselves as independent overlords of their territories.[18] This was the scale of the local. It encompassed a spatiotemporal range, which could simultaneously incorporate Cuttack, an ancient Hindu (Rajput) India, and a feudal Europe.[19] From here, Stirling proceeded to a meticulous grounding of this frame in the lands of Cuttack.

Orissa was under one of those regional sovereigns, Stirling observed, who became independent of the mighty emperor. He argued that the land tenures currently existing in the area denominated Rajwareh showed that this region was the abode of a number of military chieftains, among whom lands were distributed by the gajapati, the great sovereign of Orissa. Stirling noted that the principle of administrative independence existing between the emperor and the regional sovereigns was reproduced in the relation between the gajapati and his subordinate chiefs as well. Thus, he pointed out, "these Chiefs may be safely considered as de facto proprietors of their possessions . . . that is to say they held them hereditarily, exercised uncontrollable territorial jurisdiction within their limits, and appropriated the entire revenues, subject to the condition of performing Military service, or other offices and duties, at the court of their superior Raja, the Gajapati."[20] In Stirling's opinion, however, the other part of Cuttack, the Mughalbandi, was under the direct authority of the gajapati and consequently of his successors, like the Mughals, Marathas, and English.

Property and political power was viewed as an interconstitutive complex by Stirling. The various proprietary relations characterizing the lands of the Rajwareh and the Mughalbandi were seen as deeply imbricated in different forms of political power. The chiefs inhabiting the Rajwareh, Stirling's "feudal lords," were variously known as Khandait, Bhuyan, Poligar, Sawant, Sirdar, and finally, zemindars. Stirling noted that these chiefs "held their situations hereditarily, and were in the habits of mortgaging or even selling the whole or shares of them, with the sanction of the ruling power."[21] But he further pointed out that this never implied a right of property in the soil itself. That right, he argued, can be imagined to have belonged only to the actual cultivators of the soil under the ancient Hindu government, but he did not find any traces of it in Cuttack. Further, almost echoing the discussion in the *Fifth Report*, he noted that such a right was existent in Canara and Malabar (regions in the south of British India), adding, "I have never yet been able to discover any well authenticated instance of the *sale* or *mortgage* of land by a Malguzari ryot of the province."[22]

Stirling now turned to the Mughalbandi and its proprietary forms. The Mughalbandi, under the Mughal administration, ceased to be the territory of the gajapati and came under the direct management of the Mughals. Stirling remarked that the ministers of Akbar, however, did not change the system of revenue management in that area; they only translated the Oriya names into Persian ones. The revenue officers of the state here were known as chowdris, talukdars, vilaity canoongoes, mokuddums, and other names. Describing the nature of their attachment to the land, Stirling noted: "Amongst the chief of their duties were the collection of the Government Revenue assessed on their several divisions, the control of Police, the adjustment of disputes relating to the Pergunnah generally, and the enforcement of all the government orders and instructions relative to the assignment and proportion of lands."[23] Against the performance of such tasks, the revenue officers received certain perquisites on the natural resources and a certain percentage on the revenue of that area.

Such a neat differentiation between chiefs of petty principalities and revenue officers of the state collapsed totally with the introduction of the British government and its principles of land administration. Henceforth, Stirling argued, "all parties whose names appeared in the public accounts of the preceding administration as answerable for or entrusted with the collection of the public dues, were forthwith acknowledged not only as Zemindars, but as proprietors of the land comprised in their Zemindaris."[24] He continued: "We must unhesitatingly class the Zemindari so created, as nothing higher than a Talukdari, or a mere official trust."[25] As such a practice became regular, the erstwhile chowdris and canungo talukdars styled themselves as zemindars, while the "proper Zemindars," according to Stirling, adopted the title of raja. This process of contamination reached its culmination under the British government, when every description of persons responsible for the payment of revenue marked them in the official accounts as zemindars. Thus, Stirling noted: "We may distinguish no less than seven different grades of persons holding offices and tenures connected with land, who appear in the Collector's accounts as Zemindars, and absolute proprietors of the soil."[26] These were the "ancient Zemindars (now Rajahs) . . . Zemindars of Mogul or Mahratta creation . . . Chowdhri and Canungo Talukdars . . . (Mazkuri) Mokuddums . . . Village accountants, called Serberakars, and Karjis . . . head-men (Poorsettis) of Patnas . . . holders of lands . . . called Kheridah."[27]

Stirling argued that the British government misconstrued each of these revenue officers of the state, existing in the Mughalbandi, as the absolute proprietors of lands. The confusion, he noted, existed at two levels. First, as I have already pointed out, he argued that the zemindars in the accounts of the British administrators were actually revenue managers employed by the state. The true zemindars, he further emphasized, by presenting excerpts from authoritative works in the history of India, such as the "Ayin Acberi" and Ferishteh's text, were "feudal" chiefs, possessing "a title of property, and accountable to their sovereign only for the performance of such services, military or otherwise, as the condition of their tenure imposed"[28] Second, he noted that as revenue managers, the tenure holders in the Mughalbandi held "offices connected with the land, of different degrees of authority and importance, each having its distinct duties and perquisites."[29] These offices were hereditary, and deeds of sale that made the British believe that they reflected sales of lands were actually sales of positions of management. When these offices fell into arrears, the Mughal government transferred them, by sale, to other managers. But the authority of such management was always partial, distributed among a collectivity of various other managers. That is why, Stirling argued, such deeds of sale were addressed to the entire body of proprietary interest holders, "the Amils, Mutsuddis, Chowdris, Canoongos, Mokuddams, ryots, and cultivators," and not exclusively to any individual.[30] Such addresses, he also noted, were never issued to the authentic zemindars.

As is evident, Stirling's text was an operation in disentangling the different lineages of the local. Stirling separated the Rajwareh from the Mughalbandi on the basis of the different relations between property and political power that marked these lands. Proprietary rights in the soil itself, according to his representations, could never be located in the varied repertoire of tenures in Cuttack. That kind of proprietary right, if existent at all, could only be found in those lands where the tenures reflected the mode of administration of an ancient Hindu kingdom. A proprietary right in the soil, belonging only to the peasant cultivators, however, did not exhaust the domain of property in India. For Stirling, landed property in India existed both in the soil and in the offices of revenue management. Surely, what is at stake in my discussions of the *Fifth Report*, or the Cuttack insurrection, or the minute on tenures, is the question of property. I have been arguing that the category of the local was assembled over various sites, in different manners, to make sense of property in India. What we have seen up to this point is that in various rearticulations of the category, property in India is understood as a field of infinite dispersal. There seems to be no idea of *the* proprietary right of the kind that is an exclusive, pervasive, and singular relation between land and person. Even the omnipotence of the despotic landlord state is marked in terms of a constitutive instability. Its sovereignty is always presented as supreme, yet qualified by the social practice of distribution. So we have, in Stirling's story, a vast range of diffusion of rights, from the grand sovereign, to smaller rulers, to even smaller revenue managers, village heads, and, finally, types of cultivators.

Let me now introduce some words of caution. This portrayal of property, as diffused and plural instead of unitary and singular, can easily lead to claims about difference, couched in realist terms. A significant body of scholarship on agrarian relations in colonial India has often argued, implicitly and explicitly, that absolute and divided forms of rights to land are Indian and European forms of property, essentially. This line of argument also acts as the basis of the claim that land settlements in the Company's time were products of a fundamental inability of European understandings of property to correctly recognize Indian proprietary forms. I argue that these distinctions themselves were produced by varying articulations of the local, across political economy, governance, and, as we will see later, quotidian social practice. In that sense the singular-plural opposition was immanent to the workings of the local.

Rachel Sturman makes a similar point in thinking about histories of property, in her work on liberalism. She notes, "What scholars have typically identified as the misrecognized features of Indian property—its nonabsolute, nonprivate character, and the multiple, layered, and partial claims that it bore—were also at least to some extent recognized as part of the English Common Law in Blackstone's time. . . . Moreover, these analyses reproduce the dominant Western formulation of property as a 'bundle of rights,' only in this case with the various 'sticks' held by the different owners."[31] Stirling's text, therefore, can be considered as one site in a wider field of discursive practices that construed property in India as dispersed, being embedded in multiple lineages of the fractured political. Across these sites, there was an effort to sort out these lineages in terms of their varying respectability, into a hierarchy. The upcoming sections show how this hierarchy was reinterpreted time and again, till it acquired a fixed character during the settlement of Cuttack. All along, in and out of Cuttack, within and beyond specific locales, this process invested various agrarian figures with new lineages and new identities.

Cultivators and Proprietors

As I noted earlier, right from the beginning of the nineteenth century express instructions were communicated to authorities in British India from the Court of Directors in London, about knowing in detail the various interests connected with land in the newly acquired territories of the Company. Orders from London emphasized that any decision on a long-lasting settlement could be taken only on the basis of such knowledge. I have already demonstrated that similar opinions on the issue were articulated in Cuttack, after the rebellion. But the hot seat of contention involving all questions of settlement, during the first three decades of the nineteenth century, was located elsewhere. The biggest territorial acquisition of the Company at the turn of the century was a region administratively classified as the "Ceded and Conquered Provinces." Situated in the northwest of India, this area was conquered between 1801 and 1803. It consisted of the districts of Bareli,

Moradabad, Farrakkhabad, Etawah, Kanpur, Allahabad, Gorakhpur, Saharanpur, Aligarh, Agra, and Bundelkhand.[32]

The history of settlements in this region was similar to that of Cuttack. From the time of its conquest, a series of short-term settlements were carried out under the promise of a permanent settlement in the near future. The promise was never fulfilled, however. As Imtiaz Husain notes, "The Bengal Government under Lord Wellesley had promised a permanent settlement for the Ceded and Conquered Provinces. But between 1807 and 1813 the applicability of that policy to those regions was earnestly discussed, and a radical departure from the Bengal system of land settlement emerged."[33] Subsequently, a new mode of settlement for this region was gradually assembled under the leadership of Holt Mackenzie, secretary to the Territorial Department of the Government of Bengal. In this section, I closely examine the vision of the local that informed this new model of settlement. Once again a variety of power relations between landholders of different descriptions and the state were established as the object of agrarian governance.

Here too the complex of property and political power was conceived as diffused and dispersed. It was considered to be distributed in varying capacities among the state and various kinds of landholders. It was seen as a shared domain of power where the state, the big landholders like zemindars and talukdars, and the small landholders like village headmen and cultivating peasants of various kinds all enjoyed varying degrees of proprietary rights. These proprietary rights were seen to be vested in both offices of revenue collection and the soil itself. But at the same time, there was an urge to fashion this welter of rights along the lines of a perfect ryotwar condition, by extracting the figure of the cultivating peasant and investing him with superior proprietary rights. His superiority over others in this matrix was argued for on the basis of the respectability of his lineage in the hierarchy of the local. He was viewed as the surviving form of that proprietor, who, in ancient times, shared the right of property in the soil with the state. Even in the North-Western Provinces, like Cuttack, however, the cultivating peasant proprietor could rarely be found in his pristine, ancient, original form. In most cases he was seen as embodying a history of loss, as an absent presence. His full presence, therefore, could be only be recovered by the operation of the local, which made visible the loss through traces left in time and space.[34]

In 1819, Mackenzie wrote a memorandum on the land and people of the Ceded and Conquered Provinces, reflecting on the past settlements in the region and putting forward a detailed plan for a future one. Mackenzie noted that the memorandum was written in response to the concerns expressed by the Court of Directors, which wanted to obtain "not merely . . . more ample information . . . respecting the general nature and the resources of the districts . . . and the quality and value of the produce; but . . . a full and particular detail of all local tenures and usages."[35] In presenting his vision of a settlement, Mackenzie seemed to be following a perception similar to Stirling that proprietary rights in land are plural and partial. So it was imperative to protect each, because superior holders have the tendency of usurping the rights of inferior ones. Thus, he emphasized the "importance of . . . ascertaining the nature and extent of the rights, interests, and privileges of the various classes of persons connected with the land, and . . . if such a course be not followed, all will be sacrificed to the Sudder Malgoozar, whose interest in the land, or the revenue of the land, if left undefined, is not naturally conceived to be that of absolute and exclusive property, and whose means of destroying or evading the rights of his inferior tenants are so powerful."[36]

Difference, however, had its own role to play in the Ceded and Conquered Provinces. The discussion on proprietary rights here grafted itself on new figures and new relationships. Mackenzie noted that in spite of the presence of big landholders, such as the talukdars, the proprietary rights of a particular form of subordinate holder, described as the village zemindars, were recognized by the administrators in this region. He pointed out that "the rights of the village Zemindars, *as the chief cultivators and sole owners of the land* . . . were fully recognized, even where the revenue of Government were received from Talukdars or other superior holders."[37] Henceforth, Mackenzie directed all his energies to disentangling the figure of the village zemindar from a complex web of relations to land. He represented most of these relations as spurious, deceitful, or subordinate, in comparison to that true relation of property in land, which he claimed to be the privilege of the village zemindar. In claiming greater authenticity for the village zemindar, he simultaneously defined many more figures, who were related to land in other, less authentic, proprietary capacities.

The talukdar, Mackenzie argued, "appears seldom to have pretended to be more than the Collector of the revenue of Government, claiming, indeed, sometimes a hereditary interest in the advantages of the office, but urging no pretension to a property in the soil."[38] These tenures, he pointed out, were created in the recent past. The village zemindars, on the other hand, "were the immemorial occupants of the soil; they cultivated generation from generation. They gave, sold and mortgaged their lands at will."[39] Originally, the proprietary right of these village zemindars was an absolute one: that is, they had a right to the soil as well as a right to their share of the income from it. But in certain situations, they had to give up this right to superior holders. These superior holders came into existence at times by the gradual purchase of individual villages from their owners. Also, whenever anyone among the leading men of the village zemindars was appointed by the government to collect the revenue from a number of villages, "he appears to have engaged in a constant struggle for the extension of his Zemindari property."[40] Thus, Mackenzie noted, wherever the talukdari tenure prevailed, the talukdar asserted the superiority of his proprietary rights, by presenting evidence of a variety of transactions, like sales, gifts, or mortgages, with the original village zemindars. But in spite of such superior claims, Mackenzie emphasized, since the zemindars had an inviolable right to the soil, even when they were forced to dispose of their property, they "would still continue to cultivate their paternal fields, and the leading men among them, preserving their influence in the village, might naturally be employed to manage it on behalf of the purchaser, in the character of a *Ryot Mocuddum*."[41]

There were other instances, however, where the village zemindars were found existing as undisturbed, sole proprietors of their lands. Mackenzie described them as putteedari tenures, where the lands of the villages were held by a multitude of sharers called putteedars. In Bundelkhand, for example, he noted that "all the persons from whom the Government revenue was collected, appear to have been Village Zemindars, themselves the cultivators of the soil."[42] He also observed that this did not necessarily mean that these village zemindars were the only cultivators of the soil. They often hired cultivators and slaves, depending on their caste and the extent of their possessions. The cultivators of the fields, Mackenzie noted, were primarily of two kinds. The khoodkasht ryot were firmly attached to their cultivating fields, possessing a prescriptive right of occupancy, dependent on the payment of a rent, based on fixed rates. The pykasht ryots, on the contrary, were traveling cultivators, without a fixed residence in those villages, the lands of which they cultivated. Mackenzie described the form of tenure these cultivators held primarily with reference to the way they were related to the village zemindars. Thus, where the village zemindars were cultivating proprietors, he considered "the only real description of Khoodkasht Ryots to be of the family of the Zemindar."[43] He further emphasized that although the khoodkhast ryots in Bengal did not currently enjoy such proprietary privileges, the way this tenure was imbricated in the authentic proprietary form of the village zemindar in the North-Western Provinces clearly provided ground for the assumption that "the resident Ryots of Bengal were originally of the same class with the Village Zemindars . . . vested with an equal right of property in the soil they occupied."[44]

Mackenzie's representations, I argue, opened up the imagination of a new form of proprietary body on land, by retaining yet reinterpreting the older inventory of the local. With the arrival of the figure of the village zemindar, the long-standing administrative imagination of the ryot, or the cultivating proprietor as the authentic proprietor, reflective of the ancient Hindu/Indian mode of administration, was significantly redefined. Here the logic of the local was again instrumental. Invoking it, Mackenzie could establish the village zemindar as the genuine proprietor, by locating his origin in the ryot, or peasant cultivator. Wherever he was not found as a cultivating proprietor, Mackenzie could argue, his proprietary capacities got lost over time. This time was seen as one of corruption and invasion, when the predatory habits of big landlords, or even at times fellow village zemindars, spoilt the pristine status of the proprietor ryot. Once again, the local worked to establish spatiotemporal equivalences between lands and figures. The puttedars of Bundelkhand, the village zemindars of the North-Western Provinces, the khoodkhasht ryot of Bengal, the mokuddums of Cuttack, the ryots of Canara—all were getting organized as a series, where each could substitute the other, and many more could emerge as further substitutes. But there were also closures to this series, as it was joined to a hierarchy.

For example, Mackenzie's deliberations also indicated certain political-economic preferences. While discussing the village zemindars, Mackenzie opined that it was greatly beneficial to have such a class of "cultivating yeomanry" as the payers of government revenue. He argued that it was certainly better to have such a group as rent holders than the zemindars of Bengal. "I confess I see little or no chance of the great zemindars (or hereditary collectors) ever becoming capable of taking part in any regular or good system of internal government."[45] It is evident that Mackenzie's understanding of property was shaped by a certain vision of "improvement," the agent of which was the figure of the cultivating proprietor. Practices of governance recognized and instituted property in India as fragmentary, reflecting the state of the political. This was a vision where the meaning of property was made by the nature of sovereignty. But the same practices also tried to make sense of property in terms of a productivist ethic by encouraging those forms of it that were rooted in use. As we have seen, similar moves were visible in the entangled fields of science and political economy in contemporary Britain as well. But I will turn to that later. For the moment, it is important to note that what came out of these debates was, in turn, highly important for Cuttack. The settlement of

Cuttack, as I showed earlier, was carried out under a regulation that emerged out of the settlement experience of the North-Western Provinces.

A Place for Everyone

Mackenzie's representations were to form the bulwark of the official regulation, following which the first survey and settlement took place in Cuttack between 1837 and 1843. But there was a considerable difference between Mackenzie's enunciations and the final formulation they acquired as a legislative enactment. In this section, I follow those deliberations over which the object of agrarian governance reached its most definite articulation in the first half of the nineteenth century.

It emerges from the previous section that Mackenzie conceived of the village zemindars as a collective of cultivating proprietors, found to exist in its most uncontaminated form in the putteedari tenure. Mackenzie wanted the engagements to be made with one or two representatives of the multitude of village zemindars composing the putteedari tenure. But at the same time, he proposed that the rights of the rest should be recorded in detail.[46] Arguing against a mode of settling revenue with each cultivating proprietor of the collective, he observed that "it would not perhaps be desirable to dissolve the village association by a rapid and extensive admission of the cultivators of the soil to engagements with Government."[47] These comments were in tune with the understanding that proprietary rights in India were vested in a dispersed cluster of power relationships, with a collective of cultivating proprietors embodying its most authentic form. So it was considered necessary, within Mackenzie's scheme, to record and retain this power complex and not break it down into individual, unrelated, discrete units of cultivating proprietors. It was important to maintain the relatedness of the collective, as the essential nature of power invested in proprietary rights seemed to emerge from specific equations of relatedness. I show in the next chapter how the village was identified as the quintessential *site* of this relatedness. Thus, Mackenzie's propositions, for having as the engagers of government revenue, a few of the leading men of the collective, promoting a mode of improvement with *the* cultivating proprietor as its leader, had to sit, even if uneasily, with the idea that the individual cultivating proprietor could be projected as a potential agent of improvement only as a part of the proprietary collective.

Similar opinions in favor of preserving the collective of village zemindars were presented by Charles Metcalfe, one of the leading administrators of the time and a member of the Council of the Governor-General. Metcalfe's views revolved around the question of the suitability of a ryotwar mode of settlement. The plan of settlement designed for the Ceded and Conquered Provinces closely resembled the ryotwar model. As members of the Board of Revenue noted, "The main purposes of Regulation VII of 1822 could be attained only by means of field surveys, so recorded on paper as to show distinctly how every owner or occupant of land in a village was connected, either as receiver or payer of rent, with the fields in which his interest existed."[48] Metcalfe, however, argued against a ryotwar settlement from a different perspective. He noted that it was absolutely essential to retain the method of surveying and recording, similar to the ryotwar mode. But the engagers of government revenue should be, instead of the individual cultivators, the representatives of the "village community." This method, Metcalfe argued, "would bring to light the owners of every portion of land, and the right of each member of the village community, without rendering it necessary to conclude engagements otherwise than with the village community jointly represented by their headmen."[49] He believed that it would both allow the headmen to exercise legitimate duties with respect to the collective yet preclude them from growing into usurpers of power.

This was a different vision of the ryotwar, reworked by the contention that putteedari was the most ancient and original tenure form of India. The ryot, as a coproprietor of the state, was no longer envisioned as an individual figure. Henceforth, his proprietary identity was viewed in terms of his membership in the collective. He became a ryot-in-the-collective, and his proprietary status was seen as indissociable from this collectivity. Yet at the same time, an individual ryot had to be put forward as a representative figure of this collective. Both Mackenzie and Metcalfe wanted this figure to be the engager of government revenue and the supervisor of the collective. But the possibilities of the proprietary form in India were not exhausted by these formulations. The logic of the local creatively reappeared in a text by William Bentinck. Bentinck, who was governor-general at that time, was closely involved in all these discussions around issues of settlement. In 1832, he wrote a minute that critically informed the enactment of Regulation IX of 1833, under the guidelines of which the settlement in Cuttack took place.

Bentinck, while retaining to a great extent Mackenzie's interpretation of tenures, created provisions for a significantly different deployment of its tenets. Echoing Mackenzie's representations, Bentinck noted that the "Putteedari is the original and natural tenure of all the lands in the Country."[50] He also pointed out, that the "Zemindari or Talukdari tenure is adventitious and artificial, being, generally speaking, a creation of the Moghul Government, and the Talukdar or Zemindar . . . himself being originally neither more nor less than a contractor with Government for its Revenue."[51] Yet, making a critical move away from previous constructions, Bentinck argued that even zemindari and talukdari tenures might possess authentic proprietary rights. He said that those zemindars and talukdars who acquired their tenure, in some way or the other, from the "village community" should be considered authentic proprietors. He noted that such tenures might have been created "either from the foundation of the village community having been laid by individual capital or from subsequent acquisition of the proprietary interests of those by whom or by whose ancestors the first occupation was made or from some other competent origin."[52] In this manner, by creating a scope for these tenures to become legitimately associated to the "village proprietors," Bentinck enabled the domain of proprietary rights to expand in its scope, while remaining firmly rooted within that collective, which represented its authentic form.

Also, by stating that the ryot, as a member of this collective, was endowed with true proprietary rights, Bentinck repeated the earlier tradition of representing proprietary rights in India as jointly held by the sovereign and the cultivator. For Bentinck, however, the ryot with proprietary rights was only one among the many peasant cultivators bearing the same title. He pointed out, "I am of the opinion that throughout the country there are three descriptions of ryots. The first class I consider as being to all intents and purposes proprietors of the lands which they cultivate, the second as having been originally tenants at will, but acquiring in course of time a prescriptive right of occupancy at fixed rates, and the third as mere contract cultivators."[53] Further, in describing the first kind, Bentinck, repeating earlier representations of the "ryot-proprietor," gave the example of the meerasidars of Deccan.[54] As examples of the second and third kind in the context of Deccan, Bentinck spoke of the judeed and pykasht ryots. The meerasidars, however, he observed, used to possess such proprietary rights during the ancient Hindu government. But over time, during the period of Muslim rule, their proprietary profits were entirely extracted by the state as revenue. As a result they were reduced to the status of occupant cultivators, or the ryot of the second kind in Bentinck's scheme. The threefold classification of ryots was thus reduced to a twofold one, using the recurring explanatory trope of the local.[55] So, what remained of the previous representation of the proprietary was the centrality of the ryot-as-a-member-of-the-village-collective. What got added to the scope of this authentic proprietary form were zamindars and talukdars, and a finer classification of cultivators.

The same divisions, Bentinck noted, prevailed in Cuttack as well. There were the occupant cultivators, or thanee ryots, having their residence and rates of rent fixed, subject to the payment of government revenue, and there were the migratory cultivators, or pykasht ryots. The thanee ryots, Bentinck also noted, were known as the khoodkhast ryots in Bengal. Here, Bentinck's analysis returned, after a full circle, to Mackenzie's portrayal of the khoodkhast ryots of Bengal as originally being of the same class as the proprietary ryots of the village communities. In the course of these deliberations, however, Bentinck had expanded the scope of the domain of proprietary rights, by elaborating on the various figures of the ryots, zemindars, and talukdars, as embodying legitimate, even if distant, legacies of the original collective of village proprietors. In a certain sense, therefore, Bentinck's scheme reinterpreted all these figures as ryots, of varying lineages.

Finally, keeping in line with the opinions of Mackenzie, Metcalfe, and others regarding the need to maintain the jointness of such tenures, Bentinck resolved that wherever the putteedari tenure was found, engagements for the revenue of government would be made with the headmen, as representatives of the collective. In those situations where legitimate talukdars and zemindars existed, Bentinck noted, the rights of all subordinate landholders would be recorded, in order to fix equitably the legitimate distribution of power relations among them. Bentinck's resolutions received official sanction in the enactment of Regulation IX of 1833. In keeping a place for everyone, it reinstituted the Indian property-power complex as a fractured field of sovereignty. Zemindars and talukdars had been excluded from this field since the failure of the Permanent Settlement in Bengal. With Bentinck, they reentered the folds of the local with newly discovered lineages of authenticity.[56] In four years' time, settlement operations began in Cuttack.

The New Proprietary Landscape of Cuttack

In this section, I look at administrative practices that invested the different prominent village-level figures of Cuttack with different kinds of rights. Arguments over their authentic proprietary status flew along circuitous pathways of the bureaucratic apparatus. In the course of the settlement of each and every village, these figures rose to prominence in a manner never known before. Exclusive proprietors or not, they surely emerged as lynchpins of the local in Cuttack.

In 1823, the Court of Directors argued in one of its dispatches that Mr. Kerr, erstwhile commissioner of Cuttack, "found a class of persons who are called Mourousee Moquddums, and whom he recognized as possessing a right to the soil. . . ."[57] The prospect of such a claim was immediately scrutinized using the interpretive scheme that defined the proprietary form of India. Once again, the logic of the local was triggered to apply the same piece of "empirical" evidence that was deployed in different contexts, from the *Fifth Report* to Bentinck's minute, to explain the supposedly specific situation of Cuttack. The court noted,

> The name suggests the idea of a similarity with the class of Meerasidars in some of the more Southern Provinces of India. That the foundation of the rights of these Meerasidars was laid in those of the proprietary class of ryots, known in your Provinces by the name of Khode Khast Ryots seems to be sufficiently ascertained. Where rights and prerogatives beyond those of proprietary ryots are claimed on the part of the Meerasidars they seem in all cases to have been those annexed to the head ryots, the managers of villages, and in many cases, when ages of exaction had destroyed the rights and obliterated the claims of the general class of Khode Khast ryots, the claims of the descendants of these headmen, under the title of Meerasidars, seem to be all that are recognized in existence of the rights of the proprietary ryots.[58]

This dispatch marked the beginning of a serious consideration of the proprietary prospects of mokuddums in Cuttack. As is evident, the court found in the mokuddums the only legitimate traces of those proprietary rights that belonged to the "meerasidars" or "khoodekhast ryots" in ancient times. In this way, while the peasant cultivator's ancient proprietary status was retained, it was at the same time reinterpreted as belonging in the present to only a select few of those ryots, who were perceived as its authentic legatees. Such interpretive strategies of simultaneous inclusion and exclusion of the archetypal cultivating proprietor, or ryot, in the debates over proprietary rights had significant consequences for the status of an immense variety of cultivators.

It is evident that by the 1820s it was resolved at all levels of administration that "village proprietors" were the original propertied body on land in India. As I showed earlier, there was a strong administrative urge to preserve this body wherever it was found in its authentic form. This attitude made itself visible in Cuttack as well. In 1824, an extract from a resolution in the territorial department was sent to the commissioner's office in Cuttack, which stated unequivocally, "It is in no degree the intention of Government suddenly . . . to break down the communities of Village Proprietors."[59] But it was also argued, as I noted with regard to the court's dispatch, that in Cuttack the true descendants of these village proprietors were the "head ryots," or "managers of villages." Such village managers were named variously, as mokuddums, serberakars, and pudhans in Cuttack. It must be kept in mind that in the discussion following the Paik Rebellion it was argued that the pudhan in the Rajwareh and the mokuddum in the Moghulbundee were merely different names for the same figure, that is, the village manager, possessing authentic proprietary rights in the land. Following the renewed interest in such figures, it was considered absolutely crucial to decide their proprietary status.

Pudhans were found mostly in the district of Pooree, located in the southern part of Cuttack. In 1833, Wilkinson, the collector of Pooree offered his opinion to the commissioner of Cuttack about the "privileges to be awarded to the recorded zemindars and their subordinate mokuddums or pudhans."[60] Wilkinson argued that these zemindars had purchased their situations from the mokuddums and pudhans, who, according to him, were "the proprietors of the soil of their respective villages."[61] In defining the status of these mokuddums and pudhans, who coexisted with zemindars, Wilkinson stated that they could not be considered the sole proprietors. It must be remembered that Bentinck had argued in his minute that those zemindars who acquired their proprietary rights legitimately from the village proprietors should be considered bona fide proprietors. In the same vein, regarding the apportionment of the "malikana," or the proprietary allowance, Wilkinson insisted that "the Mokuddums who pay through a zemindar cannot be considered the sole proprietors and the zemindars should have some proportion of the Malikana."[62] In fact, Wilkinson referred to Bentinck's minute in confirmation of his views. Finally, he suggested that an equal share of both the malikana and the expenses of collection should be given to each of these proprietors, where they existed together.

The situation described by Wilkinson existed extensively in Cuttack. There were two kinds of landholder in almost all mahals, or units of settlement. On the one hand, there were persons known as zemindars, who had been treated as the sudder malgoozar, or the engagers of government revenue in the years before the settlement. On the other, there were persons designated as pudhans, mokuddums, or serberakars who had been conceived, with varying emphasis, from the time of the rebellion to the present, as bearing traces of the original proprietary body of village zemindars. On the eve of the settlement, however, the critical attitude toward zemindars characteristic of Mackenzie, Harrington, and others was counterbalanced by Bentinck, who revalidated their authentic proprietary status. But despite this reinvigorated position of support for the zemindars, the landholders in Cuttack considered as proximate to the village proprietors could not be marginalized in this complex and conflicting field of administrative practices.

Old ideas of the zemindar as a supra-village landlord with exclusive proprietary rights were renegotiated in the course of the settlement in Cuttack. The Sadar Board of Revenue in Calcutta had firmly stated that the entire malikana and allowances for risks of collection "should be assured to the parties under engagements with Government as zemindars and not to any of the subordinate holders."[63] But in response to Wilkinson's proposal of an equal distribution of the malikana, the board also pointed out that the next related matter to be discussed was the particular nature of the interests of the mokuddums who existed in the estates of the zemindars. The local of the Ceded and Conquered Provinces had entered that of the Bengal Presidency. These entanglements articulated themselves when the Sadar Board remarked that if these mokuddums were found to be different from the village zemindars, or "maliks," of the Ceded and Conquered Provinces, "no proposition for dividing and allotting the net profit, need be, for a moment entertained."[64] Accordingly, the board laid down a number of points that were to be investigated in every single instance of settlement, in order to discern whether the mokuddums were maliks.

The settlement officers were asked to find out whether the mokuddums themselves put forward any claim of proprietorship. Further, they were given a set of guidelines to define proprietorship, in the form of questions about the dues the mokuddums received. "Do they receive house rent from artisans? Do they enter upon the lands of a thanee Ryot which have escheated? Do they receive rent from woods, tanks . . . or enjoy any other of the perquisites denoting the retention of proprietary right?"[65] The board also wanted the nature of inheritance of these tenures to be examined. They wanted to know what was inherited—an office or an interest in the soil itself. All these prescriptions tell us how the proprietary was being instituted at the level of individual villages and plots of land. What we will see is that, as elsewhere, here too property was understood to be both a right in offices and the soil, an index of both sovereignty and productivity. In other words, the question of productivity was considered to be that of sovereignty as well, and, therefore, one needed to be articulated in terms of the other's dispersals.

So even when they were not formally considered proprietors, the mokuddums and serberakars of Cuttack where granted significant rights as hereditary managers. Mouza Ruttadeah in Talooka Baumunpoor was claimed as a mokuddumee tenure holder. The settlement officers granted a prescriptive right of possession to the mokuddum and an allowance of 15 percent on the expenses of collection. Proprietary rights were, however, denied. A similar course of proceedings was followed in Mouza Oortee.[66] In Mouza Gowalsing, the mokuddums tried to prove their proprietary right. They produced deeds of sale showing that they had purchased lands of other villages and had annexed these lands to this village. The settlement officer, however, remarked: "Their witnesses failed to establish the validity of these documents and no proofs denoting them Maliks of the village were adduced."[67] There were situations as well where the mokuddums and serberakars were granted different kinds of rights. In Talooka Ramchunderpoor, the serberakars were considered mere managers and were granted 10 percent on the expenses of collection, as opposed to which the mokuddums were recorded as proprietors with a higher allowance of 15 percent, in recognition of their proprietary right. In a memorandum on this settlement, it was noted: "The Mokuddums stand on a different footing, they have a right of property apparently, in the soil; which having been conceded, is of course a saleable property."[68] But the same memorandum noted that because in Erdanga and Kespoor the pudhan could not prove any right, the zemindar was registered as the exclusive proprietor.

In the various villages of Talooka Rughoonathpore the mokuddums were granted proprietary rights either on the basis of original "sunnuds" (government letters) where these rights were recorded or on the oral testimonies of old villagers of the mokuddums' rights to grant rent-free lands. In some instances, existence of these rights was also inferred from the sunnuds of lakhirajdars, or holders of rent-free lands. The settlement officer noted that in Sandholessur "the original sunnud was not forthcoming but from a Goomnamah . . . and from the Sunnuds of Lakhirajdars it appears that the ancestors of the present Mokuddums purchased the mokuddumee from the former zemindar & exercised the usual rights of granting land free of rent."[69]

The settlement in Cuttack, by investing these figures, which resembled the village proprietors, with various kinds of rights, eventually secured a firm position for them in the property-power complex of British India. Undoubtedly, a number of distinctions were made between the different kinds of rights granted to these landholders. The malikana was reserved mostly for the zemindar as the sudder malgoozar, or principal engager of government revenue. But at the same time, the mokuddums in his estate were granted an equal amount of allowance, namely, 20 percent on the expenses of collection, as hereditary managers with a prescriptive right of possession vested in the office. Malikana was granted to mokuddums in those cases, albeit very few in number, where they existed as the party under engagement. Wherever these mokuddums were identified as "mowroosee," they were considered real proprietors. As I have shown, such identification was made mostly through the sunnuds of holders of rent-free lands. The final settlement papers noted: "The Mowroosee, or old hereditary Mokuddums, were doubtless the 'rightful proprietors of the soil,' and their tenures are of a heritable and transferable nature."[70] The pudhans, found mostly in southern Cuttack, were treated in a light similar to mowroosee mokuddums. Their tenures were considered hereditary and transferable in nature, and they were also allowed malikana, being the exclusive engagers of government revenue. The serberakars, however, were considered only hereditary managers. These tenures were perceived to be hereditary offices of management and were granted an allowance of either 15 or 20 percent on the "jumma (revenue payable to the government)," as expenses of collection.

It emerges clearly from this differentiation of rights that these landholders were decisively entrenched as mainstays in the economy of agrarian relations in Cuttack. The zemindar, despite being recorded as the sudder malgoozar in most cases, had his sovereignty fractured and distributed among these other landholders. The zemindar had always been the pivotal figure in the networks of power on land. But these serberakars, mokuddums, and pudhans, for the first time, riding on the wave of an overwhelming administrative admiration for village proprietors, wrenched an official sanction of their sovereignties. In Cuttack, like everywhere else, the uncontested supremacy that the zemindars used to enjoy was eclipsed. There were new players in the field of power. This differentiability was not unlimited, however. Certain principles of differentiability were newly introduced at the level of the villages. We will see in a later chapter how these principles were vigorously contested by various agrarian groups in the locality, and how some of them crystallized as formal markers of the authenticity of property in the process.

Property and Sovereignty: Richard Jones

It is time to return to political economy in contemporary Britain. In this chapter I have demonstrated how an ensemble of proprietary relations and political power got constituted as the object of agrarian governance. In the previous chapter I argued that rent was perceived to be a key marker of this domain of power. Rent emerged as the leading conceptual category over which a number of methodological debates took place, leading to a reorientation of the epistemological underpinnings of contemporary political economy. These changes established the property-power complex as the object of knowledge in political economy. Now, in exploring this object, I will read political economy in the light of British Indian agrarian governance.

In Richard Jones's scheme, the interrelation between the political-economic categories of rent, wage, and profit, constituting the sphere of distribution, was considered to be conditioned by the different arrangements of property and sovereignty in the world. In other words, Jones argued that an ensemble of property and political power determined how the different portions of the whole produce, as rent, wage, and profit, would be distributed to different groups of society. This distribution took place differently in different nations, depending upon the specific form of the ensemble prevailing in them. As I argued earlier, for Jones, distribution and production were integrally related domains in political economy. Thus, the specific mode of distribution also shaped the specific potential of production. In this manner, Jones oriented production toward property and sovereignty. These categories became integrated into one analytical field.

In the greater part of the world, Jones noted, a vast majority of the population labored on the land to secure the means of subsistence. He argued that a lack of employment and capital in nonagricultural occupations kept these laborers "confined to the cultivation of the earth by an insuperable necessity, by adamantine chains, which cannot be broken by any human power."[71] In these conditions, rents and wages determined each other. Jones pointed out that, "of the produce of the soil, a part is left in the hands of the occupier—it constituted his wages; a part goes to the owner of the soil—it constitutes his rent."[72] All of this, he argued, was linked to the fundamental absence of capital in these nations. He defined capital as "'accumulated wealth employed with a view to profit,' and only such wealth."[73] It was that division of wealth that brought out the greatest productive capacities of nations by organizing production in a specific manner. It acted as the fund from which laborers received their wages. It created those conditions of laboring where labor could be most continuous, skillful, and powerful. To summarize, capital created the best conditions for the production of wealth, by enabling the highest productive efficiency of labor.[74]

Jones argued that the absence of capital, and consequently of the most advanced form of laboring, in the greater part of the world were effects of the conditions under which production and distribution were organized there. He traced these conditions to the specific configurations of proprietary relations and political power. He noted that "when the lands of a country are appropriated, and the agriculturalists are dependent on the possession of portions of them for subsistence, political systems are generated, which inevitably secure the political and social subordination—we might almost say servitude—of the peasantry."[75] He proceeded to explain differences in the forms of these "political systems," by reconstructing the historical roots of entanglements between property and sovereignty in the careers of nations.

Jones noted that property in land could be divided into "European" and "Asiatic" forms. In the European nations land belonged to individuals as private property, while in the Asiatic ones it was the property of the sovereign. Jones emphasized that this difference emerged from the different constitutions of power that characterized the ruling groups of these nations. In Asiatic nations, the power of the state was absolute, which made the sovereign the paramount owner of all lands in his dominion. Jones attributed this form of power to the political constitution of the earliest invaders of these nations. "Wherever these Scythian invaders have settled, they have established a despotic form of government, to which they have readily submitted themselves, while they were obliging the inhabitants of the conquered countries to submit to it."[76] Contrary to this, Jones argued, the Germanic tribes established a free constitution in the European nations conquered by them. The difference between the political constitutions of the earliest invaders, which gave birth to different political systems in the two kinds of nations, had its roots in the essentially pastoral nature of one of these groups. "It may be found perhaps, in a great measure, in the different character of their original seats. Amidst the fastnesses and morasses of his native woods, the German, when not actually at war, was in tolerable security; his habits of military obedience, we know, relaxed."[77] In comparison to this, the Tartars and the Afghans, who introduced a "despotic" constitution in the Asiatic nations, never settled peacefully in the lands they occupied. Jones stated, "The task of guarding their property and lives, is a constant campaign; and their habits of military submission have no intervals of relaxation; they are born and they die in them."[78] Thus, he noted, "it is certain that the Tartars have every where either adopted or established a political system, which unites so readily with their national habits of submission in the people, and absolute power in the chiefs. . . . Throughout agricultural Asia . . . the same system prevails."[79]

It might appear that Jones, having redefined the object of political economy as an enmeshment of sovereignty and property, continued to work within the usual opposition between the European proprietary form as "free" and the Asian one as "despotic." Lawrence Krader insightfully documents in his work the long tradition of European thinking that made, and dwelt on, this opposition. This tradition, he notes, emerged in the seventeenth century: "The object of their comparative study was the form of rulership, law, and the political or moral judgment of the origins and effects of these. To these aims and means the political economy was later added."[80] These writers' focus on the political, or the nature of sovereignty, was critically embedded in their examination of property. They accounted for difference, as Europe and Asia, in terms of a theoretical principle of the relationship between the proprietary and the political. Krader puts Richard Jones within this tradition, arguing that his political economy was developed on the assumption that in India sovereignty was despotic and all property was owned by the king.[81]

Breaking off from Krader's scheme, I argue that one cannot insert Jones within a tradition that construed sovereignty in India as despotic, despite Jones's use of that category to talk about the form of property in India. Despotism continued to function, in the theoretical mobilization of the political, but as a category that was disintegrated and transformed from within. It generated new meanings for both Company governance of land and the formulations of political economy.[82] Let us now turn to Jones to see how his use of the category unpacked itself. Once the truth of distant pasts was established, he moved on to more recent pasts in order to represent the political in India as a variegated and complex field of relations of power between sovereignties/proprietors of several kinds. Through these historical excursions, he demonstrated how the despotism of power in India always remained incomplete. He pointed out that the state could never act as the absolute landlord. Instead, property in land was distributed among a number of landholders and landholding bodies of various size and status, who acquired their respective positions over time. Together, they constituted a complex calculus of power relations, which was time and again threatened by foreign conquests and the despotic possibilities of the power of the state.

For Jones, this collective composed of the state, the officers of state, like the zemindars, the potails as representatives of a collective body of proprietary power, namely, the village, and the ryots. The ryots possessed attributes of both tenant and proprietor. Their right of possessing land was hereditary and, to a great extent, permanent. Jones pointed out that the ryot was never a proprietor, in the sense of enjoying a landlord's rent from his land, or having alienable rights in the soil. In fact, while deliberating on the question of the proprietary status of ryots, Jones referred to the writings of reputed administrators of British India, like Thomas Munro and Colonel James Todd. He noted, "Sir Thomas Munro declares the ryot to be the true proprietor."[83] But he disagreed with Munro in arguing that the only right that the ryot had was of hereditary possession; he received it as "a grant from the sovereign on certain conditions; resumable at pleasure, although *practically* rarely resumed."[84] Similarly, Jones observed, the offices of zemindar and potail also became hereditary over time. Just like the British Indian administration, Jones construed various kinds of rights, either of possessing land or of possessing offices connected with land, as proprietary ones.

The same understanding of the political informed a section of his lectures on political economy at Haileybury. In this section, entitled "The Anglo-Indian Revenue Systems," Jones marked the failure of the British Indian administration to understand the political in India. He began with the blunders of the Permanent Settlement. Pointing out that the policy was "grounded upon delusions," he argued that "great ignorance prevailed at that time . . . with regard to the manifold and diversified rights connected with the soil."[85] The effect of the policy was pernicious, as it converted the revenue farmers into absolute landlords, rejecting the entire gamut of proprietary rights that coexisted with them. Jones remarked, there was, however, an attempt to correct the errors of the Permanent Settlement in Madras. He noted, echoing the way the local was mobilized to explain proprietary forms in India by administrators, that "to the southern parts of India the Mohammedans had not penetrated; and there Hindu institutions remained in their completeness and vigour."[86] Here, based on the vision of an erstwhile relation of coproprietorship between the ryot and the state, a new settlement was implemented. As Jones saw it, the political in India was still being misconstrued. Thus, he argued that the ryotwar system was "founded upon a principle just the reverse of that which was the basis of the zemindary system, but was equally false and equally fatal. The one disregarded the rights of the ryot, its framers having been deluded by a name into confounding together an infinite diversity of proprietary claims and interests; while the other swept away, suddenly and violently, a multitude of relations, linking the highest with the lowest."[87]

In this way, I argue, Jones's writings broke the stability of the category of despotism from within. The Indian proprietary form was no longer imagined as constitutive and reflective of a singular, absolute, and totalizing form of sovereignty, namely, that of the despotic landlord state. Rather, both property and sovereignty in India were represented as a plural, uneven, dispersed, and contested welter of rights. This is why Jones kept on insisting that it was a diversity of proprietary relations and not the superiority of one to the exclusion of others that defined the political in India. The British Indian administration, time and again, falsely upheld one right at the expense of others. The misperceptions continued, Jones argued, as another system of settlement was introduced. This was based on an imagination of the ancient village as the authentic seat of proprietary rights in India. But in an attempt to recreate such a putatively ancient unit of property and government, namely, the village, a new exclusive center of power was created.[88] Clearly here Jones was referring to the foregrounding of village proprietors, along with the village, as a seat of proprietary power, in the practices of governance in British India in the early decades of the nineteenth century.

Jones perceived the political of India as a distributed field of power relations flowing out of a variety of proprietary capacities. Such an understanding of proprietary forms also informed the constitution of the object of agrarian governance in British India. Here, movements of the category of the local assembled similar conceptual relations between property and sovereignty, but only in the form of a hierarchical grid. Thus, the connection between property and political power was not configured, and sealed off, by the category of despotism. In the field of political economy, despotism was posited as a possibility, or theory, that in practice was forever fractured and incomplete. In British India, practices of governance worked with the local, aiming to return to the authentic Indian political, which was presented as a co-sharing of property (and sovereignty). As these practices waded through localities, this original form of sharing was recast as an even more dispersed and plural landscape of power. For both political economy and British Indian governance, therefore, the link between form(s) of sovereignty and property went beyond the conceptual cast of despotism. But political economy in contemporary Britain, while working with its new and transformed epistemological focus, moved toward other formulations of the problematic of property. In the next section, with a discussion of John Stuart Mill, I explore these new directions.

Custom as the Political: John Stuart Mill

The category of property played a pivotal role in fashioning John Stuart Mill's political economy. As it is well known, the greatest public trial that Mill's political-economic principles faced was over the burning question of the conditions of Ireland. While the discontentment emerging from Britain's political domination of Ireland during Mill's time revolved around a host of issues, the issue of grievances over landownership was unarguably one of the most important among them. It is in this sphere that John Stuart Mill, as one of the leading public intellectuals of his day, proposed major reforms in the existing state of property in land. Mill's location in this campaign has been critically scrutinized by a number of works.[89] Other works have pointed out that the prescriptions Mill proposed for Ireland were also directed by him toward British India.[90] Recently, it has also been argued that the experience Mill gained of British India as an employee at India House, the change in his own intellectual orientation from a strong Utilitarian position in early life to a revised one inspired by his readings of romantic and conservative European thinkers, and his engagement with Ireland's socioeconomic conditions, all influenced each other in shaping his positions on contemporary issues.[91] Moving away from the perspectives of these works, I argue that in order to understand the entanglements between his imperial location and his prescriptions for Ireland and British India, it is necessary to examine the epistemological core of his political economy, which was marked by a distinct analytical linkage between production and property in land. Such an analytical primacy of the category of property, I contend, made Mill's political economy both distinctive and, at the same time, part of a critical tradition of this branch of knowledge. Like Richard Jones, Mill forged connections between property in land and political power in designing his political economy. But these connections differed crucially from Jones's reckoning of the political.

In Mill's *Principles of Political Economy*, a large section was devoted to "property," which was a completely new addition to the usual outline of such treatises on political economy written in the nineteenth century. The new entry was not a mere minor additive to the established tenets of this body of knowledge. Rather, in a manner much similar to Jones, Mill explained property as a set of conditions that decisively determined both production and distribution all over the world. He noted that property was the primary institution regulating the "different modes of distributing the produce of land and labour."[92] Since property was intimately involved with production and distribution, he believed it was essential to explore what it consisted of. "Private property," he argued, "in every defence made of it, is supposed to mean, the guarantee to individuals of the fruits of their own labor and abstinence."[93] He emphasized that property essentially consisted of "the right of producers to what they have themselves produced."[94] I argue that this integral association between property and production was foundational to his perspective on the state of property in land during his time. It is primarily on the basis of this connection that Mill established distinct conceptual linkages between landed property, production, distribution, and political power in his political economy.

Property, as Mill saw it, consisted of the right of the producer to the product. There was, however, a problem in applying this definition to landed property. Land could not be owned on the basis of this principle, as it was not produced by anybody. But at the same time, land could be made productive only by the application of labor to it. Most important, it was the natural source of mankind's fundamental means of subsistence. By relating land to his conceptualization of property and production in this manner Mill was able to argue that there are both individual and collective stakes immanent in the category of landed property. Landed property was different from the category of property in general. Mill noted that "when the 'sacredness of property' is talked of, it should always be remembered, that any such sacredness does not belong in the same degree to landed property. No man made the land. It is the original inheritance of the whole species. Its appropriation is wholly a question of general expediency."[95]

Since it was the essential source of human sustenance and a gift of nature, land was immanently collective. In that case, Mill argued, the only form of individual ownership that can be legitimately instituted in land must be of a productive capacity. In other words, individual ownership of land was "only valid, in so far as the proprietor of land is its improver. Whenever, in any country, the proprietor, generally speaking, ceases to be the improver, political economy has nothing to say in defence of landed property. . . . In no sound theory of private property was it ever contemplated that the proprietor of land should be merely a sinecurist quartered on it."[96] This was the basis of Mill's advocacy for peasant proprietorship in Ireland or in British India. Mill thought that it was an absence of this constitutive connection between property and production that characterized landownership all over the world. This absence was particularly visible in Britain, where big landlords existed as unproductive owners of lands.[97]

It was this distinctive categorization of land based on the vital association between property and production that made the political a constitutive condition of Mill's political economy. The collectivist claim immanent in Mill's understanding of land transformed the epistemological underpinnings of his political economy. Consequently, the category of production had to be accounted for in terms of its connection with property and political power. Mill noted that the institution of private property in modern Europe was "the result, not of just partition, or acquisition by industry, but of conquest and violence.... The laws of property have never yet conformed to the principles on which the justification of private property rests."[98] Thus, when Mill advocated the creation of peasant properties in Ireland by legalizing customary rates of rent, he thought he was working within political-economic postulates. He believed that state intervention in the domain of private property in land was justified due to the peculiar political-economic characteristic of landed property, which harbored the political in it. The state here stood for the general will of the community. Mill declared that "the community has too much at stake in the proper cultivation of the land, and in the conditions annexed to the occupancy of it, to leave these things to the discretion of a class of persons called landlords, when they have shown themselves unfit for the trust."[99] He clearly pointed out that an exclusive ownership to land could be granted only if the proprietor was also an improver. That is because, in this capacity, by responsibly executing the act of production, he would be fulfilling his duties toward the community's source of sustenance.[100]

Mill was reworking the Malthusian proposition in conceptualizing the link between landed property, production, and political power. To be precise, he effected a secularization of the Malthusian perception of land as a divine monopoly. Malthus did not see a problem in viewing landlords as the legitimate exclusive owners of land, because he considered them natural trustees of this divine monopoly. But for Mill, since land, as the source of the fundamental means of life, was a monopoly, it was naturally connected to the rights of a community. Thus, it could only be appropriated if it served the purposes of the community. In other words, it could only be owned if it was cultivated by the owner. The state, therefore, as a representative of the community, had the right to determine the nature of its ownership. Thus, Mill pronounced: "It is an acknowledged principle that when the State permits a monopoly, either natural or artificial, it retains the right, and cannot divest itself of the duty, to place the exercise of the monopoly under any degree of control which is requisite for the public good."[101]

Moreover, Mill argued that the state had always been the legitimate owner of land and, therefore, could always ensure that the real cultivators of land possessed proprietary rights in some form. He gave a few examples to prove his point: "In Russia, even when the cultivators of the soil were serfs out of the landed proprietor, his proprietary right in the land was limited by rights of theirs belonging to them as a collective body managing its own affairs, and with which he could not interfere.... In other cases, as in Tuscany, the *metayer* farmer is virtually co-proprietor with the landlord, since custom, though not law, guarantees to him a permanent possession and half the gross produce, so long as he fulfils the customary conditions of his tenure."[102] Mill further emphasized that although in Britain the landlords were considered exclusive proprietors of land, "the theory of the law does not acknowledge an absolute right of property in land in any individual; the fullest landed proprietor known to the law, the freeholder, is but a 'tenant' of the Crown."[103] It might appear that here Mill was speaking in the language of a long tradition of European thought, particularly its eighteenth-century form, where, following Rahul Govind, the political had still not been divorced from the economic.[104] Mill's framework, however, although different from Jones's, imagined the political as constitutive of property and production. Let us see how this link was posited.

It is evident that, like his father, Mill was trying to argue that the form of landed property prevalent in Britain was contrary to both the facts of the world and the correct principles of political economy. In Britain, and in Ireland, such a connection between property and production was long lost. Mill argued that the landlords of Britain rarely acted as responsible managers of the community's asset; they were not productive proprietors of land. The critique Mill offered of big landlords, emerging from the alliance of property and production, was combined with an influential contemporary strand of opinion in the field of the political economy of agriculture to produce his advocacy for peasant proprietorship in Ireland. Thus, Mill confidently declared that "though the self-interest of landlords frequently operates to frustrate, instead of promoting, the interest which the community has in the most effective use of the productive powers of the soil, there is another party concerned whose self-interest does work in that useful direction; and that is, the actual cultivator of the soil, if he be either a small proprietor, or a tenant on conditions which secure to him the full fruits of his labor and outlay."[105] This was the basis of Mill's campaign for granting security of tenure and, thereby, legalizing peasant properties in Ireland. As is well known, he had similar prescriptions for reforming the state of landed property in Britain.[106] He believed that the "the *principle* of private property has never yet had a fair trial in any country; and less so, perhaps, in this country than in some others."[107]

From this perspective, when Mill analyzed the state of landed property in India the category of custom emerged as a vital resource of the political. Like Richard Jones, Mill viewed the form of landed property in India as a dispersed field of power. He perceived property in India as various kinds of rights attached with land, distributed over a range of landholders and landholding bodies. These rights were of revenue collection, management, and cultivation. They were possessed, in different capacities, by the state, its hereditary officers who collected revenue, the village community, and the cultivators. Thus, in India, as Mill saw it, the state, despite being the universal landlord, had its proprietary privileges limited by a highly differentiated field of rights. But in this power matrix, he argued, custom was the only principle of determining the proprietary rights of the actual cultivators. Custom fixed the rent, thereby determining how much of the profits of cultivation would remain with the cultivators. In certain circumstances, where landownership was implicated in the collective body of the village, custom organized production by ascertaining the share of the produce, or the land itself, to be enjoyed by the individual cultivators.[108]

For Mill, custom enabled the constitutive linkage between property, production, and political power. Mill argued, "Custom is the most powerful protector of the weak against the strong; their sole protector where there are no laws or government adequate to the purpose."[109] In India, therefore, it served to protect the cultivator's proprietary right from the despotic power of the state and the predatory propensities of its officers. Custom had a political-economic function. It ensured that the cultivator had some proprietary right in land, thereby guaranteeing a productive utilization of the community's treasure.[110] Mill observed that property and production could be brought together only if the ryots, or cultivators, were converted into cultivating proprietors. In British India, he argued, such a possibility was inherent in the proprietary conditions on land.[111] But during the early period of their rule, the British failed to realize this possibility and mistakenly made the wasteful zemindars the proprietors of the land. The mistake was, however, rectified over time.[112] Interestingly, Cuttack found exclusive mention in Mill's interpretation of the history of settlement practices in British India as a progressive space inhabiting the best form of connection between property and production. Mill noted that "the revenue system of Cuttack is ryotwar; but the attempt has latterly been made to combine the advantages of the ryotwar principle, with a portion of those of the system of the North-west Provinces. . . . This mixed system of ryotwar and village management, having been successful in Cuttack, is in course of introduction into one of our latest acquisitions, the districts made over to our permanent administration by the Nizam."[113] Thus, in his scheme of things, Cuttack emerged as the most advanced, and therefore the model, form of settlement, to be replicated in the latest territorial acquisitions of the government.

Mill chose to explain the settlement practices of these parts of British India in the light of his own argument about landed property, at the center of which was the figure of the peasant proprietor. Jones understood the interrelationship of sovereignty and property in India as dispersed, and he argued that officially favoring any one of its forms at the cost of others was erroneous. Mill, while largely adopting this view, reconfigured it in terms of the imperatives of production, by institutionalizing custom as the political.[114] He supported what he interpreted the settlement practices to be—an advocacy of peasant proprietorship. But the new administrative arrangements in British India, to which Mill referred, were adopted years before he published *Principles of Political Economy*, mostly in the 1820s and 1830s. They neither anticipated nor simply reflected this preference for the peasant proprietor. As we have seen, over different geographical sites in British India, strategies of agrarian governance variously capacitated a range of agrarian groups, both village-level ones and others.

Similarly, the organization of agrarian relations in a particular locality, in this case Cuttack, was not a linear development of an unequivocal appreciation of the peasant proprietor. The specificity of Cuttack's proprietary landscape was neither restricted to nor produced from within singular, irreducible conditions in Cuttack. Its contours were decisively determined by the trope of the local. Within the local there was a productive tension between the two articulations of the political—one that wanted to keep power relations distributed, and another that tried to resuscitate the original proprietary figure, the cultivating peasant proprietor. Even then, it was not a simple addition of these two imperatives that produced the designs of agrarian power in localities. While there was undoubtedly an epistemological kinship between the political in political economy and the local in British Indian agrarian governance, neither one was a copy of the other. Nor did they influence, anticipate, or reflect each other. Yet they were woven together by strong lines of force and circuitous pathways of connection. This book argues that their visibility emerges only when they are considered as an apparatus, as a single, unified analytical field.

I have argued here that these processes established the local as the object of agrarian governance in British India over the first half of the nineteenth century. But this chapter might have hinted that the local did not consist only of relationships between individual landholding figures like zamindars, talukdars, serberakars, mokuddums, and ryots. In the critique of the Permanent Settlement of Bengal, these figures were newly discovered not as discrete individuals but as variously related members of a landholding body, namely, the village. As this chapter has shown, their pedigrees as authentic proprietors were graded on the basis of their links to the village community. Even zemindars and talukdars, who were initially considered to be corrupt outcrops of the recent past and far removed from the authentic proprietor ryot, were eventually granted some position in this hierarchy, only if they were found to have roots in the collective of village proprietors. What emerges from these contentions is the centrality of the village as a landholding body. The next chapter shows how the village played a key role in reckonings of the political, as it emerged at the same time as the seat of the local.

CHAPTER 4

Grounding Governance

Village

The previous chapter showed how discursive mobilizations of the local produced a connected geography of property in British India. Property itself was defined, and governed across these locales, as different kinds of rights to land most authentically possessed by the landholding body called "village proprietors." Evidently, apart from its ancientness, the authenticity of this proprietary form was critically defined in terms of its location in, and relation to, the village. This chapter, therefore, discusses what the village was conceived as, by practices of governance. I argued in the earlier chapters that a variegated matrix of proprietary power was established as the object of agrarian governance, which consisted of a dispersed field of relations between the state and various landholding bodies. There was a constant attempt in governmental practices to contain this dispersal by fixing the primary relation of property and power as one between the state and the village proprietors. The ways in which the latter figure was regularly reinterpreted by the strategy of the local, however, rearranged the proprietary field as a more complex set of relations between the state and different kinds of landholders (hierarchized in terms of their varying distances from the "original" village proprietor). I argue that the village was defined in the same process, to mark the universality of this property-power complex *as* a territorial economy.

As earlier, I make sense of this process by bringing together meanings of the village generated in the discursive practices of agrarian governance in several localities of British India and contemporary political economy in Britain, while visiting Cuttack at times in the light of such spiraling journeys. I discuss again several major texts and debates of governance already examined in the previous chapters, in order to emphasize that the categories of rent, property, and village were simultaneously produced, in relation to each other, over this period. Accordingly, certain sites of governance were of pivotal importance to the constitution of each of these categories. These revisitings of beaten paths are also brought into conversation with unexplored routes belonging to different kinds of locales. The chapter shows how governmental investments in knowing the depths and details of the constitution of the village produced it as a self-regulating territorial economy of power. It was perceived as the quintessential indigenous social, which shaped the nature of the sovereignty-property relation in India. Aligned with this understanding, the village was constructed in contemporary British political economy as the critical indigenous mediator of production. The nature of this mediation, or the way in which it shaped the property-power complex in India, was interpreted differently by different strands of thinking in political economy. The various strands were, however, united in foregrounding indigenous expressions of sovereignty-property ensembles as objects of political-economic knowledge and, thereby, determinants of political-economic categories.

It is well known that the village features as a central object of inquiry in the agrarian histories of South Asia. As I noted in the Introduction to this book, a range of seminal works in this field have argued that right from the beginning of the nineteenth century the East India Company's government failed to invade the agrarian interiors of the country with its categories, policies, and strategies due to the resistance of the village. This argument emerges from similar claims made in favor of the resistive capacities of villages, by studies of different regions. In outlining the nature of this resistance, these studies have typically understood the village as the most powerful seat of traditional/indigenous social relations, which refused to change in the face of the Company's governance. Either due to misrecognition or due to certain kinds of structural inabilities, this scholarship suggests, governance was unable to include, and account for, the village within its framework of reason. That is to say, these works have considered the village only as an empirical factor thrust upon the story of governance. Therefore, the conceptual status of the village, construed in this historiography as forces of tradition, has always been that of an empirical outside governance, masquerading as facts on the ground. Critically complementing this rich body of literature, I argue here that the village was produced as a category *internal* to governmental/political-economic reason over the first half of the nineteenth century in British India.

There are some notable works that highlight the governmental production of this category. Louis Dumont's essay "The 'Village Community' from Munro to Maine" can be viewed as the earliest attempt to trace a genealogy of the village. Dumont identifies three different meanings of the "village community" fashioned in the discourse of governance in the nineteenth century. "In the first phase, the village community is primarily a political society, in the second a body of co-owners of the soil, while in the third phase it becomes the emblem of traditional economy and polity, a watchword of Indian patriotism."[1] In a characteristically structural-functionalist vein, he suggests that "community," as an equalitarian principle, tied together different characterizations of the village over this period: "In the prevalent ideology of the period a 'community' is an equalitarian group. . . . Dominance, and even hierarchy, are not absolutely ignored by all writers, but they do remain on the whole in the background."[2] Contrary to this analysis, I will show how the village, in being represented as the authentic indigenous social, was always produced as a seat of conflict, intrigue, and power by the discursive practices of governance. Accordingly, political-economic articulations of governance were made sense of in terms of this network of power.

Shifting the conceptual-historical emphasis, Clive Dewey points out that "awareness of the village community was a creation of the later nineteenth century."[3] He argues that this category was produced out of shared assumptions of metropolitan British intellectuals and British Indian administrators. In these currents of thought, the village community stood as a mark of ancient, primitive societies, the essential feature of which was collective ownership of property, structured by kinship. It was imagined as the original form of all societies, as the past of Europe, and the present of India. A particularly notable figure in this world of representations of the village community was the legal scholar Henry Maine. Karuna Mantena's work presents Maine as the critical link between such representations and the imperial ideology of the late nineteenth century. The focus of this ideology, Mantena notes, was different from the liberal-reformist one that characterized the British Empire over the first half of the nineteenth century. Maine's classification of societies, based on a comparative and evolutionary method, was the foundation of this ideological shift. Mantena points out that "nineteenth century theorists such as Maine produced a distinctively *apolitical* model of traditional society . . . viewing societies as functional, cultural wholes. It was a view that stressed the internal cohesiveness and the communal/corporate orientation of native society . . . thus de-emphasizing political conflict, change, and agency."[4] The village in Maine's theoretical framework, Mantena notes, embodied such a "traditional" society.

Both Dewey and Mantena offer rich insights into the governmental production of the village. Mantena's work explains this production in relation to several other categories and imperatives of rule, thereby locating it within a far more comprehensive and complex conceptualization of the late imperial order. They seem, however, to be still sharing with Dumont the assumption that community, as a cohesive and functional whole, was the dominant mode of representing the village in governmental discourse. This chapter notes that in the first half of the nineteenth century the village was produced by governmental reason in a different way, as a network of power, woven by complex social relations inside and outside. Most important was that the nature of this network was understood in terms of its bearings on political-economic categories. Its construal and institution, by practices of governance as a seminal marker and the primary geographical site of power relations and agricultural production, were significantly different from the sociological village community of the late nineteenth century. This chapter, thus, reconceptualizes the village by bringing forth governmental investments in the category across a range of sites and practices—from administrative treatises on authentic "Hindu/Indian" polities and modes of governance, to texts of contemporary political economy, to revenue surveys, to an ideology of occupancy.

A Seat of Power

I begin, once again, with the *Fifth Report of the Select Committee on the Affairs of the East India Company*. A discussion of the *Fifth Report* is unavoidable, as it prefigured most of the debates over governance of land that pervaded the first half of the nineteenth century. In debating different models of governance, the report, for the first time in the nineteenth century, defined the village as a distinct object of agrarian governance. By favoring a ryotwari settlement over a village settlement, the report inaugurated the possibilities of considering the village as a separate, discrete unit of governance. In differentiating between the two modes of settlement, it defined what the village signified, as an administrative unit. The village was represented in the report as the most fundamental seat of various power-relations around land, in the context of a discussion on the history of land administration in the Northern Circars, a province in the Presidency of Fort St. George. The village was depicted as the most basic unit of (agricultural) production and social life, inhabited by figures performing diverse social roles, primarily associated with production and management of land. Land was the epicenter of this collective, as all occupational groups unrelated to cultivation were remunerated either by parcels of land or by a portion of the harvest. The report outlined in detail the different occupational roles existing in the village.[5]

This outline of the constitution of the village, I argue, turned out to be immensely significant for the production of the category in the discourse of governance. For example, specifically this part from the *Fifth Report*'s discussion of the village was used by Richard Jones in his lectures on political-economy at the East India College, the implications of which will be discussed later. Further, as the chapter demonstrates, the manner in which practices of governance mapped the nature of this network of power, in dealing with individual villages in different parts of the country, was, to a great extent, assembled out of this sketch. It is important, therefore, to analyze this outline carefully. To begin with, contrary to common historiographical assumptions, this description did not posit the village as a self-sufficient community, existing *outside* the domain of the state. In presenting a diversity of occupations, it foregrounded officers like the potail, the curnum, and the talliar acting as agents of the state. The report described these figures as "officers of inspection, whose business it was to keep an account of the territorial produce, and of everything connected with the rights of the ryots, and of government, as arising from the land."[6] As it is evident, these officers were seen as guardians of the main proprietary relation, that is, between the state and the ryot. They were constitutive threads of the assemblage of property and political power that the village stood for. Other members of the village, described as servants, were also tied to the state. Their remuneration, consisting of either rent-free land or portions of harvest, came from a public fund.[7] Accordingly, the report suggested that the village was, from ancient times, an administratively controlled unit of production. Land was the fulcrum of this collective, and government its grand supervisor. The village was a "simple form of municipal government."[8]

Property, production, and political power came together in framing the village. It was seen as the quintessential (Hindu) geographical marker of the property-sovereignty matrix. In fact, that is why it was viewed as being prone to abuses of power. Over time, the report noted, the public officers, originally employed in the village to protect the peasantry from the oppression of big landlords and farmers, themselves became agents of despotic power.[9] Even the company's government, in its early years, let out lands on short or long leases to individuals. These individuals subrented the territories in parcels of villages, allowing the under-renters to determine the amount and mode of collection from the villages. Quite naturally, all these under-renters became corrupt and oppressive overlords of the villages. The report noted that as soon as the company's government was in possession of greater knowledge of their territories, they entered into more specific engagements with the head inhabitants of each village. These village engagers were, in turn, supposed to enter into engagements with each ryot regarding the rents payable for each field. They were supposed to have formal contracts with the ryots, by granting pottahs, specifying the amount to be paid for particular fields. But even under this arrangement, the disposition to usurpation of power remained undisturbed. The company's government found ample evidence of "the great deceptions and frauds practiced by the village renters, in conjunction with the curnums, in order to conceal the value of lands, and the actual quality and kinds of cultivation; and also of the serious and extensive injuries inflicted on the cultivators by the former."[10]

A potential of despotism, therefore, seemed to be inherent in such village settlements. To combat it, a new mode of settlement needed to be devised. The report now turned to the ryotwari settlement. Under the ryotwari mode of settling lands, it was argued, a much more transparent, unmediated, and protective relationship could be established between the government and the principal agents of agricultural production, the cultivators. On the adoption of this principle of settlement, the government faced strong opposition from the potails, the former de facto masters of the village. But eventually the ryotwar was a great success. The report noted that it "greatly improved the situation of the cultivator, by limiting the bounds of the public assessment, and adjusting the actual demand on each person subject to such assessment, according to his ability to satisfy it; . . . and securing him in the protection of his property and rights."[11]

But the village was never abandoned as an object of agrarian governance. It was retained in a reconfigured manner. While the Court of Directors praised the strategy of implementing the ryotwari settlement, the Board of Revenue wanted to fall back upon the village settlements. In favor of the latter, the board argued that it was "as old as the age of Menu."[12] But the *Fifth Report* contradicted the board's assertion. It noted that the authentic regulative function of the village was maintained under the ancient Hindu government, when rent was collected from the cultivators, who had a partial proprietary interest in the soil. In this mode of administration, the village officers acted as mere agents of the state. But the practice of farming out the revenues of villages was introduced much later, under Muslim rule. It is this system of farming and subfarming, the report argued, which gave birth to corrupt and oppressive overlords like the zemindars of Bengal and the Northern Circars and the potails of Carnatic. Under this arrangement, the potails in the village were no longer government-appointed collectors of rents; they became petty tyrants.

The abhorrence of a village settlement, where the state's share of the rent was settled with the headmen of the village, was grounded in this perspective. Such village settlements would return, as we saw in the earlier chapters, with the remaking of the authentic proprietary figure. For the time being, however, the report managed to accommodate the ryotwar within the village settlement, which was pitted against the latter by presenting it as inclusive of the original form of the village. It was argued that, in the ryotwari mode, the village officers remained in their original roles as servants of the state. They could not exercise unrestricted power over the cultivators. Thus, the report argued that in districts under the ryotwari system, rents "were collected by the potails, in the name and for the use of government, in their natural and constitutional character, as the agents or superintendents of the villages to which they belonged, agreeably to the antient practice of the Hindoos."[13] Not only the potails, the report noted, but also, in a ryotwari area, other village officers, such as the curnums, continued to perform their original duties and enjoy their perquisites.

The *Fifth Report*'s differentiation between authentic and inauthentic forms of the village defined future governmental investments in the category. The report had already depicted the village as the most ancient and basic territorial unit of a complex network of property, production, and political power. In the coming years of the century, the specificities of this network were elaborated by practices of governance. Since relations of power in the village were entangled with conditions of agricultural production, and it always embodied tendencies of despotism, this network needed to be closely monitored. Specifically, the report prescribed the ryotwar as the ideal form of this supervision but generally it defined the task of governance as that of managing the village. This is how, with the turn of the century, the village was firmly established as a category internal to the field of governmental reason.

A Political Economy of the Village

The previous chapter showed how Holt Mackenzie identified the village zemindars as the authentic collective of proprietors in India. It might appear that the village was solely understood as the proprietary seat of these figures, especially if we keep in mind how Mackenzie identified the puttedari tenure in Bundelkhand as the purest form of this property, where villages were nothing but territories occupied by groups of cultivating proprietors co-sharing rights to lands. Property—in terms of its entanglements with sovereignty—was indeed the central object of governance, but it was envisioned beyond the primary relation between land, village zemindars, and the state, as a far more dispersed network of power relations. This network, woven around land and a range of figures associated with it, was understood as the village. For Mackenzie, therefore, mapping the property-sovereignty complex became a problem of submitting this whole network to meticulous administrative scrutiny and control. In other words, a need to know the village was already high on the administrative agenda. As Mackenzie noted, the Court of Directors was eager to "receive a full and particular detail of all local tenures and usages . . . of the constitution of the village communities and the rights and interests of the classes composing them."[14] In Cuttack as well, since the question of a long-term settlement was raised in administrative circles, the court kept emphasizing the need to know the different figures and relations that constituted the village. It is evident that by the time Mackenzie devised a plan of settlement, authorities in London were convinced that the village was the primary cluster of power relations on land in India. The idea had taken root that successful governance of land would depend on an effective knowledge of, and control over, the village.

Mackenzie believed that it was important to limit administrative interference "with the constitution of village communities."[15] But at the same time, there was the fear that the village always had the potential of becoming a playground of despotic power. To tame this potential it was necessary to preserve the village—as the fundamental organization of agrarian power in India—but only in its pristine form, where the distribution of power remained fair. Mackenzie's prescription of knowing about the members of the village was, therefore, implicated in this administrative urge of regulating its economy of power. Accordingly, Mackenzie argued: "It is of course desirable to obtain the most accurate possible information regarding them, their leading men and classes, their officers, with their respective functions, and means of support, and an explanation of the degree of force and vigor in which those institutions exist."[16] He described in detail the different items to be known in order to "complete the picture of the village community" in the course of a settlement.[17] Regarding the proprietors, he noted: "The origin and nature of their tenure should in all cases be particularly specified."[18]About the village officers, he argued that "although we are chiefly concerned with the putwarree and police, yet, as a record of the remainder, with the perquisites received by them, in addition to any land they may hold in jageer, can be made upon the spot with great ease . . . and the perquisites of the different officers must be taken into account in estimating the gains of the cultivators."[19] He wanted to record the nature of all cultivating tenures. Other than the major figures, he proposed the recording also of "hired labourers" and "slaves," if there were any, in the village. Finally, he suggested that "a specification of the persons having a voice in the management of village affairs, in the disbursement and audit of the village expenses" should be entered in the settlement record.[20] In this way, he proposed an entire format of a settlement, which was overwhelmingly concerned with the recording of power relations. This model of settlement was later implemented in Cuttack. It established the village as the theater of agrarian power, as the smallest territorial, yet most fundamental political, unit of agrarian governance in British India. With the execution of such village-centric settlements, Mackenzie proclaimed, "we might . . . soon lay the *foundation* of a greatly-improved system of administration."[21]

These concerns were reiterated in a passionate appeal to protect the village communities by Charles Metcalfe. At first glance, Metcalfe's perception of the village communities as "little republics, having nearly everything that they want within themselves, and almost independent of any foreign relations" appears to be merely the rambles of a romantic.[22] But it is important look closely at the context in which these statements were generated. Metcalfe was defending a village settlement against a ryotwari one. This is because, like Mackenzie, he believed that the authentic form of property in India was collective, not individual. His village community was, thus, primarily the authentic proprietary unit—a collective of cultivating proprietors. The ryotwari settlement, Metcalfe thought, was aimed at granting proprietary rights to individual cultivators. Such an intention was based on a categorical confusion. Thus, Metcalfe noted, "great confusion of ideas might be produced by the misapplication of English terms which is common in our official revenue language. *We talk of estates, when we mean villages, and of proprietors, when we ought to speak of village communities*."[23] As I noted earlier, with Mackenzie, Metcalfe, and their likes, the erstwhile notion of the individual cultivator being the true proprietor, along with the sovereign, underwent a reinterpretation by which the collective of cultivating proprietors, or village zemindars, were posited as the authentic proprietary group. Metcalfe's opposition to the ryotwar was informed by the same presuppositions. He believed that settlements with individual cultivators would dissolve the fabric of proprietary relations that constituted the village community.

It is evident that the formulation of the village had changed significantly since the *Fifth Report*. The report's preference of the ryotwar was rooted in the perception that proprietary rights were vested, albeit partially, in the individual cultivator. The advocacy of ryotwar was primarily based on a desire to establish an unmediated relationship between the individual cultivator and the state. The village, as an organic unit of administration, was seen as an aid in establishing and maintaining this relationship. Munro noted that the village was the most ancient unit of agricultural production and social life in India. But he asserted that although the village had its autonomy as an arena of property and power, the sovereign was the *ultimate* owner of soil in India. Burton Stein perceptively notes that by such a reinterpretation "corporate village membership is transformed by Munro to individual membership by the metaphoric equivalence of the ruler and landlord . . . it also altered the idea of 'raiyat,' who is changed from being a part of a corporate village body into an equivalent of 'tenant,' thereby generating the transcultural metaphor or analogy—Indian sovereign or East India Company to landlord, raiyat to individualized tenant. In this way, both the corporate village and the individual peasant cultivator were preserved as bulwarks against the imposition of the Bengal zamindari settlement while at the same time maintaining the purportedly direct historical relationship between cultivator 'tenant' and government 'landlord.'"[24] The ryotwari scheme was clearly more concerned with the nature of the relationship between the state and the cultivator, trying to improve, by various means, the productive potential of the latter. That is why, as Stein notes, it was able to defeat the alternative proposal of a settlement based on village leases. Stein points out that "Munro outlined and justified a plan to reduce or obliterate the resource command of all superior land-controlling men. These last included not only peasant caste leaders . . . with authority over localities consisting of many villages, but even those whose dominance was limited to one or two villages. In effect, Munro was proposing to strike at the powers and rights of any magnate by whom major decisions about the utilization of men and land were made."[25]

But with Mackenzie, Metcalfe, and the debates of the Ceded and Conquered Provinces, the village as a collective replaced the investments that had earlier gone into the figure of the cultivator. I read this shift in governmental reason as a subtle yet critical reconfiguration within the framework of a certain kind of political economy. I noted in the earlier chapters how the legitimization of ryotwar, in terms of the authenticity of the property-power complex it was supposedly grounded in, represented the workings of a reinterpreted political economy in the articulations of governance.[26] It expressed a specific formulation of the more general governmental/political-economic objective to figure out the nature of the interrelatedness of production and distribution. Informed by the same imperative, practices of governance moved away from a radical critique of rent property and the prescription of extracting the full rent. Thus, the ryotwar was ready to leave some rent property in the hands of the cultivator, by pitching the demand low and not taxing the improvements on the land carried out by the cultivator. But gradually governance construed as its object a proprietary collective (village proprietors) and a network of power (the village), in conjunction with the state, as the total sovereignty-property complex of India. The stated administrative intention now was to establish a direct relationship with the village. The government started determining the criteria for selecting bona fide members of the village. This entire process was determined by a governmental/political-economic reason, which constructed relations between property and political power as its object of knowledge. As I showed in the earlier chapters, in British India these property-power relations were understood as dispersed and distributed over various figures. The move toward the village was consistent with this understanding. It signified both the *opening* of this dispersal, into newer figures and relations, and its *closure*, as governance attempted to fix this network of power as a territorial economy.

This shift in emphasis from the individual cultivator to the village, therefore, was reflective of a certain kind of governmental engagement with questions of production (and/as distribution). Such an engagement was not limited to the administrative affairs of British India. The governmental, as a form of reason inherent in the political economic, emerged out of a much broader, and geographically dispersed, analytical space. I have discussed the critical assault launched by Richard Jones and others against the epistemological assumptions of contemporary, predominantly Ricardian, political economy. Jones analytically foregrounded distribution in political economy, demonstrating that this domain consisted of globally varying assemblages of proprietary relations and political power. This assemblage got defined as the epistemological object of this new political economy. Further, as the previous chapter showed, Jones argued that these relations of power in "Asiatic" nations were distributed over a range of landholders and landholding bodies. The category of property, in this framework, was understood as an *effect* of this matrix of power. The village, accordingly, was fashioned as a crucial vector of power in this matrix.

Commenting on the mode of power on land in India, Jones noted that the village is "the groundwork of Hindu polity."[27] Interestingly, he used the long passage from the *Fifth Report* that I examined earlier when he described the village as a conglomerate of various roles and relations of power, linked to agricultural production. He observed that the village is a "complete, compact and independent body, politic and ecclesiastic, containing within itself all the elements of government."[28] As if in conversation with the discourse of governance in British India, Jones presented the village as the fundamental fabric of power relations on land in India and, thereby, the most authentic unit of administration. In times of peace, he argued, the "Indian/Hindu" polity consisted of a network of subordinate interests ranging from the sovereign to the zemindar to the potail to the ryot. In this network, the village was tied to the government by village officers, such as potails. Jones also restated the recurrent argument in the world of British Indian governance, that in a despotic Asiatic nation such as India, the village, as a self-governed body, acted as a protective to the incursions of government. In a comparative light, he observed that "a system not very dissimilar . . . in the United States of America, is found to bind together a loosely constructed society."[29] In discussing the different forms of land settlements in British India as part of his political economy lectures at Haileybury, Jones argued that "in former days the headman had been under control and responsibility. The old village system which we had rashly destroyed, had provided checks to their power. . . . The new set of headmen turned out exceedingly avaricious and oppressive."[30] Jones thought it was illegitimate to grant these village headmen exclusive proprietary rights. This is because he understood the property-sovereignty assemblage in India as a dispersed arena of power, which could not be tilted in favor of the village if governance was to align itself with the indigenous political.

The village featured in John Stuart Mill's political economy as well. Like Jones, Mill considered the village one of the most important sites in India where property, production, and political power were knitted together, but differently, as the seat of the peasant proprietor. Mill argued that the peasant proprietor's proprietary status was embedded in a collective, which was the village. He noted, "There were . . . village communities, consisting of the reputed descendants of the first settlers of a village, who shared among themselves either the land or its produce according to rules established by custom, either cultivating it themselves or employing others to cultivate it for them, and whose rights in land approached nearer to those of a landed proprietor, as understood in England, than those of any other party concerned. But the proprietary right of the village was not individual, but collective; inalienable (the rights of individual sharers could only be sold or mortgaged with the consent of the community) and governed by fixed rules."[31] Thus, the village was not only a proprietary collective but also the embodiment of custom, which protected the peasant proprietor from the potentially despotic state and, thereby, positively conditioned its productive capacities. The centrality of the peasant proprietor in his framework made Mill envision the village as a productive unit of power. This was not so for Jones. While appreciating its power in limiting the despotic potential of government, Jones found the village to be an obstacle to the growth of productive capacities. He noted that the village, "by excluding the principle of competition," weakened the productive potential of the cultivators.[32] The construal of the village by practices of agrarian governance in British India shared the premises of these different political-economic categorizations of the village. On the one hand, it was understood as a vital ensemble of power relations on land, affecting, as a whole, the conditions of production. Seen in this way, the task of governance was to define and regulate the entire network in its authentic form. On the other hand, it was also seen as the proprietary locus of the peasant proprietor, enabling him, through custom, to emerge as the most productive figure amid the sinews of agrarian power. Accordingly, governmental practices put emphasis on securing the conditions of such productivity for this member of the village. We will now turn toward an array of practices operating in particular villages, to see how a network of power was put in *place* as an economy.

Territorial Effects

Here I show how one of the cardinal practices of agrarian governance, namely, surveying, was critically implicated in the production of the village as a cluster of power relations. From the very beginning of Company rule, surveys aimed at generating detailed information of the relationship between the land, its inhabitants, and the government. The administrative classification of types of surveys tells us that such a task was thought to be most strongly carried out by the "revenue surveys." That is why R. H. Phillimore clearly points out these constitutive connections between governance and the revenue surveys in the opening pages of one of the seminal works on the history of cartographic operations in British India. He observes that "in the train of topographical and geographical surveys, there followed the special revenue surveys, so essential to sound administration. . . . *The tiresome details of revenue surveys touch moreover on an important aspect of sociology, the relations of Government with the tillers of the soil*. . . . The civil officers of the British *raj* were pre-eminently occupied with this complicated subject."[33] None of the agrarian histories of nineteenth-century Bengal has considered revenue surveys to be an important entry point to the rationality of the practices of agrarian governance. As large parts of the Bengal Presidency were governed under the Permanent Settlement throughout the nineteenth century, it seems to be an underlying assumption of these histories that detailed revenue survey operations, like the ones in the southern or western parts of British India, were never undertaken in Bengal. This is reflective of a more general assumption framing this historiography, which associates meticulous administrative investigations of, and interest in, land with areas outside Bengal. Such histories ignore the fact that throughout the nineteenth century detailed surveys were carried out in many parts of Bengal, mostly in the temporarily settled areas, but also in some parts of the old permanently settled areas.[34]

Phillimore contributes to this understanding by highlighting how in Bengal attempts to institute detailed surveys of land and its inhabitants were aborted early, due to the establishment of the Permanent Settlement. He notes: "Surveys of the new possessions (after Plassey and in 1760 grant of provinces of Chittagong, Burdwan and Midnapore) were ordered by the local council, and encouraged from London. The first thought was to ascertain the extent of cultivated land and the value of their revenues."[35] By this time, in other parts of British India there were growing efforts to carefully define methods and objectives of surveying. For example, in the newly conquered district of Carnatic in 1790 there was a proposal for the establishment of assistant revenue surveyors under district officers. Phillimore states that "a school was provided for their professional training. . . . The first duties of the revenue surveyors was the preparation of a topographical map of the district, to which they added much information about cultivators and the possibilities of irrigation as would be helpful to the district officer." [36]In Bengal, however, elaborate surveys could not be conducted successfully. Phillimore tells us that "the detailed measurement of individual fields was a matter for which the native staff remained responsible. . . . The district officers in Bengal had never succeeded in obtaining satisfactory or trustworthy results from such measurements and in 1793 Lord Cornwallis authorized the introduction in that Presidency of the system of Permanent Settlement, which it was hoped would, amongst other advantages, obviate any interference of Government with details of revenue collection. . . ."[37]

This chapter has already noted that in the early decades of the nineteenth century the village emerged in the discourse of governance, along with the state and various kinds of proprietary figures, as an integral constituent of the sovereignty-property matrix in British India. Interestingly, during the same period, revenue surveys officially adopted the village as their geographical unit of investigation. Let us see how one of the Company officials experienced in surveying made sense of this change years later. F. C. Hirst, while describing the revenue surveys conducted in Bengal, Bihar, Orissa, and Assam during the first half of the nineteenth century, noted: "The information collected previous to 1789 regarding the limits and areas of existing estates, was incomplete, and, probably, sometimes, very inaccurate, and it is easy, therefore, to see that, early in the nineteenth century, Collectors of Districts affected by the Permanent Settlement found themselves in difficulties as to what land has actually been included in the Permanent Settlement."[38] It is evident from Hirst's statement that the surveys that were conducted in the permanently settled areas used the "estate" as their unit of operation. But the new surveys, launched in different parts of British India, based themselves on the village.[39] Hirst himself was, however, unable to explain this change. "Whether the area dealt with was permanently settled or not, it was found *convenient*, in all but very exceptional circumstances, to adopt the village recognized locally, as the *real* unit of survey. The reason assigned for this is not clear."[40] If inadequate information and inaccuracy were conceived to be the only problems of the former surveys, the change in the unit of investigation would not have been necessary. Hirst tried to explain the change in terms of administrative expediency. He argued that the village was the smallest and most generally used administrative unit. He also noted that other "ancient land divisions," like the "pergunnahs," consisting of similar tenures, soils, and customs, had fallen out of use for years. Moreover, at present, the administration of estates was based on villages.

The suggested incomprehensibility of this change gives way to clarity when we look at the discourse of agrarian governance during this time where the centrality of the village as the seat of landed power and the starting point of administration had been established beyond doubt. The change in the unit of survey, therefore, was not merely empirical and expedient, simply aligned to practical concerns of governance. The new focus of the survey was engendered by the discursive investments of governance. By mapping individual villages all over the country, the discursive categorization of the village, as a territorial economy, could be grounded in a realist effect. Such strategies of governance remain unexamined and are often uncritically accepted in terms of their effects, even in a work that deals especially with revenue surveys. Bernardo Michael's essay "Making Territory Visible," which is an important exception in this otherwise neglected area of inquiry, argues that these surveys were primarily intended to reconstruct neat territorial boundaries. By not situating these operations within the discourse of governance, this argument fails to capture the significance of the surveys. Revenue surveys, I argue, were designed to mark the power complex of land. That could only be done by basing surveys on the village, as the category had been established as the quintessential site of this power complex in the discourse of governance during this period. Michael states that discontinuous pergunnah boundaries were the main obstacles in the way of basing surveys in pergunnahs. But territorial continuity was not the main reason for adopting the village as the *real* unit of survey. The revenue surveys, with their basis in the village, came out of greater structural and political investments.[41] This will be clearer if we examine the object of knowledge in such village-based surveys.

The revenue survey was preceded by a *thak* survey, the object of which was to "demarcate finally on the ground the boundaries of all villages and estates in the area for survey."[42] The thak survey was followed by the *khasra* survey, which recorded various details surrounding each plot of land. The *khasra chitta*, or field book, noted down the *tauzi* (area) number in the collector's rent-roll in which the field fell, the name of the estate to which the field belonged, the names of the proprietor and the cultivator, the size of the field, its location with respect to the field measured last, and a description of the soil and the crops. Hirst pointed out that these details, before being entered in the field book, were "called out loudly for the information of the villagers present at the time."[43] In the Ceded and Conquered Provinces, as debates over a plan of settlement went on, Board of Revenue officials emphasized the importance of surveys. They observed, "It was the design, we believe, of the Government which enacted the settlement law of 1822, that the rights of all persons connected with the land . . . should be carefully ascertained and recorded."[44] The khasra, they argued, "seems to constitute the record requisite for the purpose."[45] The khasra was perceived to be the bulwark of the settlement, a document in which the specificities of power, organized as the village, would be carefully inscribed. It was envisioned as the archives of power. The officials remarked, "It will be seen that this paper connects every person, whether putteedar or ryot, lakherajdar or village servant, with the fields in which he has either a permanent or temporary interest."[46]

For governmental reason, the khasra signified a text of total knowledge, which would act as the basis of infallible control. By registering the configurations of power, it was supposed to aid the administration in preventing unauthorized domination. Mackenzie noted that if the *rukba*, or settlement record, was not rooted in such detailed enlistment of the relations of power, "Wyeranee villages and waste lands will . . . be gradually usurped by the neighbouring Zemindars, alluvian lands . . . will never be traced[,] . . . boundary disputes will be frequent and intricate, and the future identification of the lands now assigned for the village watchmen or other officers will be a matter of the greatest difficulty; and other lakhiraj land will probably be absorbed in the Malgoozaree."[47] Such *mouzahwars*, or village surveys, based on khasras, were carried out in most of the temporarily settled areas of the Bengal Presidency, including Cuttack.[48] They were conducted mostly by native personnel. Prominent landholders or engagers of government revenue in the villages were involved in these survey operations. But the record was finalized, as I noted earlier, in the presence of assemblies of cultivators in every village.[49] In this manner, revenue surveys established the village as the geographical core of agrarian governance in early nineteenth-century British India. The settlement record, which emerged out of the khasras, was conceived as a mirror image of the complex network of power relations to land in each village. Surveying the village was about representing territory as a topography of power. Highs and lows of this topography were then framed as an economy of power, which was set in place by defining the locations and capacities of its members, and relations between them.

Membership Matters 1: Officers and Servants

It is time to turn to membership of the village. Matters of such membership were painstakingly deliberated and sorted out in the course of settlement operations in various parts of British India over the first half of the nineteenth century. I will be taking a close look, as earlier, at the settlement affairs of Cuttack in order to depict the encounters that fixed disparate figures in their respective locations within the village. As I argued in the previous chapter, the figures reigning supreme in the village were proprietors of various descriptions. Property was indeed the gravitational center of the village. But in the discourse of governance, the village was imagined as a totality of power, arranged as an economy, distributed over a range of figures. Administration was supposed to act as a custodian of this economy, by being aligned with it, regulating its excesses. I noted in the previous section that the khasras were geared to this purpose. By registering the legitimate economy of power, the settlement record was supposed to prevent its usurpation by the dominant actors of the village. For this purpose it was important to delve into the profiles of the myriad occupants of the village. Thus, the governor-general's list of inquiries for every village began with: "A specification of the different members, forming the constitution of a village."[50] The presence of different kinds of people in the village was interrogated and reestablished in terms of the criteria for legitimate membership in this economy, by practices of governance. This section discusses an important set of figures that were styled, in accordance with their roles, as "village officers" and "village servants." Such definitions fortified their locations, enabling governance to outline the precise contours of power in the village.

Among the village officers, the *patwari*, or village accountant, was an object of continuous governmental engagement in the first half of the nineteenth century. I noted earlier that the most significant sphere of transactions between different landholders was rent, which was a crucial marker of the sovereignty-property matrix. The village accountant was perceived as a figure who could potentially act as a supervisor of this matrix. Accordingly, by the turn of the century there was a renewed interest in this office. As the Board of Revenue noted, in a letter to the governor-general in 1816: "We have not thought it necessary to prescribe to the Putwarees any particular form of accounts. . . . A specimen of the series of accounts generally kept up by the Putwarees in the district of Cawnpore was submitted to your Lordship . . . by our accountant Mr. Newnham who has long directed his attention to the study of Revenue accounts and of the village details of the territorial assessment. That series in the mutual connection of its several parts with each other appears to possess every requisite of clearness and accuracy."[51] Around the same time, the collector of Cuttack emphasized the need to retain the village and district accountants, so that the records kept in the vernacular by the former could be translated into Persian abstracts, without "the inconvenience of removing local accounts to a great distance from the places when they may be constantly required."[52] This statement indicated that a need to have the village accountant, as a recordkeeper of power, located *within* the village was being acutely felt in administrative circles.

There were other concerns as well. The figure of the patwari had to be sanitized in order to be vested with the crucial responsibility of preventing abuses of power. It had been argued in the *Fifth Report* that such village officers often, in alliance with superior landholders, became instruments of fraud and oppression. Keeping in mind such tendencies, administrators argued that the patwari had to be kept beyond the influence of the landlords. In 1827, the collector of Hidgelee, an area adjacent to Balasore, noted that he had chosen, as patwaris, individuals from the "present Bisooeis or Village Collector of Rents to make these officers the joint servants of the Ryots and the state."[53] It was suggested by officials in Cuttack that the patwaris should be paid partially in land and partially out of the rents of the ryots. Such a practice, it was argued, had been followed in Khoordah, which made these officers there, known as the *bhoees*, "equally independent of the heads of villages and of the Ryots."[54] In 1831, the commissioner of Cuttack rejected the collector's suggestion of allowing the zemindars to pay salaries to the patwaris. He remarked, "If they are to be appointed solely by the zemindars and looked upon as their servants they will assuredly carry on the system hitherto pursued, they will fabricate papers to promote the sinister interests of their employers, they will defraud the Government and oppress the Ryot. . . . The Zemindar might be permitted to select but the voice of the Village Community should be consulted previous to confirmation and the Collector should have the power of rejecting any individual proposed for the office."[55]

In this manner, it was emphasized that the appointment of the patwari should be made under the vigilance of the collector and other members of the village. The administration, however, was not in a position to totally control these appointments. For this reason, a deep sense of anxiety prevailed wherever the patwaris were seen as capable of transgressing the legitimate limits of power. As the collector of Pooree noted, "In a great portion of this District, that office is not on a proper footing, as the Mokuddums, who are the proprietors of their respective villages and interested in benefiting themselves at the expense of the Cultivator, are the Patwaris."[56] Despite these apprehensions, however, he had to be granted admission to the village. This was because the village had been construed as internal to governmental reason. Governance defined its objective as being with the economy of power that the village was supposed to embody. It had, therefore, to work within this economy, not against it.

In a different way, with the same goal of bringing this economy to an authentic shape, greater discretion was exercised in matters of appointment related to the "village police." A village officer of great importance, the village police was viewed as an organic caretaker of law and order in the village. In Cuttack, the paiks, as former members of the landlord's private army, were considered naturally suited to this role. The paiks, in their former capacities, enjoyed lands free of rent granted by the landlords. As noted in the previous chapter, the rebellion in 1817 was perceived in administrative circles to have been fueled by an extensive resumption of these lands in the early years of the Company's rule in Cuttack. Since the rebellion, the government had already adopted a more cautious strategy with respect to resumption of such lands. Moreover, once the village was established as a legitimate field of power relations, these village officers were readily preserved in their respective locations as bona fide members of this collective.

A great number of such rent-free service lands were in existence in Talooka Panchgurh, southern Cuttack. The collector noted, "Any interference with these tenures, whether held under former orders of Government or otherwise, is much to be deprecated."[57] Similarly, in pergunnah Phulwur, in the district of Balasore, large quantities of lands were held by fifty-two paiks. The settling officer recommended a full-scale resumption of these lands. The commissioner disagreed with him. He noted that the paiks currently attended the Balasore *thannah* (police station). But the earning from the land was so much less that they fulfilled their duties by rotation in groups of ten. The commissioner insisted upon retaining these men by pointing out that they were a "useful and cheap class of officers."[58] In most cases the paiks were included within the fold of the village as deserving candidates for the office of village police. In pergunnah Searee, for example, the collector noted: "The Police establishment attached to this Pergunnah consists of 2 Sirdars 6 Paiks and 3 Digwars. The office (and lands appertaining thereto) held by these individuals appears from local inquiry to have been handed down to them as their hereditary right."[59] Although paiks were preferred for the office of village police, they were not the only group who took up such responsibilities in Cuttack. In Killu Mootree, the collector remarked: "I wanted the former Paiks to undertake the Chokeedaree duty, but the office is considered so degrading that no one though many was [sic] well inclined would venture to break through the deep rooted prejudice against it, and accept the appointment. There being no low caste men in these villages fit for the office, the former Chokeedars 3 in number Mussalman and servant of the zemindar's were entertained."[60]

A variety of village servants involved in nonagricultural occupations were allowed to retain their service lands. In Balasore, for example, a settlement report noted: "The . . . Barbers, Dhobees, Blacksmiths, Carpenters have been allowed to retain their Jageers."[61] In pergunnah Saibeer, the village astrologer was allowed to retain the six *beegahs* of land that he enjoyed rent free.[62] The settlement reports of almost all villages bore testimony to such administrative strategies of maintaining an entire network of village servants as hereditary and legitimate members of the village.[63] Rachel Sturman makes an important argument about the governmental engagement with such officers and servants of the village in western India during the same period. *Vatan* was the term generally used in this region to refer to such hereditary positions of various kinds. Incumbents of these positions enjoyed rent-free lands/revenues and performed various kinds of work for the village. In the first half of the century, Sturman argues, these offices were upheld, despite their feudal character, because the government wanted to recast them as "an effective civil service." The identification of a potential in them to contribute to governance reflected the "contemporary British context of recent and ongoing reform of offices from corrupt and inefficient personal sinecures to a professionalized state bureaucracy."[64] Sturman's analysis of the centrality of the village in governance of this period is rooted in a perspective similar to mine. She teases out the epistemological basis of what has been generally understood in the historiography as a pragmatic move of governance, aimed at collaboration with the indigenous social. In presenting the governmental reason at work here solely as a managerial imperative, however, Sturman does not clarify its political-economic character. Focusing on the political-economic investments, therefore, I argue that governmental reason envisioned the village as the most appropriate indigenous form of management of the intricate interrelationships between sovereignty, property, and production.

The village, however, did not consist only of officers and servants. These functionaries owed their existence to production on land, which was carried out by a variety of cultivators. Yet the investments in the recording of the roles and functions of these figures indicate how governance understood the question of production as entangled with, and conditioned by, this entire field of power relations. The different capacities of these officers and servants were seen as crucial to the maintenance of an economy of power within which production took place. To get more acquainted with the village, it is necessary now to look at the processes by which governance marked the cultivators of land and their relations with production.

Membership Matters 2: Occupancy as Ideology

From the beginning of the nineteenth century the figure of the ryot, as the cultivating proprietor, was continuously reconfigured over myriad sites of governance. Using the spatiotemporal classificatory framework of the local, traces of the authentic cultivating proprietor were identified among a variety of landholders, ranging from the big landlords to representatives of villages. The logic of the local defined the sovereignty-property matrix in such a way that the original ryot could be discovered almost everywhere in British India. But the ryot could not remain as an undifferentiated category. Further hierarchical classificatory indices emerged in the practices of governance that differentiated between various kinds of cultivators and determined the status of the ryots in British India during this period. These hierarchies, I argue, were produced out of transformed political-economic categories and emerged as crucial constituents of the economy of power that the village stood for. In the discourse of governance, the village was considered the most fundamental unit of agricultural production around which relations of power were distributed. Surveys reflected the need to territorialize the village, as the smallest geographical unit of power and production. In tune with this imperative, during the settlement in Cuttack cultivators, and their productive potential, were differently ranked according to their territorial location with respect to the village. Occupancy was privileged over migrancy. Being physically located in the village, instead of being a visitor to it, was considered more beneficial for agricultural production.

William Bentinck, in his "Minute on Tenures," had already granted to the thanee ryots, or the occupant cultivators, a number of privileges. Their rents were fixed, their rights to grazing of cattle on waste land and use of forest produce were reserved, and they were allowed to have the lands on which their houses were built rent free. These endowments were rooted in the premium laid on occupancy in the village. These ryots were considered chief cultivators of the village. In Cuttack as well, practices of governance tried to secure their conditions of cultivation. In a letter to the commissioner, Mr. Mills, the collector of a district in Cuttack, noted: "It must be borne in mind that it is our interest to maintain the Thanee Ryots in possession of their house and lands."[65] Attaching the ryot to his lands and homestead reflected the preference for a "cultivating yeomanry" that was always articulated in the discourse of agrarian governance throughout the first half of the nineteenth century. In spite of the differences in their perspectives, Munro and Mackenzie both envisioned the peasant proprietor as the leading cultivator. As the village was foregrounded as the fundamental unit of power regarding land, however, the problem of production also got rearranged with reference to it. An assumed hereditary presence denoted a permanent and superior membership of the village. Accordingly, it both capacitated and disempowered different groups of cultivators.

E. Repton, acting collector of Balasore, emphasized that "with regard to the Thanee Ryot . . . a definite rate must be fixed, and the necessity of an interchange of Pottahs and Cabooleuts has been so frequently urged by the Court of Directors and the authorities in this country that I can hardly imagine it can be negatived."[66] Fixing the rent of thanee ryots was considered a necessary incentive for improvement. These ryots, as I have mentioned, were considered potential improvers, primarily due to their fixed, hereditary location within the village. In their improving role, they were often compared with English farmers. As R. Hunter, commissioner of Cuttack noted, "A khoodkasht ryot should, like the English farmer, be encouraged to go hand in hand with his landlord in improving his lands and if such is effected by the aid of the landlords funds."[67] It was strongly believed that fixed rates would ensure protection from exactions by superior landlords and enable agricultural improvement. Repton noted, "If the Zemindar, when the season for tilling commences, may demand an increase of rent or turn the former cultivator out, what encouragement is held out for an industrious labourer? No man will expend money in the improvement of his land, if he is thus liable to be ousted at the will of his landlord."[68]As I argued earlier, a low rate of rent was prescribed for these ryots in order to generate a proprietary status and, thus a potential for improvement.

But the village worked in a different way to shape this preference for the Thanee ryots. It gave territorial form to the assumption that occupancy was the indispensable condition for productivity. Such assumptions constitutive of the political-economic articulations of governance emerge clearly when the strategies aimed at the *pahee ryots* are considered. The pahee ryots, Ricketts, the collector of Balasore, noted, "are those tilling lands in villages in which they do not reside."[69] The settlement officer in pergunnah Searee, Balasore district, described the characteristics of pahee ryots in detail: "The Pahee Ryot has no hereditary or transferable property whatever in the land he cultivates. . . . These ryots are constantly changing their lands. Should the past season's experience induce them to think that the soil they then cultivated is not sufficiently fruitful to repay them . . . they resign their engagements at the end of the year and enter into fresh ones . . . for some more productive lands in another village."[70] The village was such an important marker of the authenticity of conditions of production (occupancy, in this case) that the same cultivator was granted different designations and awarded unequal privileges depending on his different locations, within or outside the village. It was noted in the settlement report of a particular area in Cuttack that "the Pahee Ryot is generally an inhabitant or the son of an inhabitant of one of the villages in this or a neighbouring Pergunnah in which he holds lands as a Thanee Ryot."[71] Rents of these ryots were not fixed, owing to their migratory status. Settlement officers suggested that their rents should depend on the bargains they were able to strike with the zemindar. The board concurred partially with this opinion and ordered that the formation of a detailed list of pahee ryots was unnecessary. But at the same time, since rent was perceived to be the effect of power equations between superior landlords and cultivators, it was considered essential to provide some protection to even pahee ryots. Thus, lands occupied by pahee ryots were classed at a particular rate, which was entered in the settlement record, so that the zemindars could not place illegitimate demands on them.[72]

Occupancy, as a virtue, was also central to the exaltation of the figure of the peasant proprietor in contemporary political economy. Property, in this vision, was translated as belonging. It expressed a relation of cultivation between people and objects. Property was perceived as a relation that made a person feel at one with an object, through actions of continuous care, attention, and nurturing. This is how William Thornton presented the lifeworld of the peasant proprietor. Physical residence in his property, which allowed him to devote an unwavering attention to it, defined the peasant proprietor. His proverbial industriousness and purely productive self were the effect of this *presence*. His relentless capacity to dwell on his dwelling made the man and the land, the subject and the object, inseparable from each other. Presenting evidence from several countries of Europe, Thornton brought out in vivid detail the worlds of such peasant proprietors: "One is struck with the extraordinary industry of the inhabitants . . . every shrub, every flower is tied to a stake; and where there is wall fruit, a trellice is erected against the wall to which the boughs are fastened, and there is not a single twig that has not its appropriate resting-place."[73] For example, in the whole of Switzerland, he noted: "The little spots of land, show the same daily care in the fencing, digging, weeding, and watering." The owners, he continued, "have a kind of Robinson Crusoe industry about their houses and little properties; they are perpetually building, repairing, altering, or improving something about their tenements."[74]

The same vision that celebrated the peasant proprietor, however, also denigrated another kind of producer, namely, the day laborer, or contractual cultivator. It was argued that while the former was reputed for his industry, the latter was notorious for his indolence. Once again, property was seen as constitutive of productivity. Thornton emphasized that it was the lack of a proprietary title in the case of the day laborers that generated their careless and wasteful nature. He observed: "The small farmer . . . is subject to no immediate compulsion. No one can forbid his sitting down as soon as he is tired, or taking a holiday whenever he feels inclined. . . . But although he is exempt from the same compulsion, he is stimulated to exertion by influences much stronger than any that affect the hired labourer. . . . He has little or no inducement to exert himself further; he has no certainty of gaining an increase of wages by so doing."[75]

John Stuart Mill repeated the same hierarchy. He saw the day laborer as possessing all those vices that were engendered by an unproductive existence. "Day-labourers . . . are usually improvident; they spend carelessly to the full extent of their means, and let the future shift for itself. . . . The tendency of peasant proprietors, and of those who hope to become proprietors, is to the contrary extreme; to take even too much thought for the morrow. . . . They deny themselves reasonable indulgences, and live wretchedly in order to economize."[76] Such were the inclusions and exclusions of the contemporary political-economic investments in the figure of the peasant proprietor. In a similar yet different manner, by opposing occupancy to migrancy, agrarian governance in British India privileged the thanee over the pahee ryot. The thanee was imagined as the archetypal peasant proprietor, occupying the village lands and improving agricultural production. As opposed to this, the pahee was perceived as the migrant, contractual cultivator, without a dwelling in the village and, therefore, without a productive commitment to its lands, always on the hunt for better opportunities elsewhere.

Occupancy in the village was not only an important tool for marking the productive capacity of the cultivators. For governmental reason, occupancy generally signified authenticity. The right of holding lands lakhiraj, or rent free, was also verified on this ground. The resumption laws declared: "By the orders of the Supreme Government . . . Lakherajdars who have enjoyed long possession and whose tenures have been held in good faith are on resumption of their lands to be allowed possession at half rates for thirty years."[77] In several instances, even if the lakhirajdar was unable to produce valid documents, namely, grants confirming the rent-free status of the land, simply on the basis of his physical occupation of the plot of land at that time, and certification of his conditions by witnesses from the village, the lands were not resumed.[78] Deputy collectors were instructed to choose these witnesses carefully. It was noted that only elderly people of the village, or the old occupants, could validate long occupation. It was also emphasized that these witnesses had to be either physically resident in that particular village or related to it in some official capacity. In the circular to his deputies, the commissioner observed: "Young men cannot be witnesses of what happened . . . years ago, neither do I think that inhabitants of different villages and estates can know much about the matter."[79]

Conclusion

This chapter has shown how the village was fashioned as the archetypal site of the sovereignty-property matrix by practices of governance in British India over the first half of the nineteenth century. The matrix was envisioned as an economy of agrarian power, the design of which went beyond the officially sanctioned proprietary figures. Proprietors, in being directly involved with rent ownership and agricultural production, had key roles to perform in this economy. But production was understood as embedded in a far more heterogeneous field of relations, the general maintenance of which was construed as the object of governance. Emphasizing the characteristic of the village as a circumscribed territory had the potential of addressing administrative anxieties, which had grown, since the Permanent Settlement, out of a failure to *locate* power geographically. The distaste toward big landlords, the zemindars of the Permanent Settlement, grew out of the perception that men on the spot were true players in the field of power. In order to discern such figures, visiting the spot by adopting village based surveys was considered necessary. Figures who had occupied lands within the village for a long time, in various capacities, were judged key actors of the spot. Accordingly, their interrelationships were understood as constitutive of the conditions of production—what I have conceptualized as an economy of power. Privileging village residence went hand in hand with denigrating outsiders. In contemporary political economy as well, celebration of the sedentary peasant-proprietor was tied to deprecation of the day laborer. Thus, from within the political-economic/governmental understanding that specific sovereignty-property configurations were constitutive of production, the administrative unease with "distance" in British India was suitably addressed through the category of the village.

The upcoming chapter examines evidence only from Cuttack. In it I bring out the different matters and figures at stake in a range of quotidian disputes around land in Cuttack, which emerged mostly at the end of the first half of the nineteenth century. The chapter aims to understand how these different, yet related, categories of rent, property, and village, which functioned as the bulwark of governmental reason, played themselves out in the affairs of a locality. It looks at a variety of landholders entering into complex contestations with each other and the government, in and through different kinds of uses of these categories. In the process, new equations of power surfaced in Cuttack, while the categories also underwent mutations. As I consider these occurrences, I also try to account for the formation of agrarian subjectivities at the interstices of these movements.

CHAPTER 5

Disputes in the Locality

Peasants

In this chapter I present evidence only from Cuttack, analyzing a variety of disputes around land over the first fifty years of the nineteenth century. These disputes appeared, got debated, and were adjudicated at various layers of the judicial apparatus of the district. In considering the myriad interests at stake in these legal battles, this chapter brings out how different kinds of landholders, located both within villages and outside them, made sense of their proprietary status. The previous chapters showed how governmental articulations of political economy defined the sovereignty-property enmeshment in India as a dispersed field of rights to land, the flows of which were nevertheless crucially conditioned by the village—both as a territorial unit and as a body of power. This double determination of property, by inward and outward movements with respect to the village, created a structural potential for contestation, which was creatively used by different landholders in localities. Therefore, while village-based landholders unarguably had an advantage in this framing of property, their possible gains were also always open to critical challenges. Accordingly, in Cuttack, as this chapter demonstrates, there were severe tussles between village-based and other kinds of landholders over proprietary claims.

In making these claims, each group tried to posit a relationship of directness between itself and the government, in the process characterizing the rival group as an "intermediary." All of these groups used the governmental construal of the sovereignty-property interrelationship in India as a co-sharing of proprietary rights between the sovereign and the ryot (reconfigured as the village zemindar) to justify their claims. In the process, the idea of mediation and the figure of the intermediary gained a new currency in the locality. Every group tried to resist the challenge of the multiplicity of claims by marking others as intermediaries, as inauthentic obstructions to the lost yet recoverable intimacy of the government and the ryot. We have already seen how the critique of the Permanent Settlement in governmental discourse had unleashed a search for the authentic relationship between sovereignty and property in India since the turn of the century. This chapter argues that in battles of the locality the same governmental logic was creatively redeployed to establish new hierarchies, figures, and relationships of agrarian power.

These were also processes of subjectification. The chapter takes a close look at the various movements effected by different kinds of landholders in a locality to produce themselves as proprietary subjects. These movements can be seen as lines of force that worked upon, with, against, and around the governmental/political economic framings of the categories of rent, property, village, and the local. The locality, as the book argues, was only one node of the apparatus of political economy, as the latter assembled itself across a huge variety of localizable and nonlocalizable sites. Political-economic categories, as governmental techniques, went through a series of transformations, or localizations, over these different sites. Subjects of property can be conceived of as complex effects of these multiple transformations. We find these effects in the everyday conflicts of the locality, folding within themselves different scales, intensities, and motions of the apparatus. Thus, following Deleuze's reading of Foucault's *dispositif*, I argue that it is as these folds that subjects shaped up in the apparatus. As Deleuze notes: "Foucault discovered lines of subjectification. . . . The discovery of this new dimension arose out of a crisis in Foucault's thought, as if it had become necessary for him to redraw the map of social apparatuses [*dispositifs*], to find for them a new orientation in order to stop them from becoming locked into unbreakable lines of force which would impose definitive contours. Leibniz gave exemplary expression to this state of crisis which sets thought on the move again when one thinks a resolution has been found: we thought we were in port, but we were cast back out into the open sea."[1]

There was a relentless striving to achieve directness, or immediacy, in the exercise of agrarian power in a locality. This chapter argues that it was shared by all actors, ranging from the government to the individual ryot. It kept reappearing in various guises in different disputes, engendering complex, often contradictory alliances and shifting targets. It often fought against the framing of dispersed power but at times also mobilized the latter toward its own ends. Claims of immediacy produced a volatile juridical terrain, as the category of the intermediary was put to multiple uses by different kinds of landholders. Zemindars used it to depict village-level landholders as obstructions in the path of a direct relation of power between zemindars and ryots. But there was already a negative predisposition toward zemindars in the discourse of governance, which marked these claims as deceitful. The village-level landholders also couched their claims in the idiom of the authenticity of directness, demanding proprietary capacities superior to the zemindars. Interestingly, the figure of the "farmer" emerged as the determining principle of authenticity in these debates. The classical political-economic construal of the farmer as the agrarian capitalist, or ideal improver, was entirely discarded here. In these debates the farmer was refigured as the inauthentic subject of property, exhibiting a negative image of "improvement." He was understood as the rapacious contractual leaseholder, from whom all other agrarian actors tried to distance themselves.

Further, there were attempts to universalize the local from within the locality. Assertions of directness by mokuddums were not always lodged within local genealogies. Cuttack mokuddums often argued for their proprietary legitimacy in terms of a general classification of tenures, going beyond a particular locality. They wanted their proprietary capacities to be judged in the light of regulations pertaining to tenures like *patnis*, existing in other parts of Bengal. The logic of the local, in this way, was reused by landholders in a locality to reconfigure the category of property through new geographies of comparability and universality. Even the government invoked such similarities, without necessarily being able to always establish credible registers of comparison. Finally, we also see that the category of intermediary failed to generate any stable, fixed referent, as a variety of agrarian actors—zemindars, lakhirajdars, mokuddums, pudhans—all directed the term farmer toward each other to claim greater authenticity, and more immediate forms of authority in the intricate web of power relations in the locality.

In the process there were continuous reconfigurations of political-economic categories, from the Ricardian formulations to the Jonesian ones, from the administrative practices of the Bengal and Madras Presidencies and the North-Western Provinces to John Stuart Mill's engagement with property, from the government's search for real proprietors to varied alliances between different landholders in battles over acquiring directness of power in Cuttack. These were all moments of *localization*, whereby the sovereignty-property interrelationship was performed and created at every successive site of reconfiguration, indicating the limits of its constituent categories and opening up fresh pastures for further change. The local, therefore, was not a single, bounded geographical locality but an analytical possibility invested in a variety of sites, textual or otherwise, within which sovereignty-property relations got organized, revealed their limits, and generated new reorganizations.

Entanglements

When Bhuwanee Purshaud, the proprietor of *talukas* Tulpuda and Juggernauthpore fell into arrears of revenue in 1811, C. S. Waring, the collector, argued that it was a *benamee* purchase and, therefore, the amount should be recovered from his brother Ram Kanoy, the real proprietor. In order to prove his contention, Waring cross-questioned a number of persons who were involved in these talukas in different capacities. These questions tried to establish Ram Kanoy as the real proprietor in terms of his physical presence, and involvement in the affairs of the talukas. Waring examined Ruseekchurn Maintee, the *tehsildar* (native revenue-collector) of Tulpuda, Laloo Maintee, an erstwhile servant of Bhuwanee Purshaud, Kisooree Maintee, who expected to be employed by the two brothers, Nitye Naik, a ryot of Tulpuda, and Sobah Sing, an inhabitant of that area. Waring's queries tried to establish the specific nature of the sovereignty-property interrelationship in this territory. Rent, as I have argued earlier, was fashioned by the discursive practices of governance as the primary entry point into this interrelationship. Waring, thus, began his investigation by asking who was in charge of the collection of rent from the talukas. In answer to this query, Ruseekchurn, the tehsildar, who carried out the collections, said that he "sent it to Ram Kanoy & received receipts from him."[2] Nitye Naik, the ryot, noted that it was collected by Ram Kanoy's servants. Kissoree Maintee pointed out that the serberakars and ryots made payments to Ramkanoy, and finally Soobah Sing also came up with the same response.

While this set of responses seemed to vindicate Waring's suspicion that Ramkanoy, as the receiver of rent, was the real proprietor of the talukas, answers to other questions left the matter unresolved. On being asked, "Whom did the Ryots know as the proprietor," Ruseekchurn replied: "They took Pottahs from Bhuwanee Purshaud but sent the revenue to Ram Kanoy."[3] He further remarked that he used to obey the orders of Ramkanoy. Waring, in order to confirm his suspicion about the real seat of authority, wanted to know why he did so, despite being a servant of Bhuwanee Pershaud. In reply, Ruseekchurn argued that although Bhuwanee Pershaud was the real proprietor of the talukas, "Ramkanoy being the elder brother of Bhowanee Pershaud & manager of all their affairs, I therefore obeyed him."[4] It is by invoking such a familial domain of authority, marked by brotherhood, trust, and mutual cooperation that most of Waring's respondents maintained both positions—of Bhuwanee Purshaud being the real proprietor and Ram Kanoy being the key operator in the affairs of the talukas—as mutually consistent.[5] This mode of persuasion also allowed them to agree with the statement by Nitye Naik (the ryot) that the ryots considered Ram Kanoy to be the real proprietor.[6] The respondents seemed to suggest that the ryots falsely understood the person with whom they had immediate and more regular contact, especially in relation to the payment of rent, as the real proprietor. Interestingly, Nitye Naik, the sole spokesman of the ryots, appeared to have reached a different conclusion about the real proprietorship from a perspective similar to that of the zemindary servants. Even Nitye Naik claimed to know that the talukas were jointly governed, due to a familial intimacy between the two brothers. But he reversed the proprietary authority in this familial domain, remarking: "Ram Kanoy was the proprietor & Bhowanee Purshaud was his confidential manager."[7]

The Board of Revenue, after going through Waring's inquiries, noted: "[We] do not consider the Benamy purchase alleged to have been made by Ramkanoy as sufficiently established to enable them to enforce payment from him & they accordingly direct that you confine Bhuwaneepershaud in the Dewanny Jail unless he shall discharge the arrears due from the lands purchased in his name."[8] Waring's assumption of the illegality of this proprietorship, I argue, was informed by the way the category of property was being framed in the governmental practices of that time. Waring tried to make sense of proprietorship in terms of rent reception, the most important marker of direct control over land. This was also compatible with the more general governmental understanding at this time that the zemindars were hardly real proprietors, as they had no control over the rents of their lands. This kind of critique of the Permanent Settlement, which considered the policy to be a failure *in practice*, would soon be recast by another form of critique, which dismissed it as being erroneous *in theory*, giving rise to a renewed debate on authentic proprietorship in land.

The board's refusal to admit Waring's claim, I argue, does not, however, necessarily unsettle this framing of property. The reckoning of proprietorship as direct control of lands, seen in the practice of rent reception, is vindicated at the level of the board by representing Ramkanoy as an extension of Bhuwanee Purshaud, in familial terms. Thus, the apparent contradiction generated by the use of the proprietor-manager distinction by different figures of the taluka in opposite ways was resolved by the government by considering

Ram Kanoy's practice of rent reception as a familial responsibility, consistent with Bhuwanee Purshaud's status as the real owner of those rents. It was not only rent that defined the problem of directness and the category of property. A crucial index of authentic proprietorship, which became established in governmental practices later, can be seen operating in determining directness in the early years of the nineteenth century. When Kaleesunker Ghose, proprietor of taluk Kishenpur in pergunnah Ankora asked for help from the government in getting possession of certain villages in *mouza* (a cluster of villages) Govindpur, which he argued was part of his estate, and unjustly withheld by Koonjbeharry Chowdree, the Sudder Dewanny Adawlut rejected his application. The court order noted that "the disputed villages remain in the possession of the person by whom they were then enjoyed (Koonjbeharry Chowdree) and that Kulee Sunker should be referred to establish his claim by instituting a regular suit."[9] This made the collector report in detail on the settlement of Ankora, which was at the root of this dispute.

The collector noted that in the year 1811 taluka Kishenpoor, the property of Koonjbeharry Chowdree, was sold for the recovery of arrears of revenue and purchased by Bhyrubsunker Chowdree and Rajchunder Shome. "Shortly after the purchase," the collector continued, "these persons conceiving they had not received possession of all the lands included in the sale presented a petition . . . when the assistance usually afforded to purchasers at public sales was applied for to the Zillah court thro' the Government Vakeel, this assistance I believe was not afforded and Bhyrubsunker Chowdree did not obtain possession of the villages."[10] The next year, they disposed of the property to Kaleesunker Ghose, the present proprietor. But in the matter of acquiring possession of the disputed portions, even he "was no more fortunate than his predecessors."[11] In the light of these circumstances, the collector argued that Kaleesunker would not be authorized by the existing regulations to acquire the disputed villages unless his claim were supported by a separate suit instituted for the same property by the person from whom he purchased Kishenpoor. The central question to be answered in this entanglement, as the collector succinctly put it, was "'What is Kulee Sunker entitled to as purchaser at private sale of Kishenpoor'"[12]

The collector argued that Kalee Sunker could not be entitled to a property that was sold by a person who never took possession of it, because the seller, in the first place, could not have sold a property without his own claims on it being established. He asserted: "If Kalee Sunker purchased lands by private sale and does not get possession of all, he must look to the vender for remuneration, the vender cannot refer him to Government because he purchased those lands at a Public Sale, it was the duty of the latter during the period he held Kishenpoor to have called upon Government to put him in possession of all the lands and not to have disposed of them before he got possession of all he conceived included in his purchase."[13] What was it that engendered such complex entanglements in a simple case of successive transfers of a piece of landed property? I argue that the complexity was generated because the category of property was being reframed in governmental discourse, and its new bearings had not yet crystallized. In this reframing, the abstraction of title was as important as the concreteness of possession—both qualities understood from within juridical terms. Thus, Kulee Sunker's claim was never admitted, because he was not considered to possibly have a property right in something that he did not "possess." So the sale and purchase of a property right in these lands, to begin with, was considered null and void. Property did not remain only an abstract relation to land, conceived in terms of a titular right to transferability or alienability of land as a commodity, but rather was made contingent on the concreteness of possession.

Questions of possession—as concreteness and directness of power—determining the category of property became increasingly important and pervaded disputes throughout the first half of the nineteenth century. In the 1840s, a conflict arose over the rent of a certain amount of land in mouza Jutni, pergunnah Khoorda. Seewuck Barick, the rent payer, argued that in 1806 Pudolab Mahapater executed a *kubooleut* (agreement) with the government for a certain portion of land in mouza Jutni and held undisturbed possession of it, with his son Minjugdeb, until 1841. Seewuck paid rent for a portion of this land to Pudolab until his death in 1849. After this, he was supposed to pay the rent to his son when Huree Raotra and his brothers claimed the rent. They argued that the land was originally Pudolab's but after a *butwarra* (partition) in 1836 became theirs. The judge, however, ruled out their claim. He noted, "It is quite evident that a family dispute existed . . . regarding the right to the land in mouza Jutni since 1836 A.D. . . . and although it is alleged that Pudolab . . . executed a deed or relinquishment of his right in the 33 batees, 2 mauns and 4 biswas . . . in Jutni and other mouzas, the document or deed filed in the suit does not altogether bear out the allegation."[14] He was more convinced of the absence of any butwarra, by the fact that the dispute had been brought earlier to the deputy collector who in 1843, that is, seven years after the alleged butwarra had recorded Minjugdeb as the proprietor "in succession to his father, Pudolab . . . on the grounds of their *ascertained possession*."[15] From Huree Raotra's subsequent petition to be put in possession, the judge also inferred that for all these years Huree Raotra was not in possession of these lands. Once again, it is evident that the issue of possession played a deciding role in judging the authenticity of contending claims to property and rent. Huree Raotra and others presented quite a few documents to establish their proprietary status. This included a kubooleut issued by them in the name of Seewuck Barick, as well as a *ladavee* (deed of relinquishment) showing the butwarra. But actual possession was considered a greater evidence of proprietary status. In the discursive practices of governance, possession became a sign of complete presence, without which the category of property seemed to remain hollow and incomplete.

That is why in 1852 when Brindaban Oopadya claimed property rights in a portion of land in *chuck* (square) Sardung, mouza Meerpore, his claims were dismissed, and the lands were settled with Puhlad Das. Brindaban put forward a plaint against the decision of the deputy collector, stating that when in 1838, in execution of a decree against him, some lands in Meerpore were sold, the purchaser, Puhlad Das, falsely represented that the entire mouza was sold and managed to get possession of the lands that belonged to Brindaban. The *moonsiff* (native judge), however, refused to accept Brindaban's claim, noting: "It was fully proved from the evidence of the witnesses examined before the court, and the *pottahs*, *poutees*, and *bisoduns* granted by the zemindar to the defendant from 1246 to 1249 [the Bengal calendar, equivalent to years 1840–1843 A.D.,] . . . that the defendant had been in possession for upwards of twelve years."[16] He dismissed the suit on the ground of lapse of time.

Against this decision, Brindaban filed an appeal, further pointing out that he had not appealed earlier because in 1839 although Puhlad was awarded the value of some fish that Brindaban took from a pond situated in chuck Sardung, this did not prove Puhlad's possession of those lands, as Puhlad's claim to the rent of the lands surrounding the pond was not admitted. The judge admitted that there was a flaw in the sale of these lands. He also noted that the sale could have been canceled, had the plaintiff applied for a reversal of this decision in time. But in the light of the present circumstances, he argued, Brindaban "has himself solely and entirely to blame for allowing his property to pass from his hands."[17] The judge upheld the decision of the moonsiff on the same ground of continuous possession by the defendant for a period of more than twelve years since the property came under dispute. Once again, despite the dispute over Puhlad's claim to proprietary rights over the lands around the pond, the merits of possession determined the fate of proprietorship. Even though the government admitted its own mistake in allowing the property right of the disputed lands to slip out of the hands of the true owner, it overruled everything on the basis of what was perceived to be the greatest vindication of property right, namely, the reality of continuous, undisturbed possession for a certain period of time. The disputes discussed in this section, I argue, expressed a growing consensus over the category of possession as constitutive of property. These contentions displayed that property as a gamut of rights and relations around land had to be continuously recast in the image of a directness of power and presence. Governance, here, signified a relentless striving toward full presence. Possession seemed to offer that promise of presence, which was, however, as I show in the subsequent sections, never guaranteed in that battlefield of power relations called land.

Battles of the Locality

In the years following the completion of the settlement, incessant battles were fought over control of land in the judicial amphitheaters of Cuttack. Claims to possession of land, in a variety of ways, by a range of landholders flooded the courts in the district. As I demonstrated in the previous chapters, by the time of the settlement in Cuttack, a map of sovereignty had been established, in which different kinds of proprietary interests in land were distributed over a number of figures. But despite these emplotments, possession was never stable. It relentlessly churned conflicts between different agrarian groups in the locality. Governmental practices tried to steer through the contestations and settle the issue of possession according to its calculus of legitimacies, in the process opening up space for newer articulations of the sovereignty-property complex.

As I noted earlier, the principles of settlement in Cuttack were informed by a range of debates that took place in different times and at different sites over the nature of the sovereignty-property interrelationship in India. Big landlords like the zemindars and talukdars were objects of criticism in this proprietary imaginary. The ryot, as a member of the collective of village proprietors, was perceived as the authentic proprietor of the soil and foregrounded as the most privileged figure in the proprietary matrix. These reformulations, however, did not destroy the rights of the old zemindars and talukdars. But they surely created a new dynamics of power concerning land. The zemindars and talukdars suddenly found themselves in tough combats with village proprietors of various sorts. As the rights and interests of the latter became more sharply defined and a critical attitude developed in administrative circles toward bigger landlords, the grounds of sovereignty, property, and possession in Cuttack started experiencing tremors and settlements of new kinds.

The serberakars and mokuddums of Cuttack became the immediate enemy of the zemindars. Official recognition of their rights made them strong contenders in the dispersed matrix of power concerning land, and zemindars utilized every opportunity to get rid of these figures from their estates. Such strategies by the zemindars can be read as yet another form of attempts to institute directness as the modality of agrarian power. Establishing direct control or possession over land, as we will see, amounted to an unambiguous and undivided ownership of rents. Of course, a certain portion of the rents was owned by the government. The conflict was, therefore, over the determination of the other figure, who could legitimately own the rent and have a direct control over land (jointly with the government). Each struggled with the other to become this figure. The reconfigurations of the sovereignty-property equation had surely weakened, for the zemindars, the prospect of acquiring such legitimacy. But they had not yet lost their privileges. Accordingly, reclamation wars had to begin in the nineteenth division of the Bengal Presidency.

The potential for contestations was opened up by a decision of the government passed against the serberakars of Puttamoondee in 1844. As discussed earlier, the government had established a set of criteria for judging the authenticity of the proprietary status of serberakars, mokuddums, and pudhans in Cuttack. In Puttamoondee, the government pointed out that serberakars could not claim proprietary rights, because they held land from the zemindars as *moostajirs*, or farmers.[18] This ruling introduced one more type of landholder into the sovereignty-property field as another level of distinction against which the authenticity of the proprietary figures of Cuttack had to be established. Moreover, since the figure of the moostajir, or *ijaradar* (farmer), embodied the possibility of resembling or of being different from the putatively authentic proprietary figures, it became the rallying point for reclamation strategies on both sides. Henceforth, zemindars always tried to prove that the village-level landholders in their estates were mere farmers, devoid of superior proprietary rights.

The definition of the farmer, therefore, became of crucial importance in these conflicts. The government understood the farmer as a contractual and short-term leaseholder of lands, lacking ancientness, authenticity, and, consequently, legitimate proprietary capacities. So if the zemindars could prove that the landholder, whose title was in dispute, held the lands on the basis of varying, short-term "farming kubooleuts," as they did in Puttamoondee, his claim over rents and, thereby, to a proprietary status was rejected. Governmental distrust of farmers, as impermanent stakeholders, and, therefore, as an extortionist, parasitic presence on the land, was part of the critique of the Permanent Settlement and the search for ancient, authentic proprietors (improvers). Much earlier, in Cuttack itself, this attitude became visible when, during the Paik Rebellion, the illegitimate collections and generally rapacious conduct of the tehsildar of Khoordah was identified as one of the major grievances of the inhabitants leading to the uprising. Unlike Ricardian political economy, where farmers were considered to be agrarian capitalists, governmental rationality in British India construed this figure of the farmer as an enemy of agricultural improvement.

The category of the farmer, however, like most categories of Ricardian political economy, was never entirely discarded. Rather, it was reconfigured and incorporated within the search for authentic proprietors/appropriate improvers. There were different attempts to invest in the same figure the improving zeal of a farmer and the ancient indigenous authenticity of a proprietor. For example, in describing the meerasidars (the putative proprietary cultivators), Thomas Munro argued that they were ideal agents of improvement because they possessed the capacities of proprietors, farmers, and cultivators. Again, in the debates surrounding the Bengal Rent Act of 1859, as Andrew Sartori has pointed out, ryots, or peasant cultivators, were viewed as capitalist improvers.[19] Here also indigeneity was mobilized in the service of contemporary political economy, as the categorization of the ryot as a proprietor and an improver was considered to be rooted in the ryot's productive function of mixing labor with the soil. All of this was understood to be based on "custom." It is evident from Sartori's argument that in this debate the ryot was classified as both farmer and proprietor. But in Cuttack, the farmer was differently imagined. In the disputes between zemindars and mokuddums, which crucially revolved around the figure of the farmer, the farmer was perceived as a contractual improver, different from and inferior to improving agents like the village-level landholders, who were also ancient proprietors. The interweaving of property and sovereignty, assembled across multiple sites during this period, represented the farmer in terms of certain radical reconfigurations of classical political-economic categories. In a changed form, it was neither a combination of Lockean and Ricardian categories, as Sartori understands it, nor able to cling to a more classically Ricardian identity.

In Cuttack, negative predispositions toward the figure of the contractual farmer structured a number of disputes between the zemindars and various village-level landholders. In five mouzas of taluk Pandua, Dwarkanath Tagore, the zemindar, managed to prove that the landholders in his estate claiming to be hereditary mokuddums were mere ijaradars, or farmers. The decision against the proprietary claims of the latter was based on the evidence of their having exchanged farming kubooleuts of varying rents with the zemindar.[20] The claim to a surburakaree title over some mouzas in taluk Kishenpoorah was challenged by zemindar Juggernath Pershad Mullick on the same ground. Although the deputy collector, collector, and commissioner upheld the rights of the surburakar, the Board of Revenue overruled their decision. The secretary to the board noted, "The claims of all the *middlemen* in the Kishenpoorah Taluk were . . . rejected by me, on the grounds that they had held as *mere managers* for a long period on lease periodically renewed."[21] As it is evident, this judgment was based on a prevalent perception of these village-level landholders as contractual "managers" and wasteful "middlemen." It reflected, once again, an urge to establish direct forms of power on land—between the government and the zemindar, as coproprietors (sharing the rents between them), and the ryots. But the identical claim of directness was articulated by a different set of landholders—the village-level ones, namely, serberakars, mokuddums, and pudhans. These oppositions, therefore, represented different designs of the same language of directness—one voiced by the zamindars, which labeled the village-level landholders as illegitimate encroachers, short-term farmers, or middlemen, and the other by the village proprietors, who presented themselves as authentic proprietors, thereby claiming direct control and possession of lands.

Several village-level landholders were denied the status of authentic proprietors in Cuttack. Tarun Mukhopadhyay argues that the Puttamoondee judgment served an important point of reference in most of these disputes. In the dispute over mokuddum rights in mouza Danpore, Mukhopadhyay notes: "In his petition Radhamadhub quoted the decision in the Puttamoondee case. On consideration of the case the government rejected the claim to the mokuddumi right over the mouza."[22] The same strategy was adopted by the zemindar of Boorapara and Noapara. Referring to the board's order in the case of Puttamoondee, he argued against the mokuddum claims in his estates. He tried to prove that these landholders were mere farmers, and was successful in his attempt. Invoking a number of such instances, Mukhopadhyay concludes that there was a generalized dispossession of such village-level landholders in Cuttack in the years after the settlement. This point, however, can be contradicted statistically. Sakti Padhi, after a close statistical scrutiny of the tenancy structure of nineteenth- and twentieth-century Orissa, argues: "What we do find in the end is that the sub-proprietors as a group were very much able to hold on to their own: they maintained their share in the total gross rental as well as their area share in the total assessed area. Moreover, they increased their share in the gross rental that they were collecting (from 20.2 per cent to 32 per cent between 1837 and 1897) and continued to get the same preferential treatment vis-à-vis the zemindars in the 1927 settlement—they were pocketing 32.1 per cent of the rent they were collecting, as compared to 15.4 per cent going to the zemindars."[23]

It is evident that in a number of such disputes the village-level landholders lost the battle with the zemindars. But they also won their rights in a considerable number of instances, which I discuss in the next section. The more important point, however, is that Mukhopadhyay misunderstands the significance of these battles. The growing number of these disputes shows that governmental practices, by redefining the relationships between zemindars and village-level landholders, established a new equation between sovereignty and property in the locality. Although the Puttamoondee verdict can be taken as exemplifying a contrary tendency, a closer look at more disputes will reveal that a generalized critical disposition toward zemindars in the administrative circles gradually depleted their proprietary privileges. As the practice adopted by zemindars of using kubooleuts of varying rents as evidence to turn the distinction between farmers and proprietors in their favor became regularized, administrators soon identified a potential for fraudulence in it. In this manner the Puttamoondee case very easily got reinterpreted against the zemindars. Administrators thought it had implanted in the structure of legislation a strong potential for deceit, which they believed necessarily lent itself to inappropriate and false uses.

This reinterpretation of the Puttamoondee verdict came out clearly even in situations where mokuddumi claims were eventually dismissed by the administrative apparatus. In Booraparrah and Noaparrah, the commissioner pointed out: "The claim to hold these villages as mokuddumi was admitted by the settling officer, the Collector, and by myself in appeal. The zemindar's plea, of the mokuddum having entered into engagements with him as farmer was overruled, because there is strong reason to believe, that the mokuddums were inveigled into the execution of these engagements. The zemindar recognized their title, as mokuddum, from the time he purchased the property in 1219 [1813 A.D.] until 1246 [1840 A.D.] when having become acquainted with the Board's orders, in the case of the Pattamoondee estate ruling, that the execution of farming documents nullified summary cognizance of mokuddumee claims, he got these mokuddums to style themselves as farmers."[24]

Thus, even though in this particular case vindication of mokuddumi claims by the district officials was overruled by the board, apprehensions about cunning zemindars remained deeply entrenched in the various echelons of governance. As my argument in earlier chapters brings out, it had to be this way, because by this time the zemindars had lost the guarantee of a privileged position in the changing matrix of sovereignty and property. The time was ripe, and the field had been opened up, for new agents. Settling the sovereignty-property enmeshment as the key object of governance was shared by all actors in the form of struggles over directness of power in the locality. While zemindars, by putting forward their own justification of authentic immediacy, won some of these battles, there was an emergent governmental disposition in Cuttack, which turned the tables against them in a greater number of situations.

Leaders of the Locality

The same Radhamadhub Banerjee, zemindar of taluk Kistopore, who managed to disenfranchise Markund Pundah from his claim to mokuddumi rights on mouza Danpore was caught up in a more complex state of affairs in the dispute over the mokuddumi rights on mouza Joomrah. In this case, the different levels of the administrative apparatus seemed to be in absolute disagreement with each other. The moonsiff dismissed the mokuddum claims, the collector reversed the moonsiff's decree, the commissioner reaffirmed the moonsiff's decision, the senior member of the Board of Revenue thought that mokuddum rights should not be upheld, but the junior member was convinced that these rights were well established. I do not know what finally happened to the case, as it was sent to the government of Bengal for the ultimate judgment. But what strikes me as more revealing than the finality is the radical potential of difference embedded in disputes of this kind, which were shaping the contours of agrarian power in the locality.

When mouza Joomrah came under settlement, Jankeebullubh Ray put forward his claims to the mokuddumi of the mouza to the deputy collector. The deputy collector, admitting his claims, submitted the case for orders of the collector. The collector, Mr. Mackintosh, dismissed these claims on the basis of certain kubooleuts that had been taken at varying jummas for the mouza. The commissioner canceled the collector's order, confirming Junkeebullubh's claims, arguing that the mouza was purchased as a mokuddumi in 1834 by the latter. Baboo Radhamadhub Banerjee appealed against this decision, saying that he had "always received Izardary Kabooleuts for the mouzas comprised in it."[25] He also pointed out that the abovementioned sale was a mistake on the part of the civil court, as the sellers in question were mere *izaradars*. He further argued that the erstwhile zemindars of this taluk were its only proprietors, which can be inferred from the fact that they granted lakhiraj lands in the mouzas. As I noted earlier, the right to grant lakhiraj lands was considered one of the most authentic markers of proprietary rights by the government during the settlement of Cuttack. This right was evaluated primarily with regard to the issue of the proprietary privileges of the village-level landlords like serberakars, mokuddums, and pudhans. But as is evident, in this renewed context of contests they were strategically used by zemindars as well. This shows, once again, that the zemindars' proprietary status was no longer guaranteed. It had to be wrenched out from a number of oppositional claims.

The zemindars, especially the absentee ones, in the context of a preference for *direct* forms of agrarian power, had lost their credibility among administrators. Responding to Radhamadhub's appeal, commissioner Mills noted: "The petitioner is a non-resident proprietor and like all of this class, in the Province of Cuttack refuses to acknowledge . . . the Mokuddumi tenure, it has been the uniform policy of these zemindars to reduce the mokuddums to the situation of farmers. . . . Dwarkanath Tagore, and other influential zemindars, have in order to attain this object goaded the mokuddums to enter into farming engagements. This practice has been more particularly followed since the Board's orders in regard to the Serberakars of Patamoondee were passed . . . and the zemindar relying on this precedent have left no means untried, to make their mokuddums hold from them as farmers."[26] Mills argued that the mere execution of a farming kubooleut should not be treated as adequate proof of the illegitimacy of claims to a superior proprietary status of village-level landholders in relation to the zemindars. Instead, he pointed out: "Each case must of course be decided on its merits but . . . I may add, that I have looked on all Moostajiri Pottahs, which purport to have been executed subsequent to the Board's orders on the Puttamoondee settlement, with much distrust and suspicion, and it is of great importance, to the protection of the mokuddum's right, that the point should receive serious consideration."[27]

Admitting Junkeebullubh's statement about the purchase of the mouza as a mokuddum to be true, the senior member of the board argued that a settlement of the mouza was subsequently concluded as a moostajir by the mutual consent of both parties. He pointed out that Junkeebullubh voluntarily executed moostajir kubooleuts in 1840 and 1841. Mr. Lowis, junior member of the board, argued in favor of the mokuddumi rights on the basis of a number of points. He noted that the mouza was entered as a mokuddumi in the papers of the recordkeeper of the Maratha government, Gopal Pundit, which certified the ancientness of the title. He further noted that moostajir tenures were not saleable, yet this mouza was sold at a public auction. Responding to the senior member's primary area of contention, Lowis pointed out that the voluntariness of Junkeebullubh in the execution of the farming kubooleuts was by no means established. He maintained: "The voluntary execution . . . besides being denied by the respondent is open to suspicion as having been given or invented after the orders in the Patamoondee settlement had set the ingenuity of all the zemindars in the province at work to destroy the under-tenures in their respective zemindaries."[28] These deliberations between different levels of the bureaucracy shows that the definition "farmer," on which hinged the sovereignty-property relations of the locality, opened itself up to many more criteria, as the established one, enshrined in the Puttamoondee judgment, became highly questionable. Preferences for village-level landholders were so strong that practices of governance even invented new grounds of legitimacy and forms of "evidence," or redefined old ones, in order to establish the rights of these figures. Facts presented in favor of the zemindars were understood to be already tinged with untruth and deceit. Thus, questions of truth and falsity in the assessment of evidence were prefigured by the structural logic of a governmental rationality—which went beyond the government and was creatively and contingently deployed by all actors, zemindars, village-level landholders, and many others.

In 1847, a dispute arose over the proprietary rights of mouza Koorkora and its under-tenure Kureempoore, part of taluk Randeah in Balasore. Gopeenath Dukhin Rae and others claimed these lands as their mokuddumi. Zemindar Anund Ballab Rae Mahashoy argued that they held the lands as mere farmers. In defense of his contention, the zemindar noted that the claims of the rival party were inconsistent. The evidence showed that when the taluk came under settlement in 1842 Gopeenath and others had claimed these lands first as mokuddums, then as serberakars, and finally again as mokuddums. The district officials were, however, convinced of the authenticity of their mokuddumi rights. As an appeal was put forward against these decisions in the civil court, the sudder ameen upheld the serberakary right of the defendants, dismissing their claims to mokuddum status. Against this decision both parties appealed, maintaining their respective original positions.

Gopeenath and others denied ever having executed farming kubooleuts. They claimed to have held possession of mouza Koorkora as mouroosee mokuddums since A.D. 1658, when it was granted to their ancestor Ramchunder Jenna, together with the title of Dukheen Rae, by the raja of Orissa. Kurreempore, they argued, was subsequently purchased. They further remarked, "Although it was true that they first claimed the right of possession as mokuddums, and afterwards as serberakars before the settlement officer, they were inveigled into doing so by the plaintiff, and when they discovered that he was endeavoring to deprive them of all title to the lands, they resolved on urging their original and genuine claim as mokuddums."[29] Once again the zemindar's assertions were presented as a general untruth, reflecting a standard strategy of deceit. This had become an accepted wisdom, which is why the district judge also accepted it as "self-evident."[30] But the judge ruled in favor of the mokuddumi claim on the basis of a number of other kinds of evidence. He traced the ancientness of the title from a variety of documents. These were (1) a *farakhuttee* (a deed of dissolution of partnership) executed in 1766 by Neeladhury Jena, described as one of the shareholders who relinquished his rights in the mokuddumi in favor of Radha Churn Dakhin Rae, which bore the seals of both the pergunnah cazee and the zemindar; (2) a *sunud* (land-grant deed), drawn by Joogul Kishore Ray Mohasoy, one of the former zemindars, in the name of Nursing Jena; (3) a *talpotro pottah* (a palm-leaf land deed) granted in 1804 by Kishen Pershaud Ray Mohasoy; and (4) the copy of Gopal Pundit's *jumma-wasil-bakee* (an account showing the amount of collections and outstanding balances) papers. The judge noted that all these documents "were filed before the settlement officer, and in all of them the ancestors of the applicants are styled *mokuddums*."[31] To this list, he also added a *hookumnamah* (order), issued by the ancestors of the mokuddums, conjointly with other local landlords and officers of the pergunnah, like the *chowdree* (village headman), *canoongoe* (district accountant), and *gomashtah* (clerk), declaring the grant of certain rent-free lands for the worship of village idols and maintenance of fakirs and Brahmins.

This case shows that a great variety of testimonies exhibiting sovereignty-property equations in the locality were used by both the government and the village-level landholders to authenticate mokuddumi rights. New possibilities of evidence were being established to differentiate between farmers and ancient proprietors. Interestingly, the mokuddums here claimed their legitimacy as derived from the sovereign, thereby repeating the governmental understanding that the authentic indigenous sovereignty-property equation in India was originally shared between the sovereign and the village proprietors. The government, however, admitted their claims on the basis of endorsements of their mokuddum status, given by erstwhile zemindars of the region. This was in tune with the representation that in India property-sovereignty relationships were dispersed and shared between a range of landholders and the state—all forms of the these landholders being, in some way, originally traceable to the village proprietor. Ironically, former zemindars appeared as defendants of mukaddami rights, acting, in effect, against the interests of the contemporary zemindars.

The legitimacy of village-level tenures was admitted even in situations where they could not be defined in terms of any of the available categories. In 1846, a dispute emerged over a lease of mouza Saontrapore granted by Maharajah Ramchunder Deo, who at that time held the title of the ancient raja of Orissa, and also acted as the superintendent of the temple of Juggernauth. It was supposed to be a farming lease for twelve years, granted to Lalla Pursooram Rai. Lalla argued that as soon as he had collected a portion of the rents, Permessur Podhan, the zemindar, through whom the rents had been realized previously, drove away the person he had deputed for collections.

Permessur and others claimed that the raja had no right to grant the lease to anyone. Further, they argued that the right to collect rents from the mouza belonged to them, as they had held possession of it through their ancestors from time immemorial. The principal sudder ameen dismissed these contentions. He noted that in a different case Permessur's serberakary claims to Saontrapore had been rejected by the government, as the *mehal* (estate) in question was defined as government property, with the raja as its superintendent. The titles involved in this case lacked any clear definition. While Lalla described Permessur as a zemindar and himself as a farmer, Permessur claimed to be the surburakar of the mouza and argued that his title was independent of the raja's will. Permessur and others argued that when the Mahrattas granted the mehal for the support of the idol, they paid their rent to the temple authorities. Later, when it was transferred to the British government and the raja was appointed as the superintendent, they paid the rent annually to him. Unlike the previous case, here it can be seen that village-level tenure holders often denied their dependence on the will of the sovereign. Permessur and others maintained that their right to the collections from the mouza surpassed the official recognition of any particular government. Eventually the district judge upheld their rights, but still he could not name the tenure holder.

The judge noted that it was not clear "whether they are to be viewed in the light of mokuddums, serberakars, or farmers."[32] On the basis of documentary proof of their undisturbed possession since the time of the Mahrattas, however, these landholderswere granted a prescriptive right that was "superior to that of *khoodkasht* or *thanee* ryuts, though they may not possess a proprietary or transferable right in the mouza. . . . So long as they continue to pay the customary or proper rent, the rajah . . . has no power to oust them or to farm the mouza to any other party. . . . And although the appellants hold no pottah or certificate, either defining the nature of their tenure, or showing that they are entitled to possession at a fixed jumma, the non-possession of such a document can in no way prejudice their claim to possession."[33] It is evident from this case that the government, in order to maintain all forms of ancient village-level tenures, did not mind reconfiguring the established classificatory frames or, at times, even discarding them. It seemed to be not even important to be able to define the tenure according to established categories, as long as its ancientness was established.

There were many more directions in which such redefinitions went. Quotidian practices of governance even challenged the central premise of differentiation between village-level proprietary tenures and contractual-farming ones. In 1847 Hurree Naik petitioned the district court, claiming mouza Neelconna in taluk Bulbhudderpore as his hereditary mokuddum. The defendants were Rajnarain Chowdree, who had purchased half of the taluk, and other zemeendars, namely, Kasseenath Chowdree, Rughoonath Chowdree, and Koontilla Dey, who had mortgaged the other half to Rajnarain. They simply stated that the plaintiff was merely a farmer. They based their assertions on the jummabundee accounts of the mouza of 1804, where it was entered as the *ijarah* (farm) of Bhagut Maintee, some moostajir kubooleuts said to have been executed by the plaintiff in favor of the zemindar from 1831 to 1833, and an *ikrarnamah* (acknowledgment) of 1827, on account of an arrears in rent, which was supposedly signed by the plaintiff as a moostajir.

The district judge upheld the mokuddumi rights on the basis of a host of documents, issued at different times by different authorities of the locality, which endorsed the mokuddumi title. But more important, the judge did not dismiss the validity of the farming kubooleuts that the zemindars had presented in defense of their claim. Rather, he argued that "the execution of such *kubooleuts* even if they were all genuine[,] . . . cannot be considered as a relinquishment on the part of the plaintiff of his mokuddumi claim."[34] The mokuddum title, he thought, had been sufficiently established by other documents. He also pointed, "If it had been satisfactorily shown by the defendants, that the line of succession had been interrupted, or that the mouza had ever entirely lapsed from the hands of the plaintiff's family, and that on recovering possession, they executed farming kubooleuts, the case would be different. . . . It has been satisfactorily proved that the plaintiff and his ancestors have been in undisturbed possession[, which] . . . in my opinion amply refutes the defendant's assertion that the plaintiff was only a farmer or tenant at will."[35] Interestingly, what we see here is that the earlier form of critical engagement with these disputes, which was structured primarily in terms of a perceived falsity, or possibility of deceit, inherent in the problem, had changed into an outright reinterpretation of the problem, based on the rejection of the central premise of distinction between farmers and mokuddums, namely, the short-term kubooleuts. Many more documents, belonging to periods of both pre-British and British governments, were considered authentic markers of mokuddum titles. These were supported by proof of undisturbed possession.

But there was hardly a consensus over documents. I noted earlier that the papers of Gopal Pundit, the central authority of revenue accounts from the Maratha period, were used in most of these disputes to prove the ancientness of mokuddums.[36] When this ubiquitous standard of authenticity was used by zemindars against mokuddum claims, however, it got challenged. In 1849, Sheeb Churn Saontra and Gobind Churn Saontra petitioned the district court, stating that mouza Juggernathpore in taluk Mobarackpore, Balasore, was their *mouroosee* (hereditary) mokuddumi. Oordhub Churn Das and Unoopram Mhaintee based their opposition to this claim on, among other documents, Gopal Pundit's papers where the mouza was allegedly recorded as *paikasht* (contractual). The judge upheld the mokuddumi claim after examining and challenging all the documents presented against it. With regard to Gopal Pundit's papers, he noted: "The said accounts are not only unauthenticated by any signature whatever, but it is well known that abuses of various kinds have been practiced with respect to them."[37] He stated that these papers had been accepted as important testimonials in disputes over ancient tenures, but only when supplemented by other corroborative evidence.

Such a critical interrogation of these papers was somewhere tied to the fact that in the present instance they were being used against mokuddums. It is evident that a highly favorable attitude toward such village-level landholders had become embedded in the discursive practices of governance. This produced the possibility of a fluid and dynamic field of evidence, where markers of authenticity were negotiated, changed, supplemented, and even put to contradictory uses, aimed at the protection of the rights of village-level tenures. The village-level landholders were active participants in the production of this field, not necessarily through purposive alliances with the government. This coproduction was not about particular subjective intentions; it reflected different articulations of the same rationality of governance. To add another dimension to this production, it will be interesting to see where such landholders were placed, and how they styled themselves with reference to the territorial classification of proprietary rights that were structured over various sites, in and out of Cuttack, in the first half of the nineteenth century.

We will take a quick look at that in the next section, before developing a critical perspective on the historiographical treatment of the category of undertenants, or intermediaries, as it emerges from these discussions.

Dependent Locations

It is evident that village-level landholders, such as mokuddums, serberakars, and pudhans, fought for an independent proprietary status vis-à-vis the zemindars in these disputes. Their assertions were admitted by the government, as the prevailing classificatory frame of property defined them as both legitimate and appropriate proprietors, in contradistinction to zemindars, who were seen as inauthentic proprietors and wasteful landholders. But this did not engender a radical removal of the zemindar from the shared matrix of proprietary rights in land. Practices of governance, in tune with the framing of a dispersed field of property-sovereignty relations, maintained different kinds of proprietary rights in land, while significantly redefining the position of the village-level landholders in this field. There were, however, limits to this redefinition. The superiority of village-level tenures was also circumscribed in certain situations where they remained dependent on zemindars. As and when these boundaries were drawn, the juridical category of undertenures was used to describe the village-level tenures of Cuttack. I argued in an earlier chapter that tenures specific to a locality were always debated and defined in a comparative register, which enabled the category of property to be assembled out of concurrent localizations. In the same vein, the village-level tenures of Cuttack were often recast in the light of another comparative field, which was that of intermediaries and undertenants in Bengal.

In 1849, Narain Mahapater claimed Rs. 51 as rent for a portion of land situated in mouza Irda, taluk Gujrajpore, from Mahadeb Das. Narain argued that Mahadeb cultivated the land as a pahee ryot and had not paid rent for three years. In response, Mahadeb denied that he was a pahee ryot, stating that the taluk was his zemindaree. He further pointed out that Irda was a mokuddumi mouza belonging to Kirpasindoo Swain and others, who granted him, on payment of Rs. 15, an *istemraree pottah* (by which land can be held at a fixed rent) for five mauns of land in the mouza, at an annual jumma of one rupee.[38] While the moonsiff of Cuttack rejected the evidence in favor of the istemraree pottah, the district judge accepted it, dismissing Narain's claim. Narain appealed to the Sudder Dewanny Adawlut, arguing that since he had purchased the mokudumee of Kirpasindhoo Swain, which was sold for arrears in rent, the istemraree tenure was no longer valid. As the case came back to the district court for a retrial, the judge upheld Narain's appeal, declaring that the istemraree pottah had become void by the sale of the mokuddum. He noted, "Although it is no where, that I am aware of, definitely laid down, that sales held in execution of decrees for arrears of rent, under Regulation VIII of 1831, are to have the same effect with regard to the cancelment of all leases or under tenures created by the defaulting tenant, as sales for arrears of Government revenue held under Act I, 1845, I am of opinion that with reference to the provisions of Regulation VIII of 1819, which declares that in the event of a sale of a *putnee taluk* for arrears of rent, all such incumbrances, the acts of the defaulters, become cancelled."[39]

It is worth noting that the governmental recognition of the contested proprietary form, in this case, was enabled by comparability, but of a kind different from the one we have seen so far. The decision was arrived at by comparing mokuddums of Cuttack with putnee taluks of Bengal. The judge also admitted, however, that such a comparison was difficult to make because "*mokuddumi* . . . is a superior kind of tenure to that of a *putnee taluk*, inasmuch that the zemindars themselves possess the power of creating *putnee* tenures, and they possess no such power with regard to *mokuddumis*."[40] This comparison, along with the associated reflection on its limits, showed that the governmental geography of property-sovereignty equations was often produced by multiple, overlapping, and contradictory territorial registers. To put it differently, while the general tendency was to understand mokuddums of Cuttack in terms of similar yet different authentic proprietary forms existing in other parts of British India, like the meerasidar from the south, here we see another classificatory principle in operation that made sense of mokuddums in the light of *patnees*, a form of tenure prevalent in certain older parts of the Bengal Presidency. The patnees were in turn typically identified as "under-tenures" in these parts of Bengal, as there, the zemindar was foregrounded as the most authentic and independent proprietary form for a long period. But the reconfiguration of the property-sovereignty map had established other forms of comparison as more credible by this time. Although in this case an older form survived, it remained hesitant. More important, it demonstrated that the independence of village-level tenures continued to be a contested terrain.

In positing the distinction between mokuddums and putnidars, the judge also commented on the mode in which these two undertenants were related to zemindars. He emphasized that mokuddumi, unlike putnee taluks, could not be created by zemindars. In a similar manner, the structure of dependence between mokuddums/serberakars and zemindaris got elaborated over a range of disputes in Cuttack. When Kuroonee Jenna wanted to sell a portion of his mouroosee serberakari tenure, the judge remarked that he had a right to do so irrespective of the zemindar's consent.[41] In another instance, Bhugwan Rai Singh of mouza Batban argued that when Pudlab Senapatty and others, mokuddums on his estate, failed to pay rent in 1847, he went ahead and attached their property. He further noted that once the rents due were collected directly by him, he restored the mokuddums to their positions and asked the ryots to make payments to them. But again in the following year they failed to pay the rents, and Bhugwan sued them. The principal sudder ameen of Cuttack dismissed the plaintiff's claims, arguing: "According to Regulation VIII of 1819, he had no right to dispossess the defendants and collect the rent himself."[42] The district judge, however, challenged the ameen's decision. He pointed out that the ameen had misinterpreted the legislation. He argued: "In Clause 11, Section XVIII of the said law it is clearly laid down, that when a summary suit for arrears of rent alleged to be due may have been instituted against an under-tenant, it shall be competent to the party who may have instituted it to . . . attach and collect the rent from the cultivators. And as the plaintiff asserted that he sued the defendants . . . for the rent of 1254 [A.D. 1847] . . . the first issue on which the principal sudder ameen should have required proof was whether the plaintiff did or did not sue for the rent of 1254—because if he did, his subsequent attachment of the tenure was perfectly legal."[43]

It is noticeable that in many cases mokuddums were classified as undertenants in relation to the zemindar, and the latter was allowed to independently exercise direct control over land, by claiming exclusive ownership over rents. But the mokuddums challenged these contours of dependence, by presenting counterclaims of directness. And in doing so, they consciously imbricated themselves in a wider, comparative field of land-tenures, denying the specificities of locality and claiming lineages of generality. Comparisons and reconfigurations of the local got instituted from a different direction in Cuttack when it was claimed that mokuddumi mouza Bingarpore was not an undertenant of Kotdes zemindarry. The mokuddums Damoodur and Kirtebas wished to hold it as an independent estate, paying directly and separately to the government. The plaintiffs argued that the Kotdes zemindary, in which the mouza was situated, was formerly the property of the rajas of Orissa. During their rule, the plaintiff's ancestor Gopal Das Punda acquired Bingarpore as a grant, for which he used to pay a small quit rent to the rajas. But when the Mughals came to rule the region, their nazim assessed it and converted it into a mokuddumi. The plaintiff's ancestors, at that time, retained the proprietary right and paid rent for the mouza directly to the government. After this, the Maratha rule began, during which the plaintiff continued to pay rent direct to the government treasury.

Over the several years of Maratha rule, the plaintiff's ancestors paid rent to different officials of the government, including the son of the *amil* (revenue officer), Narain Chotra, for a brief while. When the British arrived, they initially paid, as before, straight to the government. But in 1806, Narain Chotra somehow managed to pose as the zemindar of Kotdes and offered the collector one thousand *cahuns* in excess of the jumma paid by Bhugwan Das, the plaintiff's father, for Bingarpore. The collector at that time attached it, with other mokuddums and villages, to Kotdes, refusing to hear Bhugwan Das's claim to independence and separation. Subsequent to Narain Chotra's death, the plaintiffs paid rent to Ketrabas Mungraj, the zemindar, holding on to their dependent capacity, awaiting the future settlement. When they put forward the claim for separation to the settlement officer, he referred them to the civil court.

The defendant refused to admit any right of the plaintiff to hold Bingarpore independently, arguing that it was always part of the Kotdes zemindary. He also denied that the plaintiff possessed any mokuddumi title, stating: "As the Mahratta Government, which was despotic and tyrannical, conferred the entire estate, Kotdes, on his ancestors, it matters not what rights any other persons might previously have possessed therein, as they were all cancelled by the said grant."[44] This statement is suggestive. It shows that constitutive linkages between "despotism" and "property," in defining the nature of the indigenous property-sovereignty complex in India, were not drawn only by the government. They were strategically deployed by local landlords as well. In this case, the zemindar seemed to argue that since despotism, or absolute powers of the sovereign, was the foundation of property, the variety of ancient interests attached to land got overrun in the violence of its originary moment. I have shown that in governmental discourse the relation between despotism and property was understood in different ways. While James Mill characterized the actions of pre-British governments in terms of a despotic practice that destroyed all forms of property in land, several administrators, and Richard Jones, admitted despotism more as a potential than as a regularized practice, which allowed them to identify different tenures in different localities as embodying traces of a variety of proprietary rights. The zemindar in this case, however, echoing Mill's understanding, defined despotism as a successful practice of the Maratha government.

After going through the details of the case, the principal sudder ameen argued that the basis for the decision should be the provisions of Rule XI of Regulation XII of 1805, which declared that "in all cases in which the revenue of a village had for upwards of five years past, been paid direct to Government by the hereditary mokuddum, the settlement of such village should be made with the hereditary mokuddum."[45] In this instance, he pointed out that although the plaintiffs possessed the title of a mouroosee mokuddum in the mouza, and paid revenue direct to the government from 1801 to 1805, it was not proved that they did so for upward of five years prior to the date of the proclamation, which was 15 September 1804. It was found that up to 1800 they paid through the zemindars. Accordingly, the sudder ameen dismissed their claim.

Against this decision, the mokuddums argued that their claims should not be judged by Regulation XII of 1805, which was meant specifically for Cuttack. They pointed out that in this case "all other laws and regulations promulgated for the trial of civil suits in the provinces of Bengal and Orissa were applicable, and that more especially, according to Clauses 3 and 4, Section 5, Regulation VIII of 1793, their claim to separation had been established."[46] The regulation quoted by the mokuddums declared that the revenue demand should be settled with "the actual proprietors of the soil, of whatever description, whether zemindars, talukdars, or chowdris."[47] The play of generalization and localization continued. In this case, it was the mokuddums of Cuttack who refused to be classified strictly as an incomparably local form of landholders. Instead they demanded to be recognized as similar to the chowdris of Bengal, thereby also suggesting, like Harington, that provisions admitting a variety of landholders, other than the zemindars, as actual proprietors of the soil, were embedded within the regulations of the permanent settlement itself. By drawing legitimacy for such a self-representation from the permanent settlement regulations of the Bengal Presidency, these mokuddums challenged the tendency of marking them as undertenants, which emerged out of the same regulations, standing on the assumption that the zemindar was the only authentic independent proprietor. By reading the same governmental code in a different way, they resisted the pressure of other principles of comparisons and classifications in establishing sovereignty-property equations. This was the play of the local in processes of subjectification. As we will see in the concluding section, it relentlessly capacitated openings and closures in relations of power.

Different Alliances, Same Aims: The Unending Games of Power

Contests between zemindars and village-level landholders did not exhaust the field of power around land in Cuttack. There were many more disputes over proprietary privileges between these groups and landholders of other grades.

According to the particular dynamics of each dispute, alliances and enmities developed between these landholders. But once again, in each of these changing situations, superior landholders always tried to oust or disempower inferior ones, in order to achieve a direct control over land—primarily its rents. Tussles over directness, thus, did not only characterize conflicts between the more powerful landholders; they also shaped strategies of struggle between every power stakeholder in the locality. Consequently, I argue, the category of the intermediary, or undertenant, kept changing its meaning, emerging as a dynamic and contingent construction. It was not necessarily used by zemindars to refer to village-level tenures. It got reclaimed and reused by different kinds of landholders, all of whom were invested in claiming directness. In the process, the sovereignty-property interrelationship opened itself up to a series of repetitions, as revisions.

In the dispute over the proprietary right of mouza Mundalow, pergunnah Asseressur, the usual locations of power seemed to be in disarray. Here the mokuddums, contrary to their usual position, acted as rent payers to a lakhirajdar, who, in turn, was the rent receiver. The mouza was granted in 1782 to Rajesh Bhutt as a rent-free holding. He was succeeded by his son Juggunath, who, being childless, adopted a son, called Rughoonath. The latter died suddenly, of snakebite, in 1839. At this point, while Rughoonath's aunt, Nulleta Bai, claimed the mouza as her property, mokuddum Bhowree Naik argued that since "he had all along held the estate as mokuddum, upon a jumma of 1200 Kahans of Cowries, which has been paid from the date of the Lakhiraj sunnud, to the Lakhirajdar," the proprietary right should devolve to him.[48] In response, Nulleta stated that Bhowree was merely a *gomashtah*. The matter could not be settled, as opposing decisions were passed by different officials. While the deputy collector admitted the mokuddum's claim, the commissioner canceled it and ordered that Nulleeta should be put in possession as the rightful proprietor. Eventually the case was sent for further review.

Even without knowing the final judgment on the case, it is worth noting that since in this case the mokuddum was the subordinate landholder, he tried to get rid of the lakhirajdar as soon as an opportunity arose to question the latter's proprietary status. Like the zemindars, the mokuddums here reproduced the same strategy of labeling the other landholder as subordinate—the lakhirajdar, who, in this case, was posited as an intermediary vis-à-vis the mokuddums—to establish direct control over land. Interestingly, the particular constellation of power at play in this case also reformulated the category of the village. As I argued earlier, the village was imagined as an economy of power, all members of which, through different forms of relations to land, remained under the general domination of the village proprietor. The lakhirajdar was understood as one such bona fide member of the village. As this dispute revealed, however, the lakhirajdar was the proprietor of a village, and the mokuddum (usually the archetypal village proprietor), was subordinate to him.

Similar differences were visible in the village when the lakhirajdar of mouza Oopurbust wanted to oust the pudhans, claiming that they were merely contractual farmers. The village had been measured and settled in 1830 at Rs. 225-8-18, which the pudhans engaged for and paid to the lakhirajdar for eleven years. At the end of this period, the lakhirajdar petitioned the authorities to get rid of the pudhans "on the grounds of the term of their engagement having expired, and of their being only farmers, and to have new engagements taken from the ryots to pay their rent directly to himself."[49] The demand of the lakhirajdar was admitted by the deputy collector, whose decision was confirmed by the collector. Accordingly, after the new settlement the lakhirajdar increased the rents of the mouza. At this point a thanee ryot of the mouza instituted a suit against him, arguing that earlier when he paid rent to the pudhans, he had to pay less; the new settlement made him pay more to the lakhirajdar. The pudhans, in combination with the thanee ryot, claimed that the lakhirajdar was entitled only to a fixed amount of rent, that is, the "sudder jumma assessed on the village from them."[50]

Again, it is evident that the figure of the intermediary changed according to the specificities of conflict in different contexts. Here the lakhirajdar attempted to mark the pudhan as an intermediary, a "mere farmer," while the latter's claim indicated that both had equally valid, though different, forms of proprietary interests in the land. The lakhirajdar was entitled to an amount from the land that was the full rental, including the amount classified as revenue, otherwise payable to the state. But due to the existence of the pudhans he got a truncated amount, after deducting the allowances of the former. Since what is involved in this dispute is rent-free land, we must bear in mind that for this land the state did not receive its share of the rent, categorized as revenue. This share went to the lakhirajdar, who, in this dispute, therefore, wished to exercise a total and direct authority over the land, by extracting the full dues from it and, in the process, destroying the shared and plural matrix of rights that was perceived as proprietary, upheld in their respective capacities by strategies of governance. In this case the district judge eventually ruled that the pudhans also had a proprietary right in the mouza and could not be ousted. He noted that the settlement had to be formed with them, although there could be a reassessment of the assets of the mouza. He insisted, however, that under no circumstances could the lakhirajdar collect directly from the ryots. Proprietary rights were retained as plural and distributed.

This also reflected the advantages gained from such plurality by lower-scale landholders/cultivators. This case allows one to suggest, against several historians' understanding of subinfeudation, that tiers of landholding did not always exercise pressure on the cultivators, because, unlike the permanently settled regions of Bengal, in Cuttack, where village-level landholders of various kinds were recognized by the government as authentic proprietors, and the *mofussil jumma* (the village-level revenue dues) was settled with them, the difference between the sudder jumma and the mofussil jumma increased with greater numbers of such subordinate proprietors. These figures were not wasteful intermediaries; they functioned as legitimate, but partial, proprietors. This situation was known to the ryot, who could therefore mobilize it to his own advantage. The more such figures there were, the less the ryot had to pay as rent, which is why, in this case, the removal of the pudhans translated into an increase of the rent for the thanee ryot, and he united with the pudhans to resist the directness of power aimed at by the lakhirajdar.[51]

Sirajul Islam, echoing Ratnalekha Ray, explains the rise of village-level groups in the permanently settled areas of Bengal in the early decades of the nineteenth century in terms of the force of traditional social structures and processes. These groups, like the *jotedars*, *guntidars*, *mandals*, *pradhans*, and others, have been categorized by both Islam and Ray as intermediaries. Such a labeling, I argue, is based on the assumption that the zemindar was the only officially recognized sovereign proprietor in agrarian Bengal, in relation to whom all other forms of landholders were undertenants, or intermediaries, without proprietary capacities. Accordingly, Islam argues that such intermediaries were a nonproductive, extractive presence on land, and necessarily detrimental to the interests of the peasant cultivators. The growth of these groups is also seen, by both Islam and Ray, as an unintended effect of colonial misperceptions. Both scholars, therefore, view the history of agrarian relations in Bengal as a relentless struggle between the colonial state and these proliferating intermediaries. They explain the powerful position of such village-level landholders as the development of indigenous forces lying outside the discursive structure of colonial governance.

In this chapter, and the previous ones, however, I argue that village-level landholders could assume importance in the topography of agrarian power relations not as a result of the overturning of colonial governmental force by indigenous equations of landed power. On the contrary, it was a particular articulation of political-economic/governmental rationality, gaining ground in British India since the turn of the century, that guaranteed these landholders a privileged position, by marking them as authentic proprietors among a number of agrarian groups. Not only did this happen in Cuttack, or the North-Western Provinces, where the village zemindar was favored over the big landlords as the more authentic proprietor and a better improver; the same logic could also be viewed as operational in the permanently settled areas of Bengal, where, as early as 1812, with the legal recognition of the Pattani tenure in the Burdwan division, certain forms of village-level landholding became recognized juridically as authentic proprietary titles. As Islam notes, by this regulation all Pattani tenures became "heritable, transferable by sale, gift or otherwise, at the discretion of the holder and he would be treated in the courts *as if he were the zamindar.*"[52] This shows that even in the older areas of Bengal, right from the beginning of the nineteenth century, juridical measures started redefining so-called intermediaries, like *pattanidars*, as authentic proprietary landlords.

By calling these landholders intermediaries, therefore, Ray and Islam misread the formations of agrarian power in British India. They look at the changing forms of agrarian relations in the nineteenth century from the perspective of the Permanent Settlement, where the zemindar was posited as the sovereign proprietor, without taking note of the reconfigured governmental rationality that enabled the rise of village-level landholders since the turn of the century. These newly dominant landholders were now marked as authentic proprietors, which helped them make independent claims of sovereignty, against their erstwhile categorization as intermediaries. But since governmental mappings of sovereignty-property equations also created the structural possibility of maintaining multiple forms of proprietary interests on land as simultaneously authentic, efforts to institute direct control over land, by getting rid of other claims, became the defining feature of agrarian power struggles of this period. This resulted in a reconfigured and generalized use of the category "intermediary." It was no longer only used by the zemindar or the state to refer to village-level tenures. Different kinds of landholders put forward claims to authentic proprietorship, always referring to their opponents as illegitimate intermediaries.

Thus, contrary to the contention of agrarian histories of Bengal, the category "intermediary" was never fixed. It kept changing meaning, and was used by all, in order to attain direct control over land. The state, the zemindars, the village-level landholders, the lakhirajdars, the thanee ryots, and others—all of them, depending on the specific dynamics of the situation, wished to attain a directness of power and described other contestants in the field as obstructive intermediaries.[53] But this tendency was also offset by the understanding—shared by the government and local landholders—that sovereignty-property equations were dispersed and plural. These parallel forces often engendered shifting alliances between various kinds of landholders in Cuttack, destabilizing familiar equations between zemindars, farmers, mokuddums, and ryots. The case I discuss next offers such an example—of complex and layered equations between these landholders giving rise to a property intrigue that went beyond the usual calculus of power.

In 1849 Nubeen Mahapatur instituted a suit claiming possession of a 4 annas share of moqudumee mouza Bayhurpore, worth Rs. 1512-4-7. The plaintiff stated that when the mouza was advertised for sale in 1843, the mokuddums engaged to pay him Rs. 59-2 within a month, and executed an installment bond agreeing to pay the remaining amount with interest over the course of ten years. In a few years' time, by 1847, as the mokuddums failed to pay the installments, Nubeen sold an eight-*annas* (fractions of a rupee, sixteen annas is equal to one rupee) share of the mouza to others and purchased the remaining eight-annas share for himself. Thereafter he collected some rents from that portion and applied to get his name registered as the proprietor of an eight-annas share of the mouza. At this point he was told by the canoongoe of the pergunnah that Gocoolanund Mhaintee, the nephew of the former mokuddums, was in possession of the property on a lease granted by them since 1847. Nubeen's claim to the proprietary title of the mouza was dismissed by the deputy collector but later upheld by the collector on appeal.

Now the zemindar on whose estate the mouza was situated sued Nubeen for arrears in rent and, having obtained a decree, caused a four-annas share of his eight annas to be sold. In order to get the rent due from the remaining four annas, Nubeen sued the ryots, but Gocoolanund Mhaintee stated that he held the lease of one-half of the mouza. The deputy collector dismissed Gocoolanund's claim, following which the ryots appealed to the commissioner, who upheld their appeal. This led Nubeen to institute the present suit, claiming the proprietary rights over a four-annas share of the mouza. Nubeen argued, "If Gocoolanund Mhaintee had obtained a lease of the property before it was purchased by him, he would have represented the fact at the time of the sale . . . and the ryots, instead of stating that they had paid the rents . . . to the former mokuddums, when he demanded it from them, would have said that they had paid it to the ijaradar; and the ijaradar should have paid rent to him, the plaintiff, or, if he would not have accepted it, to the zemindar . . . and not having done so, it was clear that the zemindar and the former mokuddums to defraud him had prepared the ijara pottah in favor of Gocoolanund Mhaintee, and inserted his name in the putwarry papers.[54] Nubeen thought that every stakeholder in the dispersed networks of power embedded in the mouza conspired against him. From his perspective, the zemindar, the mokuddums, the farmer, and the ryots had a shared interest in preventing him from acquiring any kind of control over the mouza.

Quite obviously, the zemindar, the mokuddums, and the farmer denied these allegations of collusion. The principal sudder ameen, however, refused to accept the claim of the farmer. He noted that the ijara pottah was not a genuine document. Moreover, he argued that since the mokuddums had mortgaged the property to Nubeen, "they were restricted by the terms of the deed of mortgage from alienating or disposing of it, their granting a 21 years' lease of it was tantamount to selling the property, and consequently the lease could not be upheld."[55] The ameen decreed in favor of Nubeen, and his decision was upheld by the district judge. Conspiracy or not, it is quite evident that Nubeen faced opposition from all quarters as he tried to gain control over the mouza. Existent landholders, of different ranks, seemed to have suddenly lost the usual enmities among themselves when it came to resisting Nabeen. That is why the mokuddums, in this case, did not try to fight a farmer; neither did the zemindar get into an overt conflict with the mokuddums. Even the ryots, instead of paying Nubeen, paid the former mokuddums, despite the fact that they claimed to have leased the mouza to the farmer. Proprietary rights remained distributed, but the list of beneficiaries was rearranged. The battle here, between the government and the different landholders, was over different configurations of this dispersal. Eventually, the government validated one of these configurations as an authentic field of property. Interestingly, both the mokuddum and the ijaradar, despite usually being characterized as authentic and inauthentic proprietors, respectively, and often opposed to each other in the locality, were united here in falling out of the chosen list.

Conclusion

This chapter reiterates an important methodological point. It brings us back to a locality, and its intimate, quotidian affairs. In doing so, I wish to remind the reader that analyzing political economic/governmental rationality in British India as an apparatus or an interconnected discursive space does not require abandoning a close scrutiny of localities. In this book, however, that scrutiny is necessarily also an interrogation of the concept of the local itself that was constitutive of this rationality. The locality does not appear in this scheme as a separable element. It exists in simultaneity with various other kinds of sites, localizable or not. The motions of localizations are not caused by sites, even if, in certain instances, they occur in them. The book, therefore, travels with, to, along, and through localities. From the perspective of any one locality, such as Cuttack, this analytical strategy allows me to understand both what happened in the corridors of agrarian power in Cuttack and what happened elsewhere that was important for Cuttack. In this chapter, therefore, I have brought together a gamut of events, peoples, conflicts, and ideas occurring in a locality over the first fifty years of the nineteenth century in terms of their conversations—both congruent and incongruent—with practices outside the locality. With this, I have tracked the emergent configurations of power in Cuttack.

The chapter shows that the twin articulation of the governmental mapping of sovereignty-property interrelationships in India—of dispersal and directness of power—fought with each other in localities. The foregrounding of the figure of the village zemindar, as a reconfigured deployment of the vision of the ancient ryot as the authentic peasant proprietor, became crucial in determining in which direction agrarian power would flow in a locality. Events in Cuttack clearly bear out its implications. The governmental urge to uphold direct forms of power as authentic ones were shared by all landholders of the locality, as they tried to strike each other from the field. Each claimed authenticity in the language of immediacy, depicting the other either as an obstructive, illegitimate, intermediary or as a wasteful, inauthentic, contractual farmer. While village-level landholders were certainly favored by the government in these battles, due to another articulation of governance that construed agrarian power in India as dispersed, there could not be a total victory of the village forces over the big landlords. But the power equations of the locality certainly tended to drift toward the supremacy of the village. By the end of the nineteenth century, therefore, the village, with its attendant figureheads, became the principal field of power in a locality. The scope of the agrarian widened, its power bearers increased, and localities were characterized with new relations of power around land; the sovereignty-property equations set up over the first fifty years of the nineteenth century served as the foundation for new kinds of differentiation, heterogeneity, and diversification.

CONCLUSION

Rewriting Production

The Revenue-Production/Politics-Economics Separation

Why is this book also about agrarian production, when all that it seems to discuss is agrarian power in localities? This has been posed as a question and been answered in different ways over six chapters. But in concluding, I will restate the argument about production. My perspective on production speaks directly to the dominant historiographical characterization of agrarian affairs in the nineteenth century. I have looked at agrarian societies in British India over the first half of the nineteenth century. Almost all agrarian histories of British India view agrarian governance in this period as delinked from and also opposed to production. Governmental engagement with agrarian production, these histories argue, began in the late nineteenth century. This thematic separation of periods, therefore, provides us with a definition of what these histories consider as agrarian production. The same definition also tells us what marked the first half of the nineteenth century—something that is different from, in being antithetical to, agrarian production. In the first half of the nineteenth century, these histories argue, the government was solely interested in the extraction of revenue. The development of different models of settlement in the different regions of British India during this period reflected this agenda. These were basically programs of revenue generation from land. To execute these programs, the government created its agents of extraction in the various localities. These local collaborators emerged as the power holders of agrarian societies. In contrast to this, later came the practices of agricultural production. The government developed an entire infrastructure in order to promote methods and implements of production. The domain of production was assembled as a distinct object of knowledge and intervention over the second half of the nineteenth century, and it continued with greater vigor into the first half of the twentieth.

The clearest statement of this thematic division of the agrarian past comes from David Ludden. In the light of this argument, Ludden remarks about the early nineteenth century: "The politics of revenue overshadowed the economics of production in the Company's relation to agrarian India."[1] This statement, I argue, captures the central premise of the differentiation between "revenue" and "production." Ludden makes "revenue" equivalent to "politics," and "production" to "economics." These equivalences also suggest that his argument understands politics as something external and opposed to economics. Accordingly, Ludden locates the late nineteenth century as the point of departure for the governmental interest in production. He argues that it is with the famines in the 1860s, 1870s, and 1880s—during which departments of agriculture were opened all over the country—that the regime of governmental investment in agricultural production began. He notes, "Stimulated by riots and famines, which indicated deep distress in agrarian India, a flood of texts ensued on agricultural improvement."[2]

Agricultural "improvement" through scientific methods indeed became one of the central concerns of the government in the aftermath of a series of deadly famines during the last three decades of the nineteenth century. The first Famine Commission wrote its report after the famine in 1866, which devastated the entire region of the present-day state of Orissa, its epicenter being the Cuttack division.[3] The need to protect the country against such calamities was expressed in the report. But it was noted that without systematic information on agricultural conditions of the area, it would not be possible to institute preventive measures.[4] It was primarily with the Famine Commission Report of 1880 that a compelling need to improve an agriculturally malignant country was articulated. The report argued that an entire set of new knowledge about the conditions of people living on the land was required to design strategies of agricultural improvement. It noted that there was total absence "of trustworthy statistical knowledge as to the numbers of the people, the rates of their deaths and births, and the influence on these rates of epidemic disease or local distress, combined with an equally insufficient insight into their economical condition, and particularly an absence of agricultural statistics in an accessible form."[5] The report argued that the peasant cultivator, or ryot, was in an impoverished condition due to the pressure of providing land revenue, and his productive capacities had to be urgently energized in order to nurture the overall potential of Indian agriculture. Subsequent Famine Commission Reports, of 1898 and 1901, for example, continued with the same suggestions. The 1901 report noted that the different constituents of agriculture, like crops, seeds, implements, manure, cattle, and so on, needed to be protected and improved by the government in order to boost the productivity of the ryot.[6]

David Arnold argues that such a program of improvement can be traced to an even earlier time, to the initial decades of the nineteenth century. He notes that the establishment of botanical gardens in different parts of British India, the Agricultural-Horticultural Society of India, and the profound influence of Kew Gardens in London released a current of ideas and activities in this domain. Arnold observes, "The want of capital investment, the deficiencies of Indian livestock, the crudeness of Indian agricultural implements, the want of manuring, of hedges and enclosures—all these formed part of the litany of complaints directed against Indian agriculture."[7] Introduction of special plants like sago palm and cassava to protect India against recurrent famine and the building of canals, which were compared with the great historical monuments of Asia, from the pyramids to the Great Wall of China, all informed this project of agricultural improvement. While agreeing with Arnold, I would emphasize that it is toward the end of the nineteenth century that the task for designing a space of improvement in Indian agriculture began, following the recommendations of the Famine Commission Reports. Improvement had to be effected by and in this space. The construction of this space involved the creation of segregated, clearly identifiable constituents of agricultural production and then investing meaning in each of them in terms of a complementary relationship, directed solely toward the goal of improvement. John Augustus Voelcker, an agricultural chemist from England, was one of the most important architects of this space. In 1893, after a rigorous, even if short-term, inquiry into the conditions of land and people in the subcontinent, he brought out the "Report on the Improvement of Indian Agriculture." At the level of official discourse, this work was considered one of the seminal contributions to the promising project of agricultural improvement. Voelcker's treatise became almost a manual in shaping the directions of the project.

Voelcker's report was particularly concerned with increasing the productivity of the soil. Voelcker believed that manure would act as the magic potion for the miseries of British Indian agriculture. The report organized itself around a classificatory scheme. It was divided into chapters like: (I) "Historical Introduction," (III) "Cultivating Classes," (IV) "Climate," (V) "Soil," (VI) "Water," (VII) "Wood," (VIII) "Manure," (IX) "Grass," (X) "Fodder-Crops and Hedges," (XI) "Livestock and Dairying," (XII) "Implements," (XIII) "Crops and Cultivation," (XIV) "Agricultural Industries and Exports," (XV) "Economic and Political Conditions," (XVI) "Practical Enquiry," (XVII) "Scientific Enquiry," (XVIII) "Experimental Farms," (XIX) "Agricultural Education," and

(XX) "Agricultural Departments."[8] These were the elements of agriculture, each of which was examined closely, arranged in a complementary relation to others, and finally oriented toward the grand telos of improving the productivity of the soil. These were the beginnings of the productivist regime in the governance of British Indian agriculture. It became one of the defining dimensions of nation building in the twentieth century, as nationalists of various kinds built their critique of colonial rule around the issue of agricultural improvement. Ludden writes, "Economic nationalism used data on agrarian conditions against the Raj. Nationalists built empirical artefacts from official statistics and joined debates about policy, using measures of progress, as others had done before. . . . Congress agreed with government that agricultural progress required programs such as catalogued by the Royal Commission. Amid oppositions to empire, therefore, a unified paradigm for agrarian studies stretched across the political spectrum."[9]

But in this entire discourse of improvement, production was understood as a domain of economics, while politics was considered as something external to it, obstructing its smooth operation. Agrarian production, which should have been an economic matter, it was argued, was turned into a sphere of the political by shrewd strategies of revenue collection of the British government, which created wasteful, unproductive power brokers in the localities as collaborators of this project. This was an argument shared by different positions, from colonial officials, to nationalist actors, to historians of agrarian India. Let us take the case of irrigation in late nineteenth-century Cuttack. Cuttack was the only area in eastern India where the British invested significantly in irrigation. This investment needs to be seen in the context of Arthur Cotton's vision of canal networks becoming the driving force behind the improvement of India's economic infrastructure in the second half of the nineteenth century.[10] Cotton, no doubt, primarily viewed irrigation as a question of "public works." Ravi Ahuja has argued quite convincingly that the prevalent intellectual discourse on public works in Europe arose from the idea of making transport infrastructure an essential part of the production process, in order to reduce overall costs of production and increase productivity. But the questions of irrigation and productivity were also closely tied to ideas of agricultural improvement during this time.

The irrigation project, however, was considered to be a big failure by the authorities by the beginning of the twentieth century. It suffered great financial losses, as the government kept trying new means to persuade people to avail themselves of the benefits of irrigation canals and embankments. Rohan D'Souza explains the failure of this project in terms of a misfit between colonial capitalism's extractive needs and the natural hydrological complexity of the Orissa delta. He argues that due to the unique hydrological character of the delta, floods were beneficial for the lands in Orissa's deltaic plains. The colonial operations of flood control, by being insensitive to the delta's natural rhythm, turned a "flood-dependent" landscape into a "flood-vulnerable" one. D'Souza points out that the rapacious colonial concerns of revenue generation disturbed the natural ecological arrangement for agriculture in deltaic Orissa.[11] This is how he reinforces the analytical separation between "revenue/politics" and "production/economics." Based on this assumption, he argues that there was a difference between the ecologically insensitive revenue concerns of the local colonial bureaucracy and the ecologically conscious scientific-developmentalist concerns of specialists or colonial engineers. In the latter category, he places Captain Harris—one of the colonial engineers working on flood protection in the valley—who according to D'Souza had a more "organic" understanding of the delta. This division, I argue, is incompatible with what I have shown in this book as the political economy of production, which, in a reconfigured manner, made local power internal to, and a constitutive component of, the category of production. D'Souza does not recognize the fact that the organic understandings of specialists were also geared toward making the delta productive, albeit in a manner which is more suited to its hydrological peculiarity. In fact, it was thescheme of Arthur Cotton, another such "specialist", that inaugurated the revenue-exploiting project in the delta. Such separations between "revenue concerns" and revenue-disinterested "specialist science" appear in the study by D'Souza because he de-links production from the local politics of revenue extraction instead of considering production as immanent to local power in political economy.

David Washbrook's characterization of early nineteenth-century agrarian governance is rooted in a similar argument. As I noted in the Introduction, Washbrook argues that the governmental treatment of landed property, as embodied in property laws and models of settlement, reflected a pragmatic strategy to collect revenue by building networks of local agents. He defines the need for this collaboration primarily in terms of the contradictory tendencies within law of promoting market enterprise and preserving older social forms at the same time. He also points out that the Company state deliberately maintained the social relations within which the agrarian economy was organized earlier in order to secure extraction of surplus and reproduce the conditions of production. This strategy resulted in a stunted growth of property rights and a capitalist market around land.[12] Peter Robb, on the other hand, argues that collaborative arrangements in this period were necessary because of a weak administrative structure of the Company state, lack of knowledge of the complex social relations on land, and resilience of locally dominant social forces. But an incapability to penetrate effectively into local structures went hand in hand with a desire to establish private property and capitalist market relations over land. Robb differs from Washbrook here in the sense that he indicates the presence of an active will on the part of the Company state in the early nineteenth century to transform agrarian conditions along lines of capitalist improvement. He argues that the Company state "had strong motives to promote agriculture as the norm, and to order land and people, by force if necessary. There were means enough to encourage private property; there were sales laws, resumption proceedings, and a pro-landlord bias in government. . . . Washbrook believes that this private property was effectively delayed until the later nineteenth century. But for Bengal and Bihar it seems possible to trace an earlier grafting of Western concepts on to longer-term forms of land control."[13]

Such disagreements, however, do not unsettle the historiographical consensus about the agrarian affairs of this period, which posits an opposition between political economy underlying governance and "traditional" social forms of land control constitutive of local power. This opposition continues to shape the developmental discourse of the nation. In the nationalist agenda, it is presented even more aggressively, where the development warriors are seen as ready to wage war against their most formidable enemies, namely, the local powers. It is a veritable war. In the Planning Commission of 1976, one of the bodies which had agricultural development as its prime objective was called the Task Force on Agrarian Relations. It observed, with martial zeal, that local power structures are "insurmountable hurdles in the path of the spread of modern technology and improved agricultural practices."[14]

Liberalism: Another Look

Karuna Mantena's work on Henry Maine covers significant theoretical ground in building a critique of the historiography that is based on this opposition. Mantena argues that the late nineteenth-century imperial strategy of "indirect rule," by which there was a governmentalized reinvigoration of the traditional cultural and social structures of India, was not a practical/pragmatic accommodation with on-the-ground social realities. She correctly observes that "imperial historiography has shown a marked tendency to emphasize local developments and local (imperial and native) actors as the primary agents that both propel imperial expansion and shape governance patterns.... Indirect rule is thus rendered a rarefied name for a political necessity, a practical institutional solution that accommodated itself with 'facts on the ground,' that is, with local conditions and structures of power. In the self-understanding of imperial administrators, indirect rule was likewise conceived of as emblematic of the practical, anti-ideological orientation of British imperial policy."[15] On the contrary, Mantena notes, the shift to indirect rule was a distinctly ideological one that marked a move away from the earlier universalism of the liberal, Benthamite, utilitarian variety toward a culturalism produced primarily out of nineteenth-century social theory and evolutionary anthropology. These intellectual currents and their conceptualizations of "native society" became the ideological basis of late nineteenth-century imperial governance by indirect rule. This ideological foundation, Mantena argues, is rendered invisible and re-presented as "practical necessity" by imperial actors and a certain strand of imperial historiography.

Neeladri Bhattacharya also argues that culturalism was the ideological basis of late nineteenth-century colonial governance with regard to the processes of the governmental codification of custom in the agrarian society of Punjab. He highlights the analytical importance of the governmental presentation of the "local" in the drives of codification. As I argued in my chapter on the "village," Neeladri also shows how "village elders," not the "pundits," the authorities on canonical Hindu texts, were considered the key to an understanding of custom. But more important, he correctly observes that it was not only a question of "understanding" local society, by depending on it blindly. It was a case of acquiring legitimacy to represent it with greater authenticity than itself. Thus, Bhattacharya notes: "To assert sovereign power the masters had to transcend their crippling reliance on native knowledge-brokers and claim their own superior right to represent local tradition."[16] While his essay "Remaking Custom" makes important points about the governmental production of the local in agrarian societies, it still does not deal directly with the question of the relation between production and local power.[17]

A collection of essays edited by M. Desai, S. H. Rudolph, and A. Rudra, *Agrarian Power and Agricultural Productivity in South Asia*, tries to tackle this problem conceptually, over a range of studies on the past and present of agrarian South Asia. The volume offers rich and insightful essays on the relation between power and productivity in agrarian societies. But it remains committed to the historiographical orthodoxy in understanding power and productivity as analytically separate, antithetical categories. It argues that classical political economy is devoid of an understanding of power and "indigenous" social forces. It emphasizes that from James Mill to John Stuart Mill classical political economy has been an ahistorical, abstract, form of knowledge premised on a notion of "universal history," taking the European experience of commercialization and industrialization as the standard for evaluating the rest of the world.[18]

In this book, all along, I have tried to argue that "production" and "power" are not opposites. They are both part of discursive practices of political economy and agrarian governance. Classical political economy in early nineteenth-century Britain did not consist only of universals rooted in the European experience of economic development. It was not a dehistoricized discourse. It was constituted by abstractions, but of a different order. These abstractions took indigeneity and local interrelations between property and political power in different nations of the world as legitimate explanatory categories of political economy. With this reinterpretation, the local became the new universal of political economy.

Accordingly, I have tried to read practices of agrarian governance in British India as informed by a governmental rationality that mapped localities in terms of their differences from, and resemblances to, an original, ancient, Hindu/Indian political. I have argued that the dynamics of events in agrarian localities worked within these frameworks. They undoubtedly challenged the general articulation of the political, but only in order to produce newer forms of it. This method, I have argued, enables us to understand the formation of agrarian societies in different localities in terms of internal workings of political economy. This perspective makes us look at the development of specific power equations in localities, like the rise to dominance of village-level landed elites in Cuttack, without a total dismantling of erstwhile big landlords, and the privileging of the rights of resident peasants, along with a denial of the claims of itinerant ones, as productions of a specific articulation of a sociologized discourse of political economy.

The governmental rationality that worked in the nineteenth century to produce agrarian localities in terms of such specific, concrete strategies of intervention, generating from within them arrangements of power consistent to a political economic imaginary, can be described, following Foucault, as the true principle of liberalism. It is a political technique that works, as Foucault argues, "in a sphere complementary to reality . . . within reality, by getting the components of reality to work in relation to each other, thanks to a series of analyses and specific arrangements."[19] He further observes that it is "this fundamental principle that political technique must never get away from the interplay of reality with itself is profoundly linked to the general principle of what is called liberalism. The game of liberalism—not interfering, allowing free movement, letting things follow their course . . . basically and fundamentally means acting so that reality develops, goes its way, and follows its own course according to the laws, principles, and mechanisms of reality itself."[20]

In a similar vein, I argue that local power was a constitutive condition of political economy as liberalism in nineteenth-century British India. The question of production in agrarian societies was internal to that of power. The local placed difference at the heart of European liberalism. This indicates that the problem of "difference" need not be necessarily traced in the domain of "culture," in defining coloniality. Returning to Partha Chatterjee's seminal conceptualization of the "rule of difference," which contends that universalism constructs difference as its outside—something that prevents/limits its spread—I argue here that universalism constructs difference as its inside, as constitutive of its self-limiting character. Chatterjee notes that the discourse of Western universalism produces exceptionalism as, and at its limit. Rethinking this formulation, I propose that it is not as its limit but as its constitutive principle that "exceptionalism/difference" figures in the local. This is also to argue that it is not enough to show that difference is constructed; one needs to take difference out of its particularist rendition altogether.[21] A careful reading of the local tells us that the project of metropolitan universalism did not become a deferred one due to the rule of "colonial difference." Its deferrals were built within its universality, as the art of government was constituted by the self-limiting principle of difference.

NOTES

The following abbreviations appear in the notes.

BDR	Balasore District Records
BJC	Bengal Judicial Consultations
BRC	Bengal Revenue Consultations
BRP	*Board of Revenue Proceedings*
CDR	Cuttack District Records
IOR	India Office Records
OSA	Orissa State Archives
PP	Parliamentary Papers
SBOR	Sadar Board of Revenue
SBORP	*Sadar Board of Revenue Proceedings*
WBSA	West Bengal State Archives

Introduction

1. I turn to Gilles Deleuze's concept of the "abstract machine" here. Deleuze argues that processes of "signifiance" and "subjectification" are produced by an "abstract machine of faciality." He describes this machine as a force that creates a face, with all its features, walls, and holes. "Concrete faces cannot be assumed to come ready-made. They are engendered by an *abstract machine of faciality*, which produces them at the same time as it gives the signifier its white wall and subjectivity its black hole. Thus the black hole/white wall system is, to begin with, not a face but the abstract machine that produces faces according to the changeable combinations of its cogwheels. Do not expect the abstract machine to resemble what it produces, or will produce" (Gilles Deleuze and Félix Guattari, *A Thousand Plateaus: Capitalism and Schizophrenia* [London: Bloomsbury, 2013], 197). By the "abstract machine of faciality," Deleuze is indicating, as he does with most of his concepts, a topological dynamic. In the present book, the "local" is used in a similar sense, as a force that enables the continuous construction, dissolution, and reconstruction of concrete formations. These formations, as I gradually discuss, are multiple, like political economy, scientific method, liberal governance, landed property, and peasant groups—all tied together in being produced by the local.

2. Deleuze and Guattari, *A Thousand Plateaus*, 14. My book wishes to release these uses of the local, visible in both colonial governmental practices and a certain kind of historiography. It attempts to rethink the local as a "model that is perpetually in construction or collapsing, and of a process that is perpetually prolonging itself, breaking off and starting up again" (ibid., 21).

3. This potential can be read as the lines in an apparatus. These lines, Deleuze argues, have four characteristics. There are lines that determine conditions of visibility and enunciation.

There are lines of force that generate continuous dynamism within the apparatus. Finally, there are lines of subjectification, which are points of breakage and fracture in the apparatus. They generate subjectivities that "escape from the powers and the forms of knowledge of one social apparatus in order to be reinserted in another, in forms which are yet to come into being" (Gilles Deleuze, "What Is a Dispositif?" in *Michel Foucault Philosopher*, ed. Timothy J. Armstrong [New York: Routledge, 1992], 162).

4. "Introduction" in *Tensions of Empire: Colonial Cultures in a Bourgeoisie World*, ed. Frederick Cooper and Ann Laura Stoler (Berkeley: University of California Press, 1997), 1.

5. "We treat metropole and colony in a single analytic field, addressing the weight one gives to causal connection and the primacy of agency in its different parts" (ibid., 4).

6. This relapsing is particularly evident in Richard Drayton's work, which can be also taken as an early attempt to rewrite South Asian agrarian history in the light of imperial formations. In narrating the links between the emergence of botanical science, imperial rivalries over control of science, and its application in colonies and an agrarian nationalism in Britain, Drayton throws up images of an imperial theater of "improvement." But his history remains trapped within the model of a diffusionist relation between the metropole and the colony. Ultimately, it becomes a history of Kew Gardens in the context of the Victorian "revolution in government." See Richard Drayton, *Nature's Government: Science, Imperial Britain, and the "Improvement" of the World* (New Delhi: Orient Black Swan, 2005).

7. In the more recent body of work on imperialism, often referred to as "new imperial histories," the reconceptualization of space and place is still embedded in a geographical understanding of these categories. This scholarship has indeed generated an immensely enriching empirically and theoretically diversified field of research. But in engaging with the analytical problem of space/place, it has chosen to mark its point of departure from older studies of imperialism in terms of a move away from "nation-centred historical models, with sometimes a suggestion that notions of imperial cultures as global networks should be put in their place." Such a move, it has argued, decenters the "metropole" or any such fixed origin of social formations. See Stephen Howe, ed., *The New Imperial Histories Reader* (New York: Routledge, 2010), 2. My book learns from these historical moves but places its own engagement with the problem of space differently. In understanding the local as an "abstract machine," I argue that spaces and places, at the level of the empire, nation, region, or locality, were generated by this machine as concrete features. Therefore, for my purposes, these geographies, in themselves, do not exist as objects or subjects of history, either separately or in unison. Their specificities can be grasped only along with, and as effects of, the practices in which they become spaces.

8. See J. K. Samal, *History of Modern Orissa* (Kolkata: Firma KLM, 1989); K. M. Patra, *Orissa Under the East India Company* (New Delhi: Munshiram Manoharlal, 1971); N. R. Patnaik, ed., *Economic History of Orissa* (New Delhi: Indus, 1997); and T. K. Mukhopadhyay, *The Agrarian Society of Orissa: Nineteenth Century* (Kolkata: Progressive, 2008).

9. None of the seminal works on agrarian Bengal considers temporarily settled areas of the presidency. See Ratnalekha Ray, *Change in Bengal Agrarian Society:1760–1850* (New Delhi: Manohar, 1979); Sirajul Islam, *Bengal Land Tenure: The Origin and Growth of Intermediate Interests in the Nineteenth Century* (Calcutta: K. P. Bagchi, 1988); and Sugata Bose, *Peasant Labor and Colonial Capital: Rural Bengal Since 1770* (Cambridge: Cambridge University Press, 1993).

10. John Stuart Mill, "Memorandum of the Improvements in the Administration of India During the Last Thirty Years," in *The Collected Works of John Stuart Mill, XXX—Writings on*

India, ed. J. M. Robson, M. Moir, and Z. Moir (Toronto: University of Toronto Press, 1990 [1858]), 127–28.

11. One of the major strands of this internal critique was articulated by a group identified by Boyd Hilton as the "Christian economists," who "assailed what they took to be its dominant, anti-landlord, anti-clerical, and viciously secular formulation by Ricardo and the *Westminster Review* radicals" (Boyd Hilton, *The Age of Atonement: The Influence of Evangelicalism on Social and Economic Thought, 1785–1865* [Oxford: Oxford University Press, 1988], 37). In a similar vein, Harro Maas argues that political economists, like William Whewell and Richard Jones at Cambridge and Richard Whately at Oxford, critiqued Ricardianism from perspectives deeply rooted in natural theology (Harro Maas, "'A Hard Battle to Fight': Natural Theology and the Dismal Science, 1820–50," *History of Political Economy* 40 [2008]: 143–67). There are two other extreme and opposed evaluations of the contemporary impact of Ricardian principles. One of them is put forward by Keynes, who argues: "Ricardo conquered England as completely as the Holy inquisition conquered Spain" (cited in Mark Blaug, *Ricardian Economics: A Historical Study* [New Haven: Yale University Press, 1958], 1). In radical opposition to this view, Schumpeter holds that "the Ricardians were always in the minority, even in England, and it is only Ricardo's personal force which, as we look back, creates the impression that his teaching . . . dominated the thought of the time. . . . The opposite is nearer the truth" (cited in ibid., 2). Mark Blaug reinterprets both positions by stating that in the process of the popularization of the views of Ricardo, carried out by his ardent devotees, his ideas underwent substantial modification. He notes that "as Ricardian economics was disseminated, the Ricardianism which conquered England would probably not have received Ricardo's personal endorsement. A series of amendments and defences thrown up against criticism soon covered and in the end almost buried the original doctrine" (ibid., 1).

12. Eric Stokes, *The English Utilitarians and India* (Delhi: Oxford University Press, 1989), 81.

13. As Stokes notes, in the hands of Mill "the law of rent provided . . . both a coherent policy for the demarcation of public and private rights in the land, and a clear criterion of assessment" (ibid., 92).

14. Ibid., 15.

15. For a different perspective on Burke that analyzes his emphasis on cultural and historical specificity as the mark of a philosophy tolerant and appreciative of difference, in contrast to the exclusivist, aggressive universalism of thinkers commonly viewed as liberals, like the Millses, and thereby more genuinely liberal than the latter, see Uday Singh Mehta, *Liberalism and Empire: A Study in Nineteenth-Century British Liberal Thought* (Chicago: University of Chicago Press, 1999). Another work that investigates the "imperial" dimension in the thought of major eighteenth- and nineteenth-century British and French thinkers is Jennifer Pitts, *A Turn to Empire: The Rise of Imperial Liberalism in Britain and France* (Princeton: Princeton University Press, 2005).

16. David Arnold provides an important critique of the binary between a reforming, improving utilitarianism and a preserving romanticism. He argues that the romantic imagination acted as a complementary vision to the utilitarian ideologies of "improvement." Although the romantic strain in colonial imaginations of landscape adored nostalgia and cried out loud for the lost glory of a golden past and a return to the primitive state of nature, its ideal of a perfect communion of man with nature was couched entirely in terms of a vision of agriculture that would create order out of a chaotic and disarranged nature by techniques of improvement. See David Arnold, *The Tropics and The Traveling Gaze: India, Landscape, and Science, 1800–1856* (New Delhi: Permanent Black, 2005), 74–109. For a similar critique, see Neeladri Bhattacharya,

"Pastoralists in a Colonial World," in *Nature, Culture, Imperialism: Essays on the Environmental History of South Asia*, ed. David Arnold and Ramachandra Guha (Delhi: Oxford University Press, 1985), 49–86.

17. Lynn Zastoupil, *John Stuart Mill and India* (Stanford: Stanford University Press, 1994), 3.

18. Ibid., 182.

19. See Laura Snyder, *The Philosophical Breakfast Club: Four Remarkable Friends Who Transformed Science and Changed the World* (New York: Broadway Books, 2011); and Richard Yeo, *Defining Science: William Whewell, Natural Knowledge and Public Debate in Early Victorian Britain* (Cambridge: Cambridge University Press, 1993), 3–27.

20. See Jan Golinski, *Making Natural Knowledge: Constructivism and the History of Science* (Chicago: University of Chicago Press, 1998), 1–12.

21. Richard Jones, *An Essay on the Distribution of Wealth and on the Sources of Taxation* (London: J. Murray, 1831), vii.

22. Richard Jones's location in contemporary political economy has not been adequately conceptualized. In the light of disciplinary traditions of economics, Jones has been classified as a historical/institutionalist economist. See Salim Rashid, "Richard Jones and Baconian Historicism at Cambridge," *Journal of Economic Issues* 13 (1979): 159–73; and William L. Miller, "Richard Jones's Contribution to the Theory of Rent," *History of Political Economy* 9 (1977): 346–65. References to Jones are scanty in the histories of British India. It is only from a revised position in his later work that Stokes argues that Jones's theory of peasant rents had a brief and temporary influence on agrarian governance, which was eventually swept away by the persistence of the Ricardian framework. See Eric Stokes, *The Peasant and the Raj: Studies in Agrarian Society and Peasant Rebellion in Colonial India* (Cambridge: Cambridge University Press, 1978), 94–97. Chris Bayly, along similar lines, notes that Jones's theory had a minor impact, as it made officials in the North-Western Provinces reduce the rent burden on the cultivators. See C. A. Bayly, *The New Cambridge History of India, II.1: Indian Society and the Making of the British Empire* (Cambridge: Cambridge University Press, 1988), 129. More specifically, regarding debates over rent during the tenancy legislation in late nineteenth-century Bengal, Peter Robb observes that Jones's analysis of the category influenced some reformers. He notes that these reformers rejected the Ricardian-Malthusian definition of rent rooted in market competition and natural fertility, arguing, following Jones, that rent emerged out of power. See Peter Robb, *Ancient Rights and Future Comfort: Bihar, the Bengal Tenancy Act of 1885 and British Rule in India* (London: Routledge, 1997), 197. The only person to devote substantial conceptual attention to Jones is William Barber. But even he analyses Jones's work in terms of its self-styled inductivism, arguing that Jones, intuitively, had a more realistic understanding of Indian society. Moreover, he also concludes that Jones's ideas had almost no relevance for agrarian governance in British India. See William J. Barber, *British Economic Thought and India, 1600–1858: A Study in the History of Development Economics* (Oxford: Oxford University Press, 1975), 194–210.

23. Clive Dewey observes a resurgence of the peasant cultivator in the debates over agricultural improvement in nineteenth-century Britain. Dewey puts together an entire tradition in political economy, consisting of William Thornton, Richard Jones, J. S. Mill, and Alfred Marshall, championing the cause of the peasant proprietor. See Clive J. Dewey, "The Rehabilitation of the Peasant Proprietor in Nineteenth-Century Economic Thought," *History of Political Economy* 6 (1974): 22.

24. Further, even empirically, Richard Jones cannot be considered an advocate of the peasant proprietor. Although Jones developed an elaborate classification of peasant rents, he never

argued that the peasant proprietor was a superior improver. While discussing the Company's revenue policy, as part of his political economy of indigeneity, he noted only that the rent burden on the cultivators should be lightened in order to improve production. On the contrary, as David Martin's essay suggests, he was critical of their improving capacities. Martin notes that the Prussian historian Friedrich von Raumer "called on Richard Jones at Haileybury, where he tried, without success, to shake the English economist's criticism of small farmers" (David Martin, "The Rehabilitation of the Peasant Proprietor in Nineteenth-Century Economic Thought: A Comment," *History of Political Economy* 8 [1976]: 300).

25. See Abram L. Harris, "John Stuart Mill: Servant of the East India Company," *Canadian Journal of Economic and Political Science* 30 (May 1964): 185–202; R. D. C. Black, "Economic Policy in Ireland and India in the Time of J. S. Mill," *Economic History Review*, n.s., 21 (August 1968): 321–36; and S. B. Cook, *Imperial Affinities: Nineteenth-Century Analogies and Exchanges Between India and Ireland* (New Delhi: Sage, 1993).

26. Cook problematizes the Britain-India, empire-colony model by introducing Ireland into the field of exchange. He argues that this field was shaped by multilateral circuits. "Far from simply serving as a conduit for direct one-way transfers from suzerain to possession, the empire was a community of units that related to each other in different ways alternatively as transmitters, mediators and receivers of policy and opinion" (Cook, *Imperial Affinities*, 18). But he retains the metropole-colony distinction, in identifying clear pathways of influence from one to another.

Ranajit Guha's work, which analyzes the policy of permanent settlement in Bengal in the light of contemporary debates between physiocratic and mercantilist currents of metropolitan thought, is a path-breaking and pioneering example of a diffusionist perspective on British India. See Ranajit Guha, *A Rule of Property for Bengal: An Essay on the Idea of Permanent Settlement* (Durham, N.C.: Duke University Press, 1996). Robert Travers's book displays a more recent use of a similar approach, which argues that practices of governance in eighteenth-century British India were underpinned by contemporary British political ideas about the "ancient constitution." See Robert Travers, *Ideology and Empire in Eighteenth-Century India: The British Bengal* (Cambridge: Cambridge University Press, 2007). Some other similar examples of diffusionist approaches are Martha Mclaren, *British India and British Scotland, 1780–1830: Career Building, Empire Building and a Scottish School of Thought on Indian Governance* (Akron, Ohio: University of Akron Press, 2001); and Robert Travers, "British India as a Problem in Political Economy: Comparing James Steuart and Adam Smith," in *Lineages of Empire*, ed. Duncan Kelly, 137–160 (London: Oxford University Press, 2009).

27. My reading of Mill's political economy locates it as yet another, different, articulation of ongoing changes in the meanings of certain classical political economic categories, like production and distribution. I do not examine Mill's difference from the classical framework in terms of its self-representations, which has been done by a number of notable works. Samuel Hollander and Laura Snyder carry out such an exercise by analyzing Mill's methodological relationship with the program of induction, as espoused by Whewell. Accordingly, both try to measure how much Mill and Whewell were tilted toward inductivism or deductivism, in formulating their own methodologies. While Hollander argues that both incorporated some element of each methodology, Snyder writes: "In the end . . . Mill characterized political economy as the geometrical science of his father and Bentham, without successfully uniting the inductive element of the Coleridgian method" (Laura J. Snyder, *Reforming Philosophy: A Victorian Debate on Science and Society* [Chicago: University of Chicago Press, 2006], 309). See also Samuel Hollander, "William Whewell and John Stuart Mill on the Methodology of Political Economy,"

Studies in the History and Philosophy of Science 14 (1983): 127–68. In these works, Mill's political economy is contextualized in terms of the methodological vocabulary it offers—built on the deductive-inductive opposition—to characterize itself. I, however, understand this methodological engagement in Mill as part of a different conceptual transformation—the recasting of political economy as modern liberal governmental rationality. I argue that by accepting the self-evident inductive-deductive binary as the appropriate level of analysis, the works discussed above fail to capture the invisibilized consensus between these apparently opposed methodologies—which I analyze as different ambitions of universalism.

28. Andrew Sartori makes a similar argument about the deployment of category of custom in debates over the Bengal Rent Act of 1859. But he traces the political economic articulation of custom and its linkage to a reinterpretation of "rent" to a Lockean discourse of property rights. See Andrew Sartori, "A Liberal Discourse of Custom in Colonial Bengal," *Past and Present* 212 (August 2011): 163–97.

29. Thomas Metcalfe, for example, argues that the Company's government was forced to settle revenues with village-level landholders in the North-Western Provinces, as they didn't encounter big landlords, like those of Bengal, in this region. Thomas R. Metcalf, *Land, Landlords, and the British Raj: Northern India in the Nineteenth Century* (Berkeley: University of California Press, 1979), 54. I have already noted that the move away from big landlords in agrarian governance during this period was consciously explained across various levels of the imperial bureaucracy in the language of local difference. The emergence of this understanding in governmental practice, I argue, signified a new articulation of political economy. That is why, in the North-Western Provinces, as the chapters in the book demonstrate, despite the prevalence of big zemindars, the government settled revenues with village-level land controllers. Metcalfe's framing of the local as the empirical particular that challenged the universality of metropolitan abstractions is mirrored in several other studies of the making of agrarian proprietary relations in different regions of British India during the first half of the nineteenth century. As classic examples of this perspective, see J. Rosselli, "Theory and Practice in North India," *Indian Economic and Social History Review* 8 (1971): 134–63, and Neil Rabitoy, "System v. Expediency: The Reality of Land Revenue Administration in the Bombay Presidency, 1812–1820," *Modern Asian Studies* 9 (1975): 529–46.

30. Linked with the kind of argument described above, another set of works contend that the rise of the village-level landholders was due to the "misrecognition" of local indigenous conditions by metropolitan frames. These histories further emphasize that the conditions were so strong that they could successfully resist those unsuitable frames. That is why, in Bengal, attempts to make big landlords proprietors—in the model of improving farmers of the British countryside—failed, as real proprietary power had been enjoyed by the village-level land controllers since precolonial times, and they continued to exercise it, defeating the transformative intentions of the Company's government. See Ratnalekha Ray, *Change in Bengal Agrarian Society: 1760–1850* (New Delhi: Manohar, 1979); and Sirajul Islam, *Bengal Land Tenure: The Origin and Growth of Intermediate Interests in the Nineteenth Century* (Rotterdam: Comparative Asian Studies Programme, 1985). Similar arguments have been made by scholars with regard to the southern and western parts of British India, where the local—as the authentic indigenous form of proprietary power residing in the village—has been viewed as resistant to European categories of agrarian governance. See Neil Charlesworth, *Peasants and Imperial Rule: Agriculture and Agrarian Society in the Bombay Presidency, 1850–1935* (Cambridge: University Press, 1985); Nilmani Mukherjee and Robert Eric Frykenberg, "The Ryotwari System and Social Organization in the Madras Presidency," in *Land Control and Social Structure in Indian History*, ed.

R. E. Frykenberg (Madison: University of Wisconsin Press, 1969), 217–26; and R. E. Frykenberg, "Village Strength in South India," in *Land Control and Social Structure in Indian History*, ed. R. E. Frykenberg (Madison: University of Wisconsin Press, 1969), 227–48.

31. The analytical temptation of the pragmatist thesis does not escape even Eric Stokes—someone who classically inaugurated the possibility of positing a consistency between metropolitan thought and local practice. He revises this position in one of his later works, arguing that while colonial policy cannot be "reduced entirely to a near-sighted pragmatism," "the last word appeared to lie with *local* society irrespective of *European* intentions and attitudes" (Stokes, *The Peasant and the Raj*, 9, 33), emphasis mine.

32. David Washbrook argues that while the permanent settlement of Bengal aimed at enabling the individual to accumulate capital and wealth through a free operation of the market, subsequent legislations in North and South India qualified these rights by upholding the customary privileges of the tenants, or the village-based corporate groups. In this manner, the early Raj reinforced existing, local, indigenous power relations. Thus, "actual rights to possess and use the land remained part-conditioned by this context and dependent on the customs and norms of the local agrarian community" (D. A. Washbrook, "Law, State and Agrarian Society in Colonial India," *Modern Asian Studies* 15 [1981]: 664).

33. Although Neeladri Bhattacharya argues that there was a dialectical relationship between state policies and local reality, as both changed in the process of negotiating each other, his framework ultimately falls back upon analytically isolable domains of the (indigenous) "social" and its outside, the colonial state (Neeladri Bhattacharya, "Colonial State and Agrarian Society," in *Situating Indian History: For Sarvepalli Gopal*, ed. Sabyasachi Bhattacharya and Romila Thapar [Delhi: Oxford University Press, 1986], 106–45). A similar argument about the formation of an agrarian society in South India over processes of negotiation between colonial officials and peasant producers can be found in David Ludden's work. See David Ludden, *Peasant History in South India* (Delhi: Oxford University Press, 1989).

34. Peter Robb examines various aspects of the constitution of agrarian relations in the eastern Indian region of Bihar in terms of an interactive model. But even the intended dynamism of such a framework has to rest on these reigning binaries, as he argues that the tenancy debates in Bihar represented the "peculiar combination of British colonialism . . . with Indian rural society" (Robb, *Ancient Rights and Future Comfort*, 102). For a similar yet more complex argument, which uses the framework of "dialogue" to analyze the reconstruction of South Indian agrarian society in the colonial period but also tries to hint at its limit by suggesting that the exchange of ideas and practices involved in this process cannot be categorized as either "Western" or "indigenous," see Eugene F. Irschick, *Dialogue and History: Constructing South India, 1795–1895* (Berkeley: University of California Press, 1994).

35. Jon E. Wilson, *The Domination of Strangers: Modern Governance in Eastern India, 1780–1835* (Basingstoke: Palgrave Macmillan, 2008), 108.

36. This kind of analysis assumes a hierarchized binary between a direct, unmediated, essential truth, or the being-as-presence, and its derived, displaced, secondary representation. It is this binary that, as Derrida notes, "has necessarily dominated the history of the world during an entire epoch, and has even produced the idea of the world, the idea of world-origin, that arises from the difference between the worldly and the non-worldly, *the outside and the inside*, ideality and nonideality, universal and nonuniversal, transcendental and empirical, etc." (Jacques Derrida, *Of Grammatology* [Baltimore: Johns Hopkins University Press, 1976], 8), emphasis mine.

37. Michel Foucault, *The Order of Things: An Archaeology of the Human Sciences* (New York: Vintage, 1994), 237. Keith Tribe carries out a Foucauldian treatment of early nineteenth-century classical political economy, arguing that "at the beginning of the nineteenth century, a novel discursive formation came into being, one whose structure is constituted by a specific conjunction of concepts of capital, profit, exchange, production and distribution. This event marks the birth of economic discourse." See Keith Tribe, *Land, Labour and Economic Discourse* (London: Routledge and Kegan Paul, 1978), 5. In his doctoral dissertation Tribe put forward a critique of the universal assumptions immanent to the conceptualization of agrarian production in Ricardian political economy, based on his analysis of the centrality of the category of rent in it. He argues that it "is the radical a-historicity of Ricardian economics, which establishes the primacy of agrarian capitalism at the cost of an inability to establish a concept of the different systems of production and the distinct relations of production that they set to work" (Keith Tribe, "Ground Rent and the Formation of Classical Political Economy: A Theoretical History" [Ph.D. thesis, University of Cambridge, 1976], 239). This "a-historicity," I argue, was questioned within the field of Ricardianism, as the debate over method in political economy placed the problem of history/difference at the heart of the reconstituted object of political economy.

38. Foucault, *The Order of Things*, 239.

39. Ibid., 254.

40. Foucault points out that "the mode of being of economics is no longer linked to a simultaneous space of difference and identities, but to the time of successive productions" (ibid., 255).

41. Michel Foucault, *The Birth of Biopolitics: Lectures at the Collège de France, 1978–1979* (New York: Palgrave Macmillan, 2008), 2.

42. Ibid., 10.

43. Ibid., 13.

44. Keith Tribe, in an essay on the teaching of political economy at the East India College in Haileybury, notes that Richard Jones, who succeeded Malthus to the professorship of political economy at the college, taught the subject in a way that "coincided closely with the objectives of the College in training future administrators" (Tribe, "Ground Rent and the Formation of Classical Political Economy," 344). Further, in support of this argument, Tribe notes that both Whewell, in his review of Jones's book, and Jones himself defined the object of political economy to be the same as that of governance. "Political economists . . . take for granted the identity of their problems with the common questions of practice and legislation" (Whewell on Jones, cited by Tribe, 343). "Our subject then is, to a great extent, the mother science on which the philosophy of constitutional legislation rests; as does in a great measure the philosophy of jurisprudence" (Jones, cited by Tribe, 343). See Keith Tribe, "Professors Malthus and Jones: Political Economy at the East India College, 1806–58," *European Journal of the History of Economic Thought* 2, no. 2 (1995): 327–54.

45. This condition of a dispersed field of proprietary rights has usually been understood within the binaric frames of agrarian histories of nineteenth-century South Asia as reflective of a gap between the metropolitan ideal of the category of property (absolute) and its local, indigenous reality (divided). Even Stokes explains this dispersal as an effect of the failure of the Company failure to incorporate the social reality to its juridical categories. "The legal description of society failed to fit the economic and sociological" (Stokes, *The Peasant and the Raj*, 3). This field of dispersal, where sovereignty (in the form of proprietary control) was distributed between the state, as a centralizing agency, and other, overlapping, localized agencies of power, has been explained as the quintessential indigenous/precolonial form of sovereignty by Burton Stein in

an influential essay. Stein argues that the early colonial state shaped its rule by simply adopting this indigenous form of sovereignty, whereas the late colonial state broke off from it by making sovereignty absolute and centralized. Once again, even this argument hinges on the absolute-divided, central-local, and European-indigenous binaries. It uses them to essentialize both colonialism and indigeneity. See Burton Stein, "State Formation and Economy Reconsidered: Part One," *Modern Asian Studies* 19, no. 3 (1985): 387–413. My contention is that this matrix of dispersed sovereignty-property relations did not signify the essence of an indigenous society in British India. Rather, it was assembled in complex ways by rationalities of modern liberal governance. For a brilliant set of arguments that problematize, from a different perspective—that of global histories of jurisprudence—this deeply entrenched notion of a "theory-practice" gap in the histories of agrarian South Asia, see Faisal Chaudhry, "A Rule of Proprietary Right for British India: From Revenue Settlement to Tenant Right in the Age of Classical Legal Thought," *Modern Asian Studies* 50, no. 1 (2016): 345–84; and Faisal Chaudhry, "Property and Its Rule (in Late Indo-Islamicate and Early Colonial) South Asia: What's in a Name?" *Journal of the Economic and Social History of the Orient* 61, nos. 5–6 (2018): 920–75.

46. It will be useful here to return to one of Foucault's lectures, where he famously discusses the changing relationship between the ideas of "economy" and "government" in Europe between the sixteenth and eighteenth centuries. The anti-Machiavellian literature of the sixteenth century introduced a typology of government, embedded in society and organized as its different levels. Central to this typology was the level of the family, where governance meant the introduction of "economy" in the management of individuals, goods, and wealth in the family. This economy, or the management of resources, then got extended as the general principle of government at the level of the territorial state. Nineteenth-century political economy, I argue, signified this coming together of economy as form and object in governmental reason. Local was the category that performed this operation within the discourse of governance, as the general principle of self-limitation (Michel Foucault, *Security, Territory, Population: Lectures at the Collège de France, 1977–1978* [New York: Palgrave Macmillan, 2007]).

47. Foucault, *The Birth of Biopolitics*, 39.

48. Ibid., 43, emphasis mine.

49. Ibid., 40.

50. As an example of one of the older studies using this distinction, see Thomas R. Metcalf, *Ideologies of the Raj* (Cambridge: Cambridge University Press, 1995), and for its sustenance in even the more recent works in this field, see U. Kalpagam, *Rule by Numbers: Governmentality in Colonial India* (New Delhi: Orient Blackswan, 2015).

51. Thus, for Mantena, the practical and the local are not categories external to networks of knowledge and governance; rather they are constitutive components of a specific articulation of imperialist sociology. See Karuna Mantena, *Alibis of Empire: Henry Maine and the Ends of Liberal Imperialism* (Ranikhet: Permanent Black, 2010). An extended discussion of this work is taken up in the Conclusion of my book, as I comment on the enduring traces of early nineteenth-century governmental strategies in the agrarian futures of the nation.

52. See Andrew Sartori, *Liberalism in Empire: An Alternative History* (Berkeley: University of California Press, 2014), 6. My book learns from Sartori's critical contributions but is also aware of its own differences from some of them. Sartori notes, in making clear his philosophical-political commitments, that "the issue is not whether there is an outside to liberal abstractions, but rather why we should normatively or ontologically privilege that outside over liberal abstractions" (ibid., 26). It is here that I chart a different imperative for this work, that of

unpacking investments that go into the positing of such an outside to liberal abstractions—in colonial archives and historiographic practice.

53. For a comprehensive and critical summary of works examining the interfaces between empire and Western political theory, see Jennifer Pitts, "Political Theory of Empire and Imperialism," *Annual Review of Political Science* 13 (2010): 211–35.

54. Imperial power is conceptualized by Frederick Cooper and Jane Burbank as a contingent and flexible set of practices, continually shaped and reshaped by various factors, like interimperial rivalries, local resistance, customs of rule, and others. They argue that contrary to the understanding of sovereignty as unitary and absolute in canons of Western political theory, imperial practice produced sovereignty as shared, layered, and overlapping. See Jane Burbank and Frederick Cooper, *Empires in World History: Power and the Politics of Difference* (Princeton: Princeton University Press, 2010). Similarly, Lauren Benton characterizes imperial sovereignty as plural, layered, and uneven, emerging out of complex encounters between "a fluid geographic discourse and open-ended legal politics." Benton argues that the entire imperial world was a zone of "legal anomaly," where metropolitan frames of classification and strategies of rule broke down in the face of local singularities. See Lauren Benton, *A Search for Sovereignty: Law and Geography in European Empires, 1400–1900* (Cambridge: Cambridge University Press, 2010), 23. In both works, it is evident that the local still functions as a point of exception. It remains the inscrutable outside of metropolitan theory, engendering the singularity of imperial practice. It defies the canonical ideal of sovereignty in the actuality of the imperial encounter. What I argue in this book is that this very unevenness of sovereignty in colonial locales/agrarian societies of British India was indeed produced by the local. But the category was immanent to the rationality of governance, operating across, and thereby unifying, heterogenous sites; it was not the imperial outside of metropolitan forms.

Chapter 1

Note to epigraph: Gilles Deleuze, "What Is a Dispositif?" in *Michel Foucault Philosopher*, ed. Timothy J. Armstrong (New York: Harvester Wheatsheaf, 1992), 162.

1. This reading of rent also points toward a critique of the relationship Eric Stokes sets up between utilitarianism in Britain and agrarian governance in British India. Stokes argues that "the core of utilitarian philosophy, its professed scientific foundation, was the new political economy developed by Ricardo. At the heart of Indian administration lay the land revenue system. The one was to react upon the other with results of deepest importance for Indian society." Eric Stokes, *The English Utilitarians and India* (Delhi: Oxford University Press, 1989), 81. This chapter shows that with the epistemological turn in political economy, the relationship between political economy and British Indian agrarian governance did not remain restricted to Ricardianism/Utilitarianism. Even in this changed conceptual context, however, rent remained one of the critical markers of this relationship. This new governmental career of rent was built upon a critique of its Ricardian articulation. Henceforth, rent signified one of those strands of local power that tied together the indigenized analytical vocabulary of political economy.

2. William Whewell, "Review of Richard Jones's *An Essay on the Distribution of Wealth and on the Sources of Taxation*," *British Critic, and Quarterly Theological Review* 10, no. 19 (July 1831): 52.

3. See Laura J. Snyder, *The Philosophical Breakfast Club: Four Remarkable Friends Who Transformed Science and Changed the World* (New York: Broadway Books, 2011).

4. Richard Yeo, *Defining Science: William Whewell, Natural Knowledge and Public Debate in Early Victorian Britain* (Cambridge: Cambridge University Press, 1993), 56.

5. Whewell, "Review," 52.

6. Richard Jones, *An Essay on the Distribution of Wealth and on the Sources of Taxation* (London: J. Murray, 1831), vii.

7. Laura Snyder, "The Mill-Whewell Debate: Much Ado About Induction," *Perspectives on Science* 5, no. 2 (1997): 159–98.

8. Laura Snyder, "It's *All* Necessarily So: William Whewell on Scientific Truth," *Studies in History and Philosophy of Science* 25, no. 5 (1994): 803.

9. As cited in Yeo, *Defining Science*, 94.

10. Robert E. Butts, "Induction as Unification: Kant, Whewell, and Recent Developments," in *Kant and Contemporary Epistemology*, ed. Paolo Parrini (Dordrecht: Kluwer, 1994): 273–90.

11. Whewell, "Review," 55.

12. As Yeo writes, "It is important to realize that in this period the word 'empiricism' was more often used to suggest a preference for fact over theory" (Yeo, *Defining Science*, 183). Harro Maas has insightfully brought out the differences between Whewell and Jones over the theoretical scope of induction. Maas argues that Whewell, in classifying the sciences, found political economy to be occupying a problematic position. Political economy, he thought, could not move from classification to explanation, which were different stages of induction. Jones's work, he felt, only completed the task of classification. While Maas's argument is mostly persuasive, I believe there is room for further analysis of Jones's political economic scheme on this issue. I am inclined to suggest that Jones did come up with an explanatory framework for political economic categories, one that merged seamlessly with the rationality of governance, as the later chapters of this book demonstrate. But to understand the nature of this framework one needs to step out of the Whewellian definition of induction, particularly the way it differentiated between classification and explanation. See Harro Maas, *William Stanley Jevons and the Making of Modern Economics* (Cambridge: Cambridge University Press, 2005): 37–71.

13. J. R. McCulloch, "Review of Richard Jones's *An Essay on the Distribution of Wealth and on the Sources of Taxation*," *Edinburgh Review* 54, no. 107 (September 1831): 85.

14. Ibid., 86.

15. Ibid., 87, 90.

16. William Whewell, ed., *Literary Remains, Consisting of Lectures and Tracts on Political Economy of the Late Rev. Richard Jones* (London: J. Murray, 1859), xii–xiii.

17. See "Richard Jones to William Whewell, 3 November, 7 November 1831," nos. 42, 43, *Whewell Papers*, Add. Mss. C 52, Wren Library, Trinity College, Cambridge.

18. Jones, *An Essay on the Distribution of Wealth*, 183.

19. "William Whewell to Richard Jones, 1 July 1832," in *William Whewell, D.D. Master of Trinity College, Cambridge: An Account of His Writings with Selections from His Literary and Scientific Correspondence, Volume 2*, ed. I. Todhunter (London: Macmillan, 1876), 142. Samuel Hollander argues that with time Whewell expressed doubts about the possibility of developing an inductive method of inquiry in the moral and political sciences. He did not have too many examples to depend upon and, therefore, constantly urged Jones to finish his work. Hollander writes, "Whewell's concern that Jones had failed to provide adequate illustrations of the proposed approach grew with the latter's failure to publish the later parts of his work on *Distribution of Wealth*. And we find him soon complaining that Jones was 'lapsing into definitions'" (Samuel Hollander, "William Whewell and John Stuart Mill on the Methodology of Political Economy," *Studies in the History and Philosophy of Science* 14, no. 2 [1983]: 142). In my opinion, Whewell was more impatient than doubtful, especially when it came to the moral and political sciences. He wanted more works to come out in these domains, so that they could further move

toward the construction of gradually ascending generalities based on inductively established fundamental premises. It is almost as if he wanted these sciences to come up with their own highly schematized tables of induction, similar to the table he had prepared for astronomy. This only shows his relentless striving toward the achievement of immutable systems of explanation, or better theory, in all fields of knowledge.

20. "As they rise from the particular to the general, they rise from what is general to what is more general. Each induction supplies the materials of fresh inductions; each generalization, with all that it embraces in its circle, may be found to be but one of many circles, comprehended within the circuit of some wider generalization" (William Whewell, *The Philosophy of the Inductive Sciences, Founded upon Their History, Volume 1* [London: J. W. Parker, 1840], 46).

21. McCulloch, "Review," 86.

22. Ibid., 87.

23. James Mill, *History of British India, Volume I, Book II*, Fifth Edition, with notes and continuation by H. H. Wilson (London: Routledge, 1997 [1858]), 208.

24. "Evidence by James Mill, 4 August 1831," *Report from the Select Committee on the Affairs of the East India Company, Parliamentary Papers* (1831): 308.

25. He put rent property ahead of "proprietary" rights based on cultivation, or on the application of one's labor to the soil (see my next note). Mill argued that "the real beneficial interest of a proprietor of land under an European tenure may be considered to be measured by the rent he can obtain for it; but in the case of the ryot, the person whom you would call the proprietor has none of the rent, nor is entitled to it" (ibid.).

26. This is how Mill made a hierarchical distinction—where the former was superior to the latter—between the following two senses of "property": (a) arising from the ownership of the rent of land and (b) arising from the right to labor on the same plot of soil for a long period of time. "The sovereigns in India had not only the *ownership*, but all the benefit of the land; the ryots had merely the privilege of employing their labour always upon the same soil, and of transferring that privilege to some other person" (Mill, *History of British India*, 224), emphasis mine.

27. James Mill, "Observations on the Land Revenue of India," Esq., Appendix No. 7, *Report from the Select Committee on the Affairs of the East India Company; with Minutes of Evidence in Six Parts, and an Appendix and Index to Each, Volume 3, Revenue, 1832*, 48.

28. Ibid.

29. Mill, *History of British India*, 226.

30. "Evidence by James Mill, 18 August 1831," *Report from the Select Committee on the Affairs of the East India Company, Parliamentary Papers* (1831): 362.

31. David Ricardo, *On the Principles of Political Economy and Taxation* (London: J. Murray, 1821), 134.

32. James Mill, *Elements of Political Economy* (London: Henry G. Bohn, 1821), 198.

33. Mill, *History of British India*, 226.

34. Stokes, *The English Utilitarians and India*, 87.

35. Ibid., 230.

36. "The whole business of philosophy consists in the endeavor to render each theory as comprehensive as possible. The whole business of philosophy, therefore, is to furnish men as completely as possible for practice; and the best philosopher is by necessary consequence the best practitioner" (ibid., 231). It is worth noting here Robert Fenn's comment on this essay. Fenn argues that "if there was any aspect of Mill's intellectual efforts for the amelioration of society

that he would have prided himself on, it would have been his emphasis on the necessary relation between correct theory and sound practice. It was not only the topic of his last published work, it clearly dominated many of his considerations regarding social reform." (Robert Fenn, *James Mill's Political Thought* [New York: Garland, 1987], 128).

37. Mill pointed out, "If philosophy shall ever discover these sequences, and it is making constant advances, all knowledge competent to human nature will be correctly summed up in a few propositions; and mistaken practice will be no longer possible" (Mill, "Theory and Practice," 232).

38. Whewell, ed., *Literary Remains*, xxii.

39. The active engagement of Jones with his contemporary political economists has been documented in the following essays: de Marchi and Sturges, "Malthus and Ricardo's Inductivist Critics," 40, no. 160 (1973): 379–93; C. J. Dewey, "The Rehabilitation of the Peasant Proprietor in Nineteenth-Century Economic Thought," *History of Political Economy* 6 (1974): 17–47; and William L. Miller, "Richard Jones's Contribution to the Theory of Rent," *History of Political Economy* 9 (Fall 1977): 346–65.

40. He succeeded Malthus in this position.

41. Whewell, ed., *Literary Remains*, 552, emphasis mine.

42. Ibid., 554

43. Ricardo, *On the Principles of Political Economy and Taxation*, v.

44. Ibid., 46.

45. In fact, Ricardo's entire analytical framework was embedded in such an inconsistent and self-destructive temporality. Rahul Govind in a recent essay also makes this point. According to Ricardo, the price of produce of the marginal land, which did not pay rent, determined the rate of "profit," which, in turn, determined "rent." But for the rate of profit to get determined from the marginal land, Govind notes, there had to be a market, which also meant that since this was the last land, produce from earlier lands must have reached the market. But how is that possible, Govind asks, given that only the last land's produce can determine the rate of profit, and rent? "This requires a miracle and thus we have the immaculate conception of the market" (Rahul Govind, "Revenue, Rent . . . Profit? Early British Imperialism, Political Economy and the Search for a *differentia specifica (inter se)*," *Indian Economic and Social History Review* 48, no. 2 [2011]: 194). I believe that what I have described as inconsistencies in the temporal narrative of Ricardo is called a "logical historicity" by Govind. He describes it as a "matrix that is "simultaneously" diachronic and synchronic" (ibid., 195).

46. Whewell, ed., *Literary Remains*, 553.

47. Ibid.

48. Ibid.

49. "After surveying the different steps and stages of the changes I have been speaking of, we shall see at once that England is much in advance of other nations. I do not by this phrase mean to take it for granted, that her position is better than theirs, but only to point out, that in arriving at our present position, we have passed through and gone beyond those at which we see other nations stationary, or through which we see them moving" (ibid., 557–58).

50. Whewell, ed., *Literary Remains*, 557.

51. Ibid., 556.

52. Ibid., 557.

53. Ibid., 559.

54. Ibid., 558–59.

55. Ibid., 570.

56. "It is not pleasant to reflect how little has been done in England to systematize statistical inquiries or to preserve and spread the information that statistics can give us. . . . We may hope surely, that mankind and their concerns will soon attract interest enough to receive similar attention; and that a statistical society will be added to the number of those which are advancing the scientific knowledge of England" (ibid., 571).

57. "Richard Jones to William Whewell, 18 February 1834," no. 60, *Whewell Papers*, Add. Mss. C 52, Wren Library, Trinity College, Cambridge.

58. Ibid., 4.

59. Jones observed, "The labourer is rarely in a condition to retain the whole produce of his exertions. In whatever state of society he exists, some tie, or some want, makes him to a certain extent dependent upon others. Those who constitute the larger proportion of the labouring class throughout the world . . . are obliged therefore to raise it with their own hands from the soil" (Jones, *An Essay on the Distribution of Wealth*, 2).

60. Ibid.

61. "A Short Tract on Political Economy Including Some Account of the Anglo-Indian Revenue Systems," in Whewell, ed., *Literary Remains*, 199.

62. Ibid., 11.

63. Whewell, ed., *Literary Remains*, 211.

64. Michel Foucault, *The Order of Things: An Archaeology of the Human Sciences* (New York: Vintage, 1994).

Chapter 2

1. For some typical examples of such readings of agrarian governance, see Thomas R. Metcalf, *Land, Landlords, and the British Raj: Northern India in the Nineteenth Century* (Berkeley: University of California Press, 1979); J. Rosselli, "Theory and Practice in North India," *Indian Economic and Social History Review* 8, no. 2 (1971): 134–63; and Neil Rabitoy, "System v. Expediency: The Reality of Land Revenue Administration in the Bombay Presidency 1812–1820," *Modern Asian Studies* 9, no. 4 (1975): 529–46.

2. A notable exception in the interpretations of the governmental deployment of rent, which does not fall back upon a pragmatist reading but at the same time differs from Stokes's exclusively Ricardian understanding of the category, can be found in Peter Robb's work on the politics of tenancy legislation in late nineteenth-century Bihar. Robb states, in the context of the debates over the tenancy legislation of the 1880s: "On rent, the reformers rejected an untrammeled role for the market and for competition on better soils, and argued for political intervention to fix levels which would secure a sufficiency of income to the tenants. For their theory, they preferred Jones to Malthus or Ricardo. Rent was regarded not as the necessary expression of economic factors creating a "net product," but as a variable originally traced to power" (Peter Robb, *Ancient Rights and Future Comfort: Bihar, the Bengal Tenancy Act of 1885 and British Rule in India* [London: Routledge, 1997], 197). But Robb does not read Jones's ideas as part of a reconceptualization of political economy, which could be then used as a possible analytical field to assess the foundations of agrarian governance established long before the tenancy debates, early in the nineteenth century.

3. *The Fifth Report from the Select Committee on the Affairs of the East India Company, Parliamentary Papers* (1812): 136.

4. Ibid.

5. Ibid.

6. Ibid.

7. A classic discussion of the heterogeneous articulations of this idea can be found in Ranajit Guha, *A Rule of Property for Bengal: An Essay on the Idea of the Permanent Settlement* (New Delhi: Orient Longman, 1981), 20–49.

8. [Harington,] *Extracts from Harington's Analysis of the Bengal Regulations* (Calcutta, 1866), v.

9. John Sullivan's note in the collection of evidence presented to the House of Commons Select Committee on the Affairs of East India Company contained a systematic review of the several positions against the Permanent Settlement. Written in 1832, the note mentioned that "the preceding Administration at home had, in the years, 1801, 1802, 1804, and 1809 evinced a disposition more and more *adverse* to any early extension of the Bengal Permanent Settlement in the Madras possessions. A similar course had been pursued in the years 1810 and 1811, and the early part of 1812, as relating to the modern acquisitions of the Bengal side of India" ("Observations on the Revenue Systems of India," in *Report from the Select Committee on the Affairs of the East India Company; with Minutes of Evidence in Six Parts, and an Appendix and Index to Each, Volume 3, Revenue,* 1832, Appendix 8, Revenue, 51).

10. Lamenting the pernicious effects of this measure, Lord Moira, the governor-general in 1815, noted: "If it was the intention of our Regulations to deprive every class but the large proprietors who engaged with Government, of any share in the profits of the land, that effect has been accomplished in Bengal. No compensation can now be made for the injustice done to those who used to enjoy a share of those profits under the law of the Empire, and under institutions anterior to all records, for the transfer of their property to the Rajahs" ("Minute by the Right Hon. the Governor-General, on the Revenue Administration of the Presidency of Fort William, Dated the 21 September 1815," ibid., Appendix 9, Revenue, 84.

11. He stated: "The causes, which have principally operated in producing insecurity and oppression to the peasants of Bengal" were principally "the omission of clear and definite rules in the Regulations of 1793, and subsequent years, for the declaring the rights and tenures of the ryots, whose rents were, in many instances, left to be adjusted by Pergunnah or other supposed local rates, no longer in existence, or ascertainable," and "a want of due enforcement of rules, which were enacted on concluding a Permanent Settlement with the Zemindars and other landholders, requiring them, within a fixed period, to adjust the rent of their tenants, and furnish them with Pottahs; the forms of which were to be approved by the Collectors" J. H. Harington, *Minute and Draft of Regulation of the Rights of Ryots in Bengal* (Calcutta: 1827), 1.

12. Interestingly, even Ranajit Guha identifies John Shore to be the earliest, and one of the most powerful contemporary critics of the Permanent Settlement. Guha notes that Shore insisted for greater rights of government to intervene in zemindars' affairs than the policy provided for. His critique was oriented toward the future, envisioning the adoption of a governmental strategy of controlling the relationship between property and production in a better manner than the Permanent Settlement, which, he thought, had sacrificed the question of productivity, in order to ensure the security of property. Guha argues that Shore's proposals of making settlements of short duration, until more knowledge of the property-production complex could be gained substantially, anticipated governmental reason of the years ahead (Guha, *A Rule of Property for Bengal,* 187–200). Following a similar logic, Harrington claimed Shore as the mark of an older tradition, which housed this (new) framing of rent and its relationship with property and production. I agree with Guha's point, even if implicit, that Shore's specific critique of the Permanent Settlement was a more general perspective on defining and governing the

property-production matrix in British India. But Guha does not read this perspective on governance in terms of its political-economic bearings. More important, the governmental mapping of property and production in the first half of the nineteenth century represented a very different articulation of political economy, which I outline in greater detail in the chapters ahead. Shore ultimately understood the zemindars to be the sole proprietary (and improving) figure in British India. But governmental reason set up a far more complex equation between property and production, in and through a variety of landholding bodies, by the end of the first half of the nineteenth century. Thus, despite Harrington's insistence, and Guha's indication, I do not consider Shore a foreteller of these governmental futures.

13. Ibid., 3.

14. Harington, "Minute and Draft of Regulation," 15.

15. Bernard Cohn's classic work represents perhaps the earliest attempt to show how the strategy of limited government, right from the time of the Company, was rooted in a series of "investigative modalities" that discursively produced various aspects of "Indian" society as objects of knowledge and governance. See Bernard Cohn, *Colonialism and Its Forms of Knowledge: The British in India* (Princeton: Princeton University Press, 1996). Cohn's argument, as noted by Nicholas Dirks in the foreword to Cohn's book, had Foucaultian-Saidian anticipations in the relationship it suggested between knowledge, power, and governance. In this chapter, by reconstructing the governmental production of the link between rent and sovereignty, I move toward a conceptualization of governance itself, in and as a certain articulation of political economy.

16. Harington, "Minute and Draft of Regulation," 23.

17. Ibid., 29.

18. Its opening lines were: "In revising the existing settlement, the efforts of the Revenue-officers should be chiefly directed not to any general and extensive enhancement of the jama, but to the objects equalizing the public burthens, and of ascertaining, settling and recording the rights, interests, privileges and properties of all persons and classes owning, occupying, managing or cultivating the land, or gathering or disposing of its produce, or collecting or appropriating the rent or revenue payable on account of land" (F. G. Wigley, ed., *The Eastern Bengal and Assam Code, in Three Volumes Containing the Regulations and Local Acts in Force in the Province of Eastern Bengal and Assam, Volume 1* [Calcutta: Government Press, 1907], 177).

19. "Letter from the Right Honorable Holt McKenzie," in *Report from the Select Committee on the Affairs of the East India Company, Volume 3, Revenue, 1832, Parliamentary Papers*, 300–301.

20. Ibid.

21. This was because the zemindars were "without any such obligation as attaches to the government of considering the general good, and as makes it our duty to restrict our demand within the legal limit, so as to be consistent with the existence of private property and the improved comfort of the people" ("Examination of Witnesses, Holt McKenzie, April 18, 1832," ibid., 226).

22. He stated that "the rule authorizing the exchequer to take as revenue one half of the produce, which in the hands of government is in a great manner nominal[,] . . . becomes in the hands of its assignees, the zemindars or revenue contractors, a real measure of demand: and those persons, in a great part of the permanently settled districts, have therefore the power of destroying the property of the inferior, just as in the unsettled districts government may, and sometimes does, destroy the property of the cultivating zemindars by an excessive demand. For I conceive that, taking the general average of the country, if more than a third be taken by government, there can be no private property in the land; that is to say, no rent" (ibid., 227).

23. "Letter from the Right Honorable Holt McKenzie," ibid., 298, emphasis mine.

24. "If the law of rent was envisaged as supplying the correct theoretic criterion of assessment, Mackenzie was extremely cautious about its application" (Eric Stokes, *The English Utilitarians and India* [Delhi: Oxford University Press, 1989], 96). This caution was prompted by the multiplicity of "local practice," which according to Stokes was understood by Mackenzie as external and opposed to the logic of political economic categories. I would, however, argue that Stokes's own readings, not Mackenzie's, betray these oppositions: theory-practice, abstract-concrete, and metropolitan-local. Let us look at one of Mackenzie's admissions (used by Stokes): "Even the bare calculation of profit and loss will vary greatly from other causes than the mere nature of the soil" (ibid., 96). I argue that this reflected Mackenzie's grounding in a different political-economic/governmental reason, which made Mackenzie understand local/indigenous forms of proprietary power as internal to, and thereby constitutive of, the categories of political-economy. It will be useful here to remember how Richard Jones, in a similar fashion, had argued that rent is caused by several factors besides the mere fertility of soil.

25. "The work of revision went on so slowly that when ten years had elapsed from the time of its initiation, it was calculated that it would take sixty more years to render the work complete" (B. B. Misra, *The Central Administration of the East India Company, 1773–1834* [Manchester: Manchester University Press, 1959], 217).

26. Ibid.

27. "Enclosure to Circular No. 190, 12 November 1833, To Commissioners of Revenue (317–51)," in *Circular Orders of the SBOR at the Presidency of Fort William; Including the Rules of Practice for the Guidance of the Board and of the Commissioners of Revenue, from the Year 1788 to the End of August 1837* (Calcutta: 1838). Also in Acc. No. 43B, *BDR, Revenue 1832–33*, OSA.

28. Ibid.

29. "Memorandum on Talooka Bishnubur, Pergunnah Bakrabad, Zillah Cuttack," in *Copies of Memoranda on Certain Settlements in Bauleah, Cuttack, Chittagong and Murshidabad Divisions by Mr. F. J. Halliday, Secretary to the Board of Revenue, Deputed to Settlement Work, 1837–1838, Sadar Board of Revenue—Settlement Proceedings*, WBSA.

30. "Memorandum on Talooka Koorkoora, Pergunnah Kowakund, Zillah Cuttack," ibid.

31. Ibid.

32. Ibid.

33. Ibid.

34. "Memorandum on Pergunnah Saibeer, Zillah Cuttack," ibid.

35. Ibid.

36. "Letter from A. J. M. Mills, Collector's Office, Cuttack, No. 4, 20 April 1838," *Sadar Board of Revenue Proceedings, Bengal*, IOR.

37. Ibid.

38. "Letter to Assistant Commissioner of Revenue, Cuttack, from J. Grant, Collector, Balasore, 25 December 1835," Old No. 506, Acc. No. 95C, August 1835 to November 1835, *CDR, Revenue*, OSA.

39. David Washbrook, "Ricketts, Henry," *Oxford Dictionary of National Biography*. https://www.oxforddnb.com/view/10.1093/ref:odnb/9780198614128.001.0001/odnb-9780198614128-e-23602.

40. Andrew Sartori, in an essay on the Bengal Rent Act of 1859, argues that the debate about custom in fixing rent was not a conflict between liberal utilitarianism and conservatism but was *internal* to the discourse of liberalism. See Andrew Sartori, "Custom and Political Economy in Bengal's 'Great Rent Case,' 1859–1865," unpublished paper (2008).

41. Henry Ricketts, *The Real Difficulties in Bengal and How to Settle Them* (London: Smith, Elder, 1861), 4.

42. Ibid., 11.

43. Ibid.

44. Ibid., 12.

45. Henry Ricketts, *The Rent Difficulties in Bengal and How to Remedy Them, The Rent Facilities in Cuttack and How to Preserve Them* (London: Smith, Elder, 1863), 7.

46. Ibid.

47. Ibid., 11.

48. Ibid., 18.

49. "Letter to the Commissioner of Revenue, Cuttack, from H. Ricketts, Collector, Balasore, 1 January 1836," Old No. 30, Acc. No. 16B, April 1825 to April 1838, *BDR, Revenue*, OSA.

50. Ibid.

51. "Extract of a Letter from the Collector of Balasore to the Commissioner for the 19th Division, Cuttack, 22 May 1834," Old No. 465, Acc. No. 93C, 16 July 1835 to 16 November 1835, *CDR, Revenue*, OSA.

52. James Alexander, "On the Tenures and Fiscal Relations of the Owners, and Occupants of the Soil in Bengal, Behar, and Orissa," *Journal of the Asiatic Society of Bengal* 14, part II (July–December 1845): 531, emphasis mine.

53. Ibid., 532.

54. Jones argued that "there are three causes which determine the productive power of the industry of nations: 1. The continuity with which it is exerted, 2. The skill with which it is exerted, 3. The power by which it is aided. . . . Hence it follows that the production of wealth depends upon the productiveness or efficiency of labour" (In William Whewell, ed., *Literary Remains, Consisting of Lectures and Tracts on Political Economy of the Late Rev. Richard Jones* [London: J. Murray, 1859], 189).

55. Ibid., 196.

56. Alexander, "On the Tenures and Fiscal Relations," 533.

57. See Andrew Sartori, "A Liberal Discourse of Custom in Colonial Bengal," *Past and Present* 212 (August 2011): 163–97.

58. Alexander, "On the Tenures and Fiscal Relations," 537.

59. Ibid., 538.

60. Ibid., 537, emphasis mine; the equivalence between "prescriptive titles" and "marketable commodities," once again, underscored that custom, as a category, was internal to the political-economic articulation of production and exchange.

Chapter 3

1. *The Fifth Report from the Select Committee on the Affairs of the East India Company, Parliamentary Papers* (1812), 47.

2. Ibid., 155.

3. Ibid.

4. "Magistrate of Cuttack (Secret) to Secretary to Government, Judicial Department, Fort William, 4 April 1817," *BJC*, IOR.

5. Authorities at Fort William in Calcutta, however, understood the chain of events at Cuttack in a different way. Right from the beginning, they seemed to discern signs of a bigger field of discontent, which went beyond the angst of one disempowered indigenous ruler. That's why,

within a month of the reporting of the insurrection, the secretary of the Judicial Department pointed out: "Although I have discovered nothing calculated to remove the suspicion, that the Rajah of Khoordah is the immediate instigator of the disturbances at present prevailing in the Southern parts of Cuttack, I lament to state that there are some grounds to believe that a much more general spirit of disaffection at present exists in that District" (Mr. Dowdeswell's minute, "Secretary to Government, Judicial Department, Fort William, 11 April 1817," *BJC*, IOR).

6. "Extract Revenue Letter from Revenue Department, Bengal to Governor-General in Council, Fort William, 17 July 1818," *Proceedings Connected with the Recent Disturbances in Cuttack, Examiner's Office, 1819, Volume 1*, IOR.

7. This insurrection in Cuttack, better known as the Paik Rebellion, has been uniformly viewed by a number of historical works as an extremely important historical event that forced the colonial authorities to correct a number of abuses in governance of the region. See K. M. Patra, *Orissa Under the East India Company* (New Delhi: Munshiram Manoharlal, 1971); Yaaminey Mubayi, "The Paik Rebellion of 1817: Status and Conflict in Early Colonial Orissa," *Studies in History* 15, no. 1 (1999): 43–74; and Binod S. Das, *Studies in the Economic History of Orissa from Ancient Times to 1833* (Calcutta: Firma KLM, 1978). Studies of the Paik Rebellion, I argue, replicate the official framing of the local, by arguing that the rebellion forced the government to implement reforms. What these works fail to realize is that the event of the insurrection was analyzed by the authorities at Fort William in terms of an overall failure in governance only because there was an emergent critical attitude already instituted within the discourse of governance at different levels of the imperial apparatus by that time. Accordingly, both the perceived problems of governance and their solution were prefigured by the category of the local.

8. "Secretary to Government, Territorial Department, 24 October 1817," in S. C. De, ed., *Guide to Orissan Records, Volume II* (Bhubaneshwar: Orissa Sahitya Akademi, 1961), 116.

9. "Report of Walter Ewer, 18 April 1818," *Proceedings Relative to the Late Disturbances in Cuttack, Volume 2*, Examiner's Office, 1819, IOR, emphasis mine.

10. Ibid., emphasis mine.

11. "W. Trower, Collector of Cuttack to Walter Ewer, Commissioner of Cuttack, 3 April 1818," *Revenue Proceedings Relative to the Late Disturbances in Cuttack, Volume 2*, 297, Examiner's Office, 1819, IOR.

12. A. Stirling, *An Account, Geographical, Statistical and Historical of Orissa Proper, Or Cuttack*, 1822, IOR, 5.

13. Ibid., 6.

14. Ibid., 56.

15. Ibid., 56–57.

16. Ibid., 57.

17. Ibid., 58.

18. Ibid.

19. Norbert Peabody argues that James Tod made similar use of the category "feudal" in describing the social and political organization of the Rajputs of Rajasthan. Peabody writes: "Tod argued that the tribes of early Europe and 'the Rajpoot tribes' had a common Scythic origin in Central Asia and, in the more recent past, the Rajputs of western India had a feudal system similar to that which had existed in parts of Europe" (Norbert Peabody, "Tod's Rajasthan and the Boundaries of Imperial Rule in Nineteenth-Century India," *Modern Asian Studies* 30, no. 1 [1996]: 198).

20. Stirling, *An Account*, 59.

21. Ibid., 65.
22. Ibid.
23. Ibid., 74.
24. Ibid., 76.
25. Ibid., 78.
26. Ibid.
27. Ibid.
28. Ibid., 77.
29. Ibid., 87.
30. Ibid., 84.
31. Rachel Sturman, *The Government of Social Life in Colonial India: Liberalism, Religious Law, and Women's Rights* (Cambridge: Cambridge University Press, 2012), 36, n. 2.
32. Imtiaz Husain, *Land Revenue Policy in North India: The Ceded and Conquered Provinces, 1801–33* (Calcutta: New Age, 1967), 3.
33. Ibid., 60.
34. Thomas Metcalf argues that the settlement policy of the Ceded and Conquered Provinces was entirely a pragmatic response to the on-the-ground reality of the area, as the landholders here were different from those of Bengal. He writes: "The British carried with them to the newly conquered territories of northern India the preconceptions derived from their quarter century's experience of Bengal. They set out to find large zemindars of the sort they were accustomed to. . . . The relative scarcity of large landholders in the Doab and Rohilkhand meant that the British had in the long run no option but to deal directly with the village-level zemindars and coparcenary communities" (Thomas R. Metcalf, *Land, Landlords, and the British Raj: Northern India in the Nineteenth Century* [Berkeley: University of California Press, 1979], 52, 54). Metcalf fails to view the policy as reflective of a shift in the administrative discourse, engendered by the critique of zemindars. The focus on village-level groups, for Metcalf, signifies a change in the logic of governance caused by the empirical conditions of difference in the locality. What he cannot see is the gradual assembling of a spatiotemporal grid, which reconfigured and accounted for such "empirical" differences in theoretical terms, thereby addressing the question of property uniformly in these "different" localities.
35. "Memorandum by the Secretary Regarding the Past Settlements of the Ceded and Conquered Provinces, with Heads of a Plan for the Permanent Settlement of Those Provinces, 1 July 1819," *Selections from Revenue Records, North-West Provinces, 1822–1833* (Allahabad: 1872), 60.
36. Ibid., 75.
37. Ibid., 88, emphasis mine.
38. Ibid., 89.
39. Ibid.
40. Ibid., 91.
41. Ibid.
42. Ibid., 92.
43. Ibid., 96.
44. Ibid., 97.
45. Ibid., 77.
46. Mackenzie suggested: "In such cases the means of all the proprietors, however small the portion of the village held by them, be recorded in the records of the Canoongoe and of the Collector's Office." *Memorandum by the Secretary*, 150. See also, Holt Mackenzie, "Memorandum, 1 July 1819," para 414 cited in Husain, *Land Revenue Policy*, 130.

47. "Memorandum by the Secretary," 127.

48. "From the Members of the Western Board to the Governor-General in Council, 3 September 1830," No. 64, *Selections from Revenue Records, North-West Provinces, 1822–1833* (Allahabad: 1872), Number III, 206–7.

49. Ibid., 222.

50. William Bentinck, "Minute on Land Tenures," enclosure to Circular No. 190, 12 November 1833, to Commissioners of Revenue (pp. 317–51), *Circular Orders of the SBOR at the Presidency of Fort William; Including the Rules of Practice for the Guidance of the Board and of the Commissioners of Revenue, from the Year 1788 to the End of August 1837* (Calcutta: 1838). Also in Acc. No. 43B, *BDR, Revenue, 1832–33*, OSA.

51. Ibid.

52. Ibid.

53. Ibid.

54. In the *Fifth Report* the ryot proprietor was discussed in terms of the same example.

55. The meerasidar of ancient times was seen as carrying in itself capacities of both landlord and farmer. Bentinck referred to a minute of the Madras Board of Revenue, which stated that the "Meerasidars every where enjoyed a Toondoowarum, or clear landlord's rent, from all the lands cultivated by their Pyacarry tenants, and both a landlord's rent and a farmer's profit from the lands which were cultivated by their own laborers or slaves" (Bentinck, "Minute on Land Tenures"). Evidently a conglomerate of contemporary political-economic categories was grafted onto the figure of the meerasidar. This was also the stated intention of the ryotwar system. Munro had argued that in a ryotwar mode of settlement "every Ryot will on his own estate be at once, proprietor, farmer, and labourer." We can see here the simultaneous use of the figure of the peasant proprietor in the light of the authentic "Indian" proprietary form of co-sharing between sovereign and ryot. Thomas Munro, "Report of the Collector of the Ceded Districts of 15th August 1807, on the Advantages and Disadvantages of the Zemindary Permanent Settlements and of the Ryotwar Settlements," *Home Miscellaneous, Papers Concerning Revenue, Administrative and Judicial Matters in India, 1792–1812*, IOR. But the figure of the proprietor ryot, as represented in the context of the ryotwar settlement, differed markedly from the one in Bentinck's scheme. For Bentinck, this proprietary ryot, as an individual peasant cultivator, had been sacrificed on the altar of history. His existence could be discerned only in the putteedari tenure, amid a collective body of proprietors. Moreover, Bentinck further asserted the authentic proprietary claims of such joint tenures, by saying that even Munro believed that the lands of the south originally belonged to such a tenure. These were the transformations of the proprietary imagination, made operative by the deployment of the local.

56. Bentinck's resolution reminds one of John Stuart Mill's comments on what Mill believed to be a typically Whiggish attitude. Mill described it as marked by "a disposition to compromise, to say a little for aristocracy, a little for the people alternatively, and always to give up so much of every important question, as to avoid an irreparable breach, either with one side or with the other" (J. S. Mill, *Autobiography* [London: 1873], 293, cited in Bianca Fontana, "Whigs and Liberals: The *Edinburgh Review* and the 'Liberal Movement' in Nineteenth-Century Britain," in *Victorian Liberalism: Nineteenth-Century Political Thought and Practice*, ed. Richard Bellamy [London: Routledge, 1990], 50).

57. "Extract of a Despatch from the Honorable the Court of Directors, 10 December 1823," Acc. No. 12B, 13 August 1821 to 25 November 1825, *BDR, Revenue*, OSA.

58. Ibid.

59. "Extract from a Resolution of Government in the Territorial Department, 21 May 1824," Acc. No. 12B, 13 August 1821 to 25 November 1825, *BDR, Revenue*, OSA.

60. "To R. Hunter, Commissioner of Cuttack, from Wilkinson, Collector, Pooree, 9 July 1833," Acc. No. 28B, June 1829 to December 1830, *BDR, Revenue*, OSA.

61. Ibid.

62. Ibid.

63. "To the Commissioner of Cuttack, from R. D. Mangles, Acting Secretary, Sadar Board of Revenue, Fort William, 12 November 1833," Acc. No. 28B, June 1829 to December 1830, *BDR, Revenue*, OSA.

64. The board stated: "The thing to be ascertained, is this, simply whether or not the Mokuddums can prove themselves to be the absolute proprietors of their villages" ("To the Commissioner of Cuttack, from R. D. Mangles, Acting Secretary, SBOR, Fort William, 18 March 1834," Acc. No. 28B, June 1829 to December 1830, *BDR, Revenue*, OSA).

65. Ibid.

66. No. 37, 12 January 1838, *SBOR—Settlement Proceedings*, WBSA.

67. Old No. 130, Acc. No. 96C, 1836, *CDR, Revenue*, OSA.

68. "Memorandum by E. Currie," No. 38, 12 January 1838, *SBOR—Settlement Proceedings*, WBSA.

69. "To Henry Ricketts, Assistant Commissioner of Revenue for Cuttack, from James Grant, Collector, Balasore, 25 December 1835," Old No. 506, Acc. No. 95C, August 1835 to November 1835, *CDR, Revenue*, OSA.

70. "Papers on the Settlement of Cuttack and on the State of the Tributary Mehals," *Selections from the Records of the Bengal Government, No. III* (Calcutta: 1851), 19.

71. William Whewell, ed., *Literary Remains, Consisting of Lectures and Tracts on Political Economy of the Late Rev. Richard Jones* (London: J. Murray, 1859), 426.

72. Ibid., 428.

73. Ibid., 556.

74. "The objects of Political Economy are . . . Laws determining the production of wealth; and . . . Laws determining the distribution of wealth. . . . There are three causes which determine the productive power of the industry of nations: 1. The continuity with which it is exerted. 2. The skill with which it is directed. 3. The power by which it is aided. Of course, the primary sources of all material wealth are the earth and the elements. Human labour gives to wealth the various shapes in which it appears; in other words, it elicits and fashions it. Hence it follows that the production of wealth depends upon the productiveness or efficiency of labor" (ibid., 189).

75. Ibid., 456.

76. Richard Jones, *An Essay on the Distribution of Wealth and on the Sources of Taxation* (London: J. Murray, 1831), 110.

77. Ibid.

78. Ibid., 112.

79. Ibid., 112–13.

80. Lawrence Krader, *The Asiatic Mode of Production: Sources, Development and Critique in the Writings of Karl Marx* (Assen: Van Gorcum, 1975), 21.

81. Krader contends that Smith and Jones were the representatives of political economy in this tradition: "Adam Smith and Richard Jones developed the classical European theory of political economy of Asia, wherein the identification of land-tax with land-rent and the despotic power of the sovereign were their common ground. Smith took his materials from various parts of Asia, with no particular country as his model, Jones had India for his" (ibid., 55).

82. Rahul Govind argues that there was a "theoretical function" of "despotism" in eighteenth-century European thought where, conceptually, questions of political authority were posited as constitutive of the categories of political economy. He further notes that this function disappeared in the nineteenth century at one level—in the discourse of political economy overwhelmingly dominated by Ricardian theory—and reappeared at another level, in practice, as a despotic institutional form, namely, the East India Company. Rahul Govind, "Revenue, Rent . . . Profit? Early British Imperialism, Political Economy and the Search for a *differentia specifica (inter se)*," *Indian Economic and Social History Review* 48, no. 2 (2011): 177–213. To put it in his words, this "theoretical function of despotism at the birth of political economy (whether in François Quesnay or Adam Smith)" was "willfully forgotten in its 'mature' phase (David Ricardo) all the while being realized, as it were, in practice: Britain in India via the East India Company" (ibid., 178).

Differing from this interpretation, my contention is that the political did not get conceptually displaced in accounting for the categories of political economy in the nineteenth century, either in European thought or imperial practice.

83. Appendix No. VIII, "Note on Ryot Rents" in Jones, *An Essay on the Distribution of Wealth*, 40.

84. Ibid., 41, emphasis mine.

85. Whewell, ed., *Literary Remains*, 283.

86. Ibid., 286–87.

87. Ibid., 287.

88. Ibid., 289–90.

89. E. D. Steele argues that the campaign Mill waged for the reform of landed property was shaped by a great degree of pragmatism. The radicalism implicit in his theorization of landed property in his treatise on political economy was continuously tempered in his other political writings, as he did not want to take on the wrath of the English aristocracy. Thus, in later editions of *Principles of Political Economy* the radical conclusions were abandoned. See E. D. Steele, "J. S. Mill and the Irish Question: The Principles of Political Economy, 1848–1865," *Historical Journal* 13, no. 2 (June 1970): 216–36. In a subsequent piece Steele argues that Mill's radicalism was actually a vindication of English nationalism and imperialism. See E. D. Steele, "J. S. Mill and the Irish Question: Reform, and the Integrity of the Empire, 1865–70," *Historical Journal* 13, no. 3 (1970): 419–50. Bruce Kinzer critiques Steele by arguing that "with advancing years and altered circumstances, Mill came gradually to moderate his hostility towards the aristocracy, but he never relinquished his view of the retrogressive character of landlord influence in English politics . . . an antipathy to landlordism combined with a genuine sympathy for the Irish peasantry to lead Mill to consider the condition of Ireland." See Bruce L. Kinzer, "J. S. Mill and Irish Land: A Reassessment," *Historical Journal* 27, no. 1 (1984): 111–12.

90. See Abram L. Harris, "John Stuart Mill: Servant of the East India Company," *Canadian Journal of Economic and Political Science* 30, no. 2 (May 1964): 185–202; and R. D. Collison Black, "Economic Policy in Ireland and India in the Time of J. S. Mill," *Economic History Review*, n.s., 21, no. 2 (August 1968): 321–36.

91. See Lynn Zastoupil, *John Stuart Mill and India* (Stanford: Stanford University Press, 1994).

92. John Stuart Mill, *The Collected Works of John Stuart Mill, Volume II—The Principles of Political Economy with Some of Their Applications to Social Philosophy (Books I–II)*, ed. John M. Robson (Toronto: University of Toronto Press, 1965 [1848]), 207.

93. Ibid., 212.

94. Ibid., 218.

95. Ibid., 227.

96. Ibid., 226.

97. Mill pointed out that "landed property in England is thus very far from completely fulfilling the conditions which render its existence economically justifiable. But if insufficiently realized even in England, in Ireland those conditions are not complied with at all" (ibid., 227).

98. Ibid., 212.

99. Ibid., 228.

100. Mill stated: "In the case of land, no exclusive right should be permitted in any individual, which cannot be shown to be productive of positive good. . . . When land is not intended to be cultivated, no good reason can in general be given for its being private property at all; and if any one is permitted to call it his, he ought to know that he holds it by sufferance of the community" (ibid.).

101. John Stuart Mill, "Leslie on the Land Question," in *The Collected Works of John Stuart Mill, Volume V— Essays on Economy and Society, Part II*, ed. John M. Robson (Toronto: University of Toronto Press, 1967 [1870]), 218. For an overview of Thomas Malthus's views on landlords and rent, see Thomas R. Malthus, *An Inquiry into the Nature and Progress of Rent, and the Principles by Which It Is Regulated* (London: John Murray, 1815); David Cannadine, "Conspicuous Consumption by the Landed Classes, 1790–1830," in *Malthus and His Time*, ed. Michael Turner and Chris Cunneen (London: Springer, 1986), 96–111; and Donald Winch, *Malthus* (Oxford: Oxford University Press, 1987).

102. John Stuart Mill, "Chapters on Socialism," in *The Collected Works of John Stuart Mill, Volume V—Essays on Economy and Society, Part II*, ed. John M. Robson (Toronto: University of Toronto Press, 1967 [1879]), 282.

103. Ibid.

104. Rahul Govind insightfully contends that this tradition was constituted by a conceptual paradox, by representing legitimate sovereignty as absolute, and thereby, failing to separate "absolute" and "despotic" power. "Henry the VIII and Queen Elizabeth are described in no uncertain terms as 'despotic' and (yet) they are said to have laid the foundations of modern English liberty. A rigorous and sustained distinction between Absolutism and Despotism is rarely maintained. . . . The very conceptualization of sovereignty is absolute and (therefore) distinguishing it from despotism required the nimbleness of an origamist." See Rahul Govind, "Revenue, Rent . . . Profit," 181–82.

105. Clive Dewey argues that it was William Thornton's defense of peasant properties, prepared on the basis of a massive pool of evidence collected from several European countries, that enabled Mill to argue that this form of property leads to the greatest productivity in land. See Clive J. Dewey, "The Rehabilitation of the Peasant Proprietor in Nineteenth-Century Economic Thought," *History of Political Economy* 6 (1974): 17–47. Mill indeed used Thornton's evidence in *Principles of Political Economy* to argue his case. David Martin's essay, however, provides a useful corrective to Dewey's point. Martin notes that Mill was equally influenced by numerous European authors, like Tocqueville and the Prussian historian Friedrich von Raumer, to name a few, in forming an opinion in favor of small properties. See David Martin, "The Rehabilitation of the Peasant Proprietor in Nineteenth-Century Economic Thought: A Comment," *History of Political Economy* 8, no. 2 (1976): 297–302.

106. As Zastoupil writes: "In the last years of his life, Mill actively promoted the idea of curbing the power of the British aristocracy by limiting its control over land. . . . Besides

allowing large estates to be broken up and sold to industrious farmers, Mill and the Land Tenure Reform Association proposed taxing unearned increases in rent from land. . . . Furthermore, aid was to be made available to small cultivators to help them acquire land" (Zastoupil, *John Stuart Mill and India*, 186).

107. John Stuart Mill, *The Collected Works of John Stuart Mill, Volume II—The Principles of Political Economy with Some of Their Applications to Social Philosophy (Books I–II)*, ed. John M. Robson (Toronto: University of Toronto Press, 1965 [1848]), 209.

108. "The government was part owner, having the right to a heavy rent. . . . The government might make over its share to an individual, who then became possessed of the right of collection and all the other rights of the state, but not those of any private person connected with the soil. These private rights were of various kinds. The actual cultivators, or such of them as had been long settled on the land, had a right to retain possession; it was held unlawful to evict them while they paid the rent—a rent not in general fixed by agreement, but by the custom of the neighbourhood. Between the actual cultivators and the state . . . there were intermediate persons with rights of various extent. There were officers of government who . . . were often hereditary officers. There were also, in many cases, village communities, consisting of the reputed descendants of the first settlers of a village, who shared among themselves either the land or its produce according to rules established by custom, either cultivating it themselves or employing others to cultivate it for them." See John Stuart Mill, "Chapters on Socialism," in *The Collected Works of John Stuart Mill, Volume V—Essays on Economy and Society, Part II*, ed. John M. Robson (Toronto: University of Toronto Press, 1967 [1879]), 281.

109. Mill, *The Collected Works of John Stuart Mill, Volume II*, 233.

110. Mill's use of the category of custom was certainly rooted to an evolutionist hierarchy. Mill believed that while competition was a mark of modern societies, custom dominated the traditional ones. But more important, within the societies he considered as traditional, he envisioned custom as a political-economic category. In a certain sense, therefore, his use of custom contained in it a critique of the traditional-modern hierarchy. Mill's reasoning implied that due to the force of custom, property and production were organized in traditional societies like India in a manner that conformed to the principles of political economy; whereas in modern ones, like Britain, such a condition was glaringly absent.

111. In elucidating this perspective, Mill quoted extensively from the writings of a historian of India. "'There was an opportunity in India,' continues the historian, 'to which the history of the world presents not a parallel. Next after the sovereign the immediate cultivators had, by far, the greatest portion of interest in the soil. . . . The motives to improvement which property gives, and of which the power was so justly appreciated, might have been bestowed upon those upon whom they would have operated with a force incomparably greater than that with which they could operate upon any other class of men: they might have been bestowed upon those from whom alone, in every country, the principal improvements in agriculture must be derived, the immediate cultivators of the soil. . . . But the legislators were English aristocrats; and artistocratical prejudices prevailed.'" Mill, *The Collected Works of John Stuart Mill, Volume II*, 284.

112. Mill observed: "In the parts of India into which the British rule has been more recently introduced, the blunder has been avoided of endowing a useless body of great landlords with gifts from the public revenue. In most parts of the Madras and in part of the Bombay Presidency, the rent is paid directly to the government by the immediate cultivator. In the North-Western Provinces, the government makes its engagement with the village community collectively,

determining the share to be paid by each individual, but holding them jointly responsible for each other's default" (ibid., 285).

113. John Stuart Mill, "Memorandum of the Improvements in the Administration of India During the Last Thirty Years," in *The Collected Works of John Stuart Mill, Volume XXX—Writings on India*, ed. John Robson, Martin Moir, and Zawahir Moir (Toronto: University of Toronto Press, 1990 [1858]), 127–28.

114. In an ambitious, erudite, and strikingly original book, Andrew Fitzmaurice pursues changes in the connections between meanings of "sovereignty" and "property" across a great variety of imperial discourses. Fitzmaurice notes that the idea of occupation was pivotal to conceptualizations of sovereignty and property, since medieval times in Europe. But the use of "occupation" in shaping these categories and their connections changed over time. During the seventeenth and eighteenth centuries occupation became de-linked from its medieval use for a theory of rights and was recast in terms of a theory of economic development. Henceforth occupation was understood, in these discourses of imperial political theory, as being functional only in the use, or the "improvement," of nature. Later, in the nineteenth century, occupation came to be defined as political control of territorially bound resources. The changing meanings of sovereignty and property, Fitzmaurice argues, were structured by these varying ideas of occupation. While discussing in detail mutations in the related ideas of occupation, sovereignty, and property in the eighteenth century, Fitzmaurice states that the sovereignty-property relation was defined both in terms of use and convention by prominent thinkers of this century, like Pufendorf, Grotius, Hobbes, Kant, Locke, and others. It is beyond the scope of my book to engage with Fitzmaurice's long conceptual history of property-sovereignty relations, but it will be useful to note that he mostly keeps British India out of his discussion. The historical field studied in my book strongly suggests that sovereignty-property relations in nineteenth-century British India were defined through complex combinations of all those meanings that, according to Fitzmaurice, were deployed in earlier centuries to define these categories. This opens up a possibility for future works to reenter these canons of Western political theory in terms of the articulations of sovereignty and property visible in the agrarian social of British India (Andrew Fitzmaurice, *Sovereignty, Property and Empire, 1500–2000* [Cambridge: Cambridge University Press, 2014]).

Chapter 4

1. Louis Dumont, "The 'Village Community' from Munro to Maine," *Contributions to Indian Sociology* 9 (December 1966): 68.

2. Ibid. In a similar light, M. N. Srinivas observes that the administrative imagination in the nineteenth century portrayed the village as a self-sufficient and unchanging whole. While characterizing this view as erroneous, he also admits that there was a grain of truth in it, as the village did enjoy a certain degree of political autonomy from the higher echelons of power. Here we see Srinivas repeating the influential governmental understanding that the "despotism" of power in India was always fractured from within. See M. N. Srinivas, *The Dominant Caste and Other Essays* (Delhi: Oxford University Press, 1987), 20–59.

3. Clive Dewey, "Images of the Village Community: A Study in Anglo-Indian Ideology," *Modern Asian Studies* 6, no. 3 (1972): 291.

4. Karuna Mantena, *Alibis of Empire: Henry Maine and the Ends of Liberal Imperialism* (Ranikhet: Permanent Black, 2010). Mantena further argues that "this model of native society as an integral whole, held together by reciprocal bonds of custom and structures of kinship, would

provide the theoretical foundation, and even a normative justification, for the late imperial ideologies of protection, preservation, and collaboration" (ibid., 14–15).

5. *The Fifth Report from the Select Committee on the Affairs of the East India Company, Parliamentary Papers* (1812): 85.

6. Ibid., 83–84.

7. Ibid., 85.

8. Ibid.

9. The report noted that anciently these public officers were posted in the village so that "the abuses and irregularity of the zemindars, renters and managers, and of the inferior agents employed in making the collections, could be prevented or restrained." But in recent times it was seen that "the official registers, instead of being checks on the zemindars and renters, had by acceding at first to their views and encroachments, from weakness or venal motives, fallen into contempt, and lost not only their authority, but their emoluments also. Some contenting themselves with the allowance attached to their offices, continued to hold them, as sinecures; while on the other hand, a few who were rich and aspiring, acquired a footing of power and consequence, little inferior to that of a zemindar" (ibid., 84).

10. Ibid., 119.

11. Ibid., 124.

12. Ibid., 157.

13. Ibid.

14. "Memorandum by the Secretary Regarding the Past Settlements of the Ceded and Conquered Provinces, with Heads of a Plan for the Permanent Settlement of Those Provinces, 1 July 1819," in *Selections from Revenue Records, North-West Provinces, 1822–1833* (Allahabad: 1872), 60.

15. Ibid., 130.

16. Ibid.

17. "Extracts from a Memorandum, Dated October 19, 1826, by Holt Mackenzie, Esq, Secretary to Government, Explanatory of the Settlements Effected Under Regulation VII, 1822, and of the Measures Necessary to Give Better Effect to Its Provisions," in *Selections from Revenue Records, North-West Provinces, 1822–1833* (Allahabad: 1872), 196.

18. Ibid.

19. Ibid.

20. Ibid., 198.

21. Ibid., 201, emphasis mine,

22. "Minute of Sir C. T. Metcalfe, 7 November 1830," in *Selections from Revenue Records, North-West Provinces, 1822–1833* (Allahabad: 1872), 218. Eric Stokes describes Munro, Malcolm, Elphinstone, and Metcalfe as romantic paternalists, who were in opposition to the aggressive Utilitarianism of James Mill, Holt Mackenzie, and others. Such divisions need to be blurred. It is evident that in the context of the settlement of the North-Western Provinces, Mackenzie and Metcalfe both emphasized the need to protect the "village zemindars." Not only did Mackenzie not fit into the Utilitarian framework, as understood by Stokes, Metcalfe did not unambiguously belong to its opposite, the romantic-paternalist school. The ryotwar mode of settlement, which according to Stokes exemplified the romantic-paternalist line of thought, was opposed by Metcalfe. Mackenzie, whom he described as an ardent supporter of the rent doctrine and its radical critique of property, argued for a sharing of rent between the state and the village zemindars. See Eric Stokes, *The English Utilitarians and India* (Delhi: Oxford University Press, 1989), 8–25 and 110–39.

23. "Minute of Sir C. T. Metcalfe, 7 November 1830," in *Selections from Revenue Records, North-West Provinces, 1822–1833* (Allahabad: 1872), 214, emphasis mine.

24. Burton Stein, "Idiom and Ideology in Early Nineteenth Century South India," in *Rural India: Land, Power and Society Under British Rule*, ed. Peter Robb (New Delhi: Oxford University Press, 1992), 50–51.

25. Burton Stein, *Thomas Munro: The Origins of the Colonial State and His Vision of Empire* (Delhi: Oxford University Press, 1989), 58.

26. Stein explains ryotwar with an instrumentalist reading of politics, not looking into its political-economic constitution. "There is nothing of sentiment for the small farmer nor historical precedent here. Munro was proposing nothing less than the completion, by administrative means, of the military conquest of the Baramahal territory . . . by stripping the ancient gauds and karaikkars of their locality resource control, and even further by limiting village heads in their command over share-cropping labour and converting them into mere subordinate revenue servants of his own subordinate tahsildars, Munro was introducing a new and very distant authority—ultimately that of London—*directly* into the South Indian—or any Indian—agrarian system, for the first time" (ibid., 59, emphasis mine).

27. William Whewell, ed., *Literary Remains, Consisting of Lectures and Tracts on Political Economy of the Late Rev. Richard Jones* (London: J. Murray, 1859), 214.

28. Jones's use of the long passage from the *Fifth Report* can be found on pages 214–15.

29. Whewell, ed., *Literary Remains*, 215.

30. Ibid., 289–90.

31. John Stuart Mill, "Chapters on Socialism," in *The Collected Works of John Stuart Mill, Volume V—Essays on Economy and Society, Part II*, ed. J. M. Robson (Toronto: University of Toronto Press, 1967 [1879]), 281.

32. Ibid., 216.

33. Colonel R. H. Phillimore, comp., *Historical Records of the Survey of India, Volume III*, 1815–1830 (Dehradun: Surveyor General of India, 1954), ix, emphasis mine.

34. Eric Stokes makes a similar assumption, on the basis of which he does not include Bengal in his discussion of the relationship between Utilitarian thought and agrarian administration in different parts of British India (Stokes, *The English Utilitarians and India*).

35. Colonel R. H. Phillimore, comp., *Historical Records of the Survey of India, Volume I*, 18th Century (Dehradun: Surveyor General of India, 1945), 1.

36. Ibid., 7.

37. Ibid., 8.

38. F. C. Hirst, *Notes on the Old Revenue Surveys of Bengal, Bihar, Orissa and Assam* (Calcutta: Thacker, Spink, 1912), 1.

39. Even Phillimore makes a similar observation: "In districts under the permanent settlement, the survey was concerned mainly with the boundaries of the estates or *mahals*, not with those of the *mauza* or village area" (Colonel R. H. Phillimore, comp., *Historical Records of the Survey of India, Volume IV*, 1830–1845 [Dehradun: Surveyor General of India, 1958], 179). It will also be useful here to remember Charles Metcalfe's comment, where he pointed out that a misapplication of English principles on agrarian categories in India made officials falsely perceive "village communities" as "estates."

40. Hirst, *Notes on the Old Revenue Surveys*, 3.

41. See Bernardo A. Michael, "Making Territory Visible: The Revenue Surveys of Colonial South Asia," *Imago Mundi* 59, no. 1 (2007): 78–95. Mathew Edney argues in his book that

there was a huge gap between "the desire and the ability to implement the perfect panopticist survey, between what the British persistently thought they had accomplished and the hybrid cartographic image of India which they had actually constructed" (Mathew Edney, *Mapping an Empire: The Geographical Construction of British India (1765–1843)* [Chicago: University of Chicago Press, 1997], xiii). Edney tells us how each local survey was supposed to put flesh on the skeleton that was being centrally assembled through the Great Trigonometrical Survey operations. But at the level of incorporation into the central knowledge bank, the attempt to impose order on the detail of the surveys was interrupted. "Whatever order was imposed on the detailed surveys came *after* the fact, when they were incorporated into the general archives. The order did not derive directly from the surveys themselves. What the British implemented was not the ideal, but only the *image* of the ideal" (ibid., 30). It is evident that Edney also works within the distinction of an outside and an inside, a pure ideal and a contaminated practice. My book is generally not interested in drawing such unadulterated binaries. Such distinctions, I argue, were part of the process of creating the field of the "political" in all its complexities. Failure to match generalities with local details was part of the process of surveying. That did not upset, or displace, the main object of the survey, namely, the matrix of power on land rooted in the village.

42. Hirst, *Notes on the Old Revenue Surveys*, 8.

43. Ibid., 48.

44. "Letters from the Board of Revenue on Deputation, dated May 26 and July 22, 1831, and from the Governor-General, dated June 14, 1831, with copy of a letter and its enclosure from the Resident and Chief Commissioner at Delhi," in *Selections from Revenue Records, North-West Provinces, 1822–1833* (Allahabad: 1872), 270.

45. Ibid., 274.

46. Ibid., 281.

47. "Memorandum by the Secretary Regarding the Past Settlements of the Ceded and Conquered Provinces, with Heads of a Plan for the Permanent Settlement of Those Provinces, 1 July 1819," in *Selections from Revenue Records, North-West Provinces, 1822–1833* (Allahabad: 1872), 68.

48. Phillimore noted that with regard to Behar, "the Sudder Board . . . at first contemplated that the survey should be mehalwar, that is, confined to a definition of estates paying revenue to Government, instead of mouzahwar, comprehending the definition of all minor tenures, similar to the survey of the North Western Provinces." After much deliberation, however, the board concurred that the survey in Behar should be mouzahwar. After this decision, there was further debate over the need to adopt *khasra* surveys in this region. "The adoption of the khasra, or native measurements, as a part of the survey . . . was also discussed. The Western Board contended that the khasra was requisite for the protection of the Government . . . as well as for the benefit of the people." Although the board rejected the idea of adopting khasra surveys for Behar, later, in 1842 some khasra surveys did happen in parts of Behar. In Orissa, Midnapoor, and Chittagong, however, Khasra surveys were carried out (Colonel R. H. Phillimore, comp., *Historical Records of the Survey of India, Volume IV*, 180).

49. In an abstract of instructions issued to canoongoes and measuring aumeens, the collector of Balasore stated that the settlement record was to be prepared "on the ground in the presence of all the people." He also stated that the assessing officer would "examine the Pottahs of the Ryots the papers of the Putwaree compare them question both parties and then assess" (Old No. 465, Acc. No. 93C, 16 July 1835 to 16 November 1835, *CDR*, *Revenue*, OSA). This

process was described in detail in the settlement papers of Cuttack. See "Papers on the Settlement of Cuttack and on the State of the Tributary Mehals," in *Selections from the Records of the Bengal Government*, No. III (Calcutta: 1851), 16–18.

50. "No. IV Letter from the Governor-General, to the Sudder Board of Revenue on Deputation, Dated Camp Pinjore, 7 April 1831," in *Selections from Revenue Records, North-West Provinces, 1822–1833* (Allahabad: 1872), 265.

51. No. 25, 23 April 1816, *BRP*, WBSA.

52. Ibid.

53. Acc. No. 48B, January 1833 to January 1835, *BDR, Revenue*, OSA.

54. Ibid.

55. "To the Secretary, SBOR, from Commissioner's Office, 27 May 1834," Acc. No. 48B, January 1833 to January 1835, *BDR, Revenue*, OSA.

56. "To R. Hunter, Commissioner of Cuttack, from W. Wilkinson, Collector, Pooree, 9 July 1833," Acc. No. 48B, January 1833 to January 1835, *BDR, Revenue*, OSA.

57. "Copies of Memoranda on Certain Settlements in Bauleah, Cuttack, Chittagong and Murshidabad Divisions by Mr. F. J. Halliday, Secretary to the Board of Revenue, Deputed to Settlement Work, 1837–1838," *SBOR—Settlement Proceedings*, WBSA.

58. Pergunnah Phulwur, Zillah Balasore, Division Cuttack, Mouza Sahoopara, ibid.

59. No. 30, Acc. No. 16B, F, April 1825 to April 1838, *BDR, Revenue*, OSA.

60. Old No. 134, Acc. No. 102C, 2 January 1837 to 22 May 1837, *BDR, Revenue*, OSA.

61. Old No. 506, Acc. No. 95C, August 1835 to November 1835, *BDR, Revenue*, OSA.

62. "Copies of Memoranda on Certain Settlements," *SBOR—Settlement Proceedings*, WBSA.

63. For one more example, see the settlement report of Talook Kurnsunkurpore, Pergunnah Sunawut, Zillah Balasore, Acc. No. 70B, Old No. 107, April 1838 to April 1839, *BDR, Revenue*, OSA.

64. Rachel Sturman, *The Government of Social Life in Colonial India: Liberalism, Religious Law and Women's Rights* (Cambridge: Cambridge University Press, 2012), 60.

65. No. 153, 14 July 1837, *SBOR—Settlement Proceedings*, WBSA.

66. No. 155, 14 July 1837, *SBOR—Settlement Proceedings*, WBSA.

67. Acc. No. 48B, January 1833 to January 1835, *BDR, Revenue*, OSA.

68. No. 155, 14 July 1837, *SBOR—Settlement Proceedings*, WBSA.

69. "To G. Stockwell, Commissioner of Revenue for Cuttack, from H. Ricketts, Collector, Balasore, 20 October 1831," "Answer to Questions, October 1831," Acc. No. 36B, *BDR, Revenue*, OSA.

70. "Reports of Settlements Made in the Bustah Division, Pergunnah Searee, Balasore Deputy Collectorship," Old No. 30, Acc. No. 16B, April 1825 to April 1838, *BDR, Revenue*, OSA.

71. Ibid.

72. "To Commissioner of Cuttack, from Collector, Pooree, 18 March 1839," Old No. 115, Acc. No. 77B, January 1839 to December 1839, *BDR, Revenue*, OSA.

73. W. T. Thornton, *A Plea for Peasant Proprietors; With the Outlines of a Plan for Their Establishment in Ireland* (London: Macmillan, 1848), 20–22.

74. Ibid., 23.

75. Ibid., 19.

76. John Stuart Mill, "The Principles of Political Economy with Some of Their Applications to Social Philosophy (Books I–II)" In *The Collected Works of John Stuart Mill, Volume II*, ed. John M. Robson (Toronto: University of Toronto Press, 1965 [1848]), 261.

77. 12 June 1838, No. 20, *SBOR—Miscellaneous Proceedings*, WBSA. In this letter, the commissioner observed, after discussing the opinions of the collectors, that 14 October 1791 should be admitted "as the date of possession since which is to be considered long possession."

78. As examples, see No. 42, 4 September 1839, Nos. 55 and 57, 17 July 1839, *SBOR—Miscellaneous Proceedings*, WBSA.

79. "Circular No. 55, to Deputy Collectors Employed in Resumption, from E. Repton, 1 September 1838," Old No. 109, Acc. No. 72B, March 1838 to January 1842, *CDR, Revenue*, OSA.

Chapter 5

1. Gilles Deleuze, "What Is a Dispositif?" in *Michel Foucault Philosopher*, ed. Timothy J. Armstrong (New York: Harvester Wheatsheaf, 1992), 161.

2. No. 47, 7 June 1811, *BRP*, WBSA.

3. Ibid.

4. Ibid.

5. Laloo Maintee, "Ramkanoy is elder brother to Bhuwanee Purshaud and manager of his affairs." Soobah Singh, "Both of them used the profits as if equally concerned" ("Deposition of Laloo Maintee, Inhabitant of Mouza Joytollung Pergunnah Balookissee, Enclosure to a Letter to Secretary to the Board of Revenue from Collector, Cuttack," ibid.).

6. Consider Laloo Maintee's statements: "Who did the Ryots consider as the real proprietor? Ramkanoy. Do you know if the ryots truly considered Ramkanoy to be the real proprietor? Yes and the Ryots (if called upon) will affirm the same" (ibid.).

7. "Deposition of Nitye Naik, ryot, Taluka Tulpuda, Mouza Sodkund," ibid.

8. No. 47, 7 June 1811, *BRP*, WBSA.

9. No. 20, 13 June 1815, *BRP*, WBSA.

10. Ibid.

11. Ibid.

12. Ibid.

13. Ibid.

14. No. 62 of 1853, 11 February 1854, *Bengal Zillah Courts' Decisions, 1854, Cuttack*, IOR, 11.

15. Ibid., emphasis mine.

16. No. 67 of 1852, 23 September 1852, *Bengal Zillah Courts' Decisions, 1854, Cuttack*, IOR, 109.

17. No. 67 of 1852, 23 September 1852, *Bengal Zillah Courts' Decisions,1854, Cuttack*, IOR, 110.

18. "Commissioner, Cuttack to Secretary to the Board of Revenue, No. 12, 19 July 1844, Board of Reenue Proceedings," cited in Tarun Kumar Mukhopadhyay, *The Agrarian Society of Orissa: Nineteenth Century* (Kolkata: Progressive, 2008), 37. Mukhapadhyay goes on to argue: "The zamindars, relying on this precedent, did everything to reduce the *muqaddams* to the position of farmers." But the present chapter shows that the same precedent also worked against the zemindars. This was because what Mukhapadhyay presents as his analysis, namely, the strategic use of this precedent by the zemindars, soon became an indispensable part of official perception in Cuttack. Accordingly, whenever this precedent was used by the zemindars in such disputes, the use was seen as necessarily fraudulent by the officials.

19. Andrew Sartori, "A Liberal Discourse of Custom in Colonial Bengal," *Past and Present* 212 (August 2011): 163–97.

20. "Extract from the Commissioner's Proceedings in the Settlement Department, No. 8, 18 March 1845, Board of Revenue Proceedings," cited in Mukhopadhyay, *The Agrarian Society of Orissa*, 38.

21. No. 36, 2 September 1845, *SBORP*, IOR, emphasis mine.

22. Mukhopadhyay, *The Agrarian Society of Orissa*, 38.

23. Sakti Padhi, *Land Relations and Agrarian Development in India: A Comparative Historical Study of Regional Variations* (Thiruvananthapuram: Centre for Development Studies, 1999), 107–8.

24. No. 20, 10 January 1845, *SBORP*, IOR.

25. No. 21, 10 June 1845, *SBORP*, IOR.

26. Ibid.

27. Ibid.

28. Ibid.

29. No. 8 of 1847, 28 March 1849, *Bengal Zillah Courts' Decisions, 1849, Cuttack*, IOR, 25.

30. Ibid., 27.

31. Ibid., 26.

32. No. 10 of 1848, 13 April 1849, *Bengal Zillah Courts' Decisions, 1849, Cuttack*, IOR, 39.

33. Ibid., 40.

34. No. 15 of 1849, 15 January 1850, *Bengal Zillah Courts' Decisions, 1850, Cuttack*, IOR, 3.

35. Ibid., 4.

36. For one among many cases where Gopal Pundit's papers were used as a definitive authority in vindicating mokuddum status, see, No. 14, 14 December 1849, *Bengal Zillah Courts' Decisions, 1849, Cuttack*, IOR.

37. No. 3 of 1850, 19 April 1850, *Bengal Zillah Courts' Decisions, 1850, Cuttack*, IOR, 76.

38. No. 7 of 1850, 2 April 1850, *Bengal Zillah Courts' Decisions, 1850, Cuttack*, IOR, 63–64.

39. No. 7 of 1850, 28 January 1851, *Bengal Zillah Courts' Decisions, 1851, Cuttack*, IOR, 13.

40. Ibid.

41. No. 55 of 1850, 17 December 1850, *Bengal Zillah Courts' Decisions, 1850, Cuttack*, IOR, 171–72.

42. No. 8 of 1851, 4 August 1852, *Bengal Zillah Courts' Decisions, 1852, Cuttack*, IOR, 72.

43. Ibid., 73.

44. No. 14 of 1850, 19 February 1851, *Bengal Zillah Courts' Decisions, 1851, Cuttack*, IOR, 17.

45. Ibid.

46. Ibid.

47. F. G. Wigley, ed., *The Eastern Bengal and Assam Code, in Three Volumes Containing the Regulations and Local Acts in Force in the Province of Eastern Bengal and Assam, Volume 1* (Calcutta: Government Press, 1907), 28.

48. No. 185, 17 August 1842, *SBORP*, IOR.

49. 14 April 1847, *Bengal Zillah Courts' Decisions, 1847, Cuttack*, IOR.

50. Ibid.

51. Sirajul Islam, *Bengal Land Tenure: The Origin and Growth of Intermediate Interests in the Nineteenth Century* (Rotterdam: Comparative Asian Studies Programme, 1985).

52. Ibid., 27, emphasis mine.

53. See Ratnalekha Ray, *Change in Bengal Agrarian Society: 1760–1850* (New Delhi: Manohar, 1979); and Islam, *Bengal Land Tenure*.

54. 6 March 1850, *Bengal Zillah Courts' Decisions, 1850, Cuttack*, IOR, 40.

55. Ibid., 41.

Conclusion

1. David Ludden, "Introduction: Agricultural Production and Indian History," in *Agricultural Production and Indian History*, ed. David Ludden (Delhi: Oxford University Press, 1994), 5.

2. Ibid., 7.

3. For a detailed description of the famine see Gorachand Patnaik, *The Famine and Some Aspects of the British Economic Policy in Orissa, 1866–1905* (Cuttack: Vidyapuri, 1980); J. K. Samal, *Economy of Colonial Orissa, 1866–1947* (New Delhi: Munshiram Manoharlal, 2000), chap. 4; and Brajabandhu Bhatta, "Natural Calamities in Orissa During the British Rule," in *Economic History of Orissa*, ed. N. R. Patnaik (New Delhi: Indus, 1997), 356–65.

4. Charles Blair, *Indian Famines: Their Historical, Financial, and Other Aspects* (Edinburgh: Blackwood, 1874), 60–62.

5. *Report of the Indian Famine Commission*, Simla, 1880, 30.

6. *Report of the Indian Famine Commission*, Calcutta, 1901, 72–73.

7. David Arnold, "Agriculture and 'Improvement' in Early Colonial India: A Pre-History of Development," *Journal of Agrarian Change* 5 (October 2005): 513.

8. John Augustus Voelcker, *Report on the Improvement of Indian Agriculture* (London: Eyre and Spottiswoode, 1893).

9. Ludden, "Introduction," 9.

10. As Ravi Ahuja points out, "Cotton had insisted in his influential book 'Public Works in India' (1854) that there was scope for choice not only between railways and irrigation but also between railways and 'cheaper' (i.e. less capital-intensive) transportation facilities and that the latter alternative was preferable in each case" (Ravi Ahuja, "Pathways of Empire: Circulation, 'Public Works' and Social Space in Colonial Orissa [c. 1780–1914]," Ph.D. diss., University of Hanover, 2007, 95).

11. Rohan D' Souza, *Drowned and Dammed: Colonial Capitalism and Flood Control in Eastern India* (Delhi: Oxford University Press, 2006).

12. D. A. Washbrook, "Law, State and Agrarian Society in Colonial India," *Modern Asian Studies* 15 (1981): 649–721.

13. Peter Robb, "Law and Agrarian Society in India: The Case of Bihar and the Nineteenth-Century Tenancy Debate," *Modern Asian Studies* 22 (1988): 321.

14. Cited in S. H. Rudolph, "Introduction," in *Agrarian Power and Agricultural Productivity in South Asia*, ed. M. Desai, S. H. Rudolph, and A. Rudra (Berkeley: University of California Press, 1984), 12–13.

15. Karuna Mantena, *Alibis of Empire: Henry Maine and the Ends of Liberal Imperialism* (Ranikhet: Permanent Black, 2010), 10.

16. Neeladri Bhattacharya, "Remaking Custom: The Discourse and Practice of Colonial Codification," in *Tradition, Dissent and Ideology: Essays in Honour of Romila Thapar*, ed. R. Champakalakshmi and S. Gopal (New Delhi: Oxford University Press, 1996), 28. For another work that argues that Henry Maine's evolutionary anthropology crucially informed the agrarian policies of late nineteenth-century Punjab, see Clive Dewey, "The Official Mind and the Problem of Agrarian Indebtedness in India, 1870–1910" (Ph.D. diss., University of Cambridge, 1972). Dewey identifies a "conservative" turn in imperial thought behind the formation of these policies trying to prevent land alienation and protect "agriculturalists." This "conservatism," however, has been reinterpreted by a host of studies, as modernist practices of producing the "social," which focused on the governmental production of ethnicity and other forms of indigeneity in the late nineteenth century, manifested in the activities of an "ethnographic state." One of the leading examples of such works is Nicholas Dirks, *Castes of the Mind: Colonialism and the Making of Modern India* (Princeton: Princeton University Press, 2001). Dirks's work argues that "caste" was produced by these governmental operations as the essence of "civil society" in India.

17. In his recent book *The Great Agrarian Conquest*, Bhattacharya demonstrates, with remarkable analytical precision, the whole gamut of governmental practices operative in the production of agrarian society in Punjab between the late nineteenth and early twentieth centuries. But even here he continues to work within oppositions that have structured the historiography this book critically engages with. So, while Bhattacharya productively borrows from Foucault the use of "depth" by the modern episteme as a discursive strategy of making the social, in examining the ethnographic plumbing of deep histories and customs in colonial Punjab, he himself relapses into distinctions like surface-depth, code-practice, and state-society, indicating that it's the latter term in the binary that stands for the "really real." "There were, however, limits to the reach of the state. Beneath the regime of codes was the reality of uncodified practices." See Neeladri Bhattacharya, *The Great Agrarian Conquest: The Colonial Reshaping of a Rural World* (New Delhi: Permanent Black, 2018), 219.

18. Rudolph, "Introduction," 1–19.

19. Michel Foucault, *Security, Territory, Population: Lectures at the College de France, 1977–78* (New York: Palgrave Macmillan, 2007), 69.

20. Ibid., 70. For Foucault, as Michell Dean argues, "politics is never, even in the most immediate or brutal action of the exercise of domination and power, without some degree of 'thought.' This is the first part of his thesis on political rationality. The second part is that this 'thought,' this political rationality, does not simply arise from the rulers consulting their 'interests,' or their capacity for rational choice, but from historically developed and modified forms of rationality. Political rationality, in this sense, is anterior to political action and a condition of it" (Mitchell Dean, *Critical and Effective Histories: Foucault's Methods and Historical Sociology* [London: Routledge, 1994], 182).

21. See Partha Chatterjee, *The Nation and Its Fragments: Colonial and Postcolonial Histories* (Princeton: Princeton University Press, 1993), especially chapter 2.

BIBLIOGRAPHY

Archival Records

Orissa State Archives, Bhubaneshwar

Balasore District Records, Judicial, 1803–1860

Balasore District Records, Revenue, 1803–1860

Cuttack District Records, Judicial, 1803–1860

Cuttack District Records, Revenue, 1803–1860

West Bengal State Archives, Kolkata

Board of Revenue Proceedings, 1803–1850

Sadar Board of Revenue—Settlement Proceedings, 1836–1843

Sadar Board of Revenue—Miscellaneous Proceedings, 1836–1843

India Office Records, British Library, London

Home Miscellaneous, Papers Concerning Revenue, Administrative and Judicial Matters in India, 1792–1812

Bengal Revenue Consultations, 1803–1850

Bengal Judicial Consultations, 1803–1850

Bengal Zillah Courts' Decisions, Calcutta, 1845–1855

Selections from Revenue Records, North-West Provinces, 1822–1833, Allahabad, 1872

Proceedings Connected with the Recent Disturbances in Cuttack, Examiner's Office, 1819 (Volumes 1–7)

Sadar Board of Revenue Proceedings, Bengal, 1838–1850

Wren Library, Trinity College, Cambridge

Whewell Papers, Add. Mss. C. 51–52

Published Primary Sources

Alexander, James. "On the Tenures and Fiscal Relations of the Owners, and Occupants of the Soil in Bengal, Behar, and Orissa." *Journal of the Asiatic Society of Bengal* 14 (July–December 1845): 527–45.

Blair, Charles. *Indian Famines: Their Historical, Financial, and Other Aspects*. Edinburgh: Blackwood, 1874.

Circular Orders of the SBOR at the Presidency of Fort William; Including the Rules of Practice for the Guidance of the Board and of the Commissioners of Revenue, from the Year 1788 to the End of August 1837. Calcutta, 1838.

Extracts from Harington's Analysis of the Bengal Regulations. Calcutta, 1866.

The Fifth Report from the Select Committee on the Affairs of the East India Company, Parliamentary Papers, 1812.

Harington, J. H. "Minute and Draft of Regulation, of the Rights of Ryots in Bengal." 1827.

Hirst, F. C. *Notes on the Old Revenue Surveys of Bengal, Bihar, Orissa and Assam*. Calcutta: Thacker, Spink, 1912.

Jones, Richard. *An Essay on the Distribution of Wealth and on the Sources of Taxation*. London: J. Murray, 1831.

Malthus, T. R. *An Inquiry into the Nature and Progress of Rent, and the Principles by Which It Is Regulated*. London: J. Murray, 1815.

McCulloch, J. R. "Review of Richard Jones's *An Essay on the Distribution of Wealth and on the Sources of Taxation*." *Edinburgh Review* 54 (September 1831): 84–99.

Mill, James. *Elements of Political Economy*. London: Henry G. Bohn, 1821.

———. *History of British India, Volume I, Book II*. Fifth edition. With notes and continuation by H. H. Wilson. London: Routledge, 1997 (1858).

———. "Theory and Practice." *London and Westminster Review* 3 (April 1836): 223–34.

Mill, John Stuart. "Chapters on Socialism." In *The Collected Works of John Stuart Mill, Volume V—Essays on Economy and Society, Part II*, edited by John M. Robson, 703–56. Toronto: University of Toronto Press, 1967 (1879).

———. "Leslie on the Land Question." In *The Collected Works of John Stuart Mill, Volume V—Essays on Economy and Society, Part II*, edited by John M. Robson, 669–86. Toronto: University of Toronto Press, 1967 (1870).

———. "Memorandum of the Improvements in the Administration of India During the Last Thirty Years." In *The Collected Works of John Stuart Mill, Volume XXX—Writings on India*, edited by John Robson, Martin Moir, and Zawahir Moir, 118–75. Toronto: University of Toronto Press, 1990 (1858).

———. "The Principles of Political Economy with Some of Their Applications to Social Philosophy (Books I–II)." In *The Collected Works of John Stuart Mill, Volume II*, edited by John M. Robson. Toronto: University of Toronto Press, 1965 (1848).

"Papers on the Settlement of Cuttack and on the State of the Tributary Mehals." In *Selections from the Records of the Bengal Government, No. III*. Calcutta, 1851.

Report from the Select Committee on the Affairs of the East India Company; with Minutes of Evidence in Six Parts, and an Appendix and Index to Each. Volume 3, Revenue, 1832. London.

Report from the Select Committee on the Affairs of the East India Company, 1831. London.

Report of the Indian Famine Commission. Simla, 1880.

Report of the Indian Famine Commission. Calcutta, 1901.

Ricardo, David. *On the Principles of Political Economy and Taxation*. Third edition. London: J. Murray, 1821.

Ricketts, Henry. *The Real Difficulties in Bengal and How to Settle Them*. London: Smith, Elder & Company, 1861.

———. *The Rent Difficulties in Bengal and How to Remedy Them, The Rent Facilities in Cuttack and How to Preserve Them*. London: Smith, Elder, 1863.

Selections from Revenue Records, North-West Provinces, 1822–1833. Allahabad, 1872.

Stirling, A. *An Account, Geographical, Statistical and Historical of Orissa Proper, or Cuttack*. 1822.

Thornton, W. T. *A Plea for Peasant Proprietors; with the Outlines of a Plan for Their Establishment in Ireland*. London: Macmillan, 1848.

Todhunter, I., ed. *William Whewell, D.D. Master of Trinity College, Cambridge: An Account of His Writings with Selections from His Literary and Scientific Correspondence, Volumes 1 and 2*. London: Macmillan, 1876.

Whewell, William. *The Philosophy of the Inductive Sciences, Founded upon Their History, Volume 1*. London: J. W. Parker, 1840.

———. "Review of Richard Jones's *An Essay on the Distribution of Wealth and on the Sources of Taxation*." *British Critic, and Quarterly Theological Review* 10 (July 1831): 41–61.

———, ed. *Literary Remains, consisting of Lectures and Tracts on Political-economy of the late Rev. Richard Jones*. London: J. Murray, 1859.

Wigley, F. G., ed. *The Eastern Bengal and Assam Code, in Three Volumes Containing the Regulations and Local Acts in Force in the Province of Eastern Bengal and Assam, Volume 1*. Calcutta: Government Press, 1907.

Voelcker, John Augustus. *Report on the Improvement of Indian Agriculture*. London: Eyre and Spottiswoode, 1893.

Secondary Works

Ahuja, Ravi. "Pathways of Empire: Circulation, 'Public Works' and Social Space in Colonial Orissa (c. 1780–1914)." Ph.D. diss., University of Hanover, 2006.

Arnold, David. "Agriculture and 'Improvement' in Early Colonial India: A Pre-History of Development." *Journal of Agrarian Change* 5 (October 2005): 505–25.

———. *The Tropics and The Traveling Gaze: India, Landscape, and Science, 1800–1856*. New Delhi: Permanent Black, 2005.

Barber, William J. *British Economic Thought and India, 1600–1858: A Study in the History of Development Economics*. Oxford: Oxford University Press, 1975.

Bayly, C. A. *The New Cambridge History of India, II.1: Indian Society and the Making of the British Empire*. Cambridge: Cambridge University Press, 1988.

Benton, Lauren. *A Search for Sovereignty: Law and Geography in European Empires, 1400–1900*. Cambridge: Cambridge University Press, 2010.

Bhatta, Brajabandhu. "Natural Calamities in Orissa During the British Rule." In *Economic History of Orissa*, edited by N. R. Patnaik, 356–65. New Delhi: Indus, 1997.

Bhattacharya, Neeladri. "Colonial State and Agrarian Society." In *Situating Indian History: For Sarvepalli Gopal*, edited by Sabyasachi Bhattacharya and Romila Thapar, 106–45. Delhi: Oxford University Press, 1986.

———. *The Great Agrarian Conquest: The Colonial Reshaping of a Rural World*. New Delhi: Permanent Black, 2018.

———. "Pastoralists in a Colonial World." In *Nature, Culture, Imperialism: Essays on the Environmental History of South Asia*, edited by David Arnold and Ramachandra Guha, 49–85. Delhi: Oxford University Press, 1985.

———. "Remaking Custom: The Discourse and Practice of Colonial Codification." In *Tradition, Dissent and Ideology: Essays in Honour of Romila Thapar*, edited by R. Champakalakshmi and S. Gopal, 20–51. New Delhi: Oxford University Press, 1996.

Black, R. D. C. "Economic Policy in Ireland and India in the Time of J. S. Mill." *Economic History Review*, n.s., 21 (August 1968): 321–36.

Blaug, Mark. *Ricardian Economics: A Historical Study*. New Haven: Yale University Press, 1958.

Bose, Sugata. *The New Cambridge History of India, III.2: Peasant Labor and Colonial Capital: Rural Bengal Since 1770*. Cambridge: Cambridge University Press, 1993.

Burbank, Jane, and Frederick Cooper. *Empires in World History: Power and the Politics of Difference*. Princeton: Princeton University Press, 2010.

Butts, Robert E. "Induction as Unification: Kant, Whewell, and Recent Developments." In *Kant and Contemporary Epistemology*, edited by Paolo Parrini, 273–90. Dordrecht: Kluwer, 1994.

Cannadine, David. "Conspicuous Consumption by the Landed Classes, 1790–1830." In *Malthus and His Time*, edited by Michael Turner and Chris Cunneen, 96–111. London: Springer, 1986.

Charlesworth, Neil. *Peasants and Imperial Rule: Agriculture and Agrarian Society in the Bombay Presidency, 1850–1935*. Cambridge: Cambridge University Press, 1985.

Chatterjee, Partha. *The Nation and Its Fragments: Colonial and Postcolonial Histories*. Princeton: Princeton University Press, 1993.

Chaudhry, Faisal. "Property and Its Rule (in Late Indo-Islamicate and Early Colonial) South Asia: What's in a Name?" *Journal of the Economic and Social History of the Orient* 61 (2018): 920–75.

———. "A Rule of Proprietary Right for British India: From Revenue Settlement to Tenant Right in the Age of Classical Legal Thought." *Modern Asian Studies* 50 (2016): 345–84.

Cohn, Bernard S. "Structural Change in Indian Rural Society, 1596–1885." In *Land Control and Social Structure in Indian History*, edited by Robert Eric Frykenberg, 53–122. Madison: University of Wisconsin Press, 1969.

Cook, S. B. *Imperial Affinities: Nineteenth-Century Analogies and Exchanges Between India and Ireland*. New Delhi: Sage, 1993.

Cooper, Frederick, and Ann Laura Stoler, eds. *Tensions of Empire: Colonial Cultures in a Bourgeoisie World*. Berkeley: University of California Press, 1997.

Das, Binod S. *Studies in the Economic History of Orissa from Ancient Times to 1833*. Calcutta: Firma KLM, 1978.

De, S. C., ed. *Guide to Orissan Records, Volume II*. Bhubaneswar: Odisha State Archive, 1961.

Dean, Mitchell. *Critical and Effective Histories: Foucault's Methods and Historical Sociology*. London: Routledge, 1994.

Deleuze, Gilles. "What Is a Dispositif?" In *Michel Foucault Philosopher*, edited by Timothy J. Armstrong, 159–68. New York: Routledge, 1992.

Deleuze, Gilles, and Félix Guattari. *A Thousand Plateaus: Capitalism and Schizophrenia*. Minneapolis: University Minnesota Press, 2013 (1987).

de Marchi, N. B., and R. P. Sturges. "Malthus and Ricardo's Inductivist Critics: Four Letters to William Whewell." *Economica*, n.s., 40 (November 1973): 379–93.

Derrida, Jacques. *Of Grammatology*. Baltimore: Johns Hopkins University Press, 1976.

Desai, Meghnad, Susanne Hoeber Rudolph, and Rudra Ashok, eds. *Agrarian Power and Agricultural Productivity in South Asia*. Berkeley: University of California Press, 1984.

Dewey, Clive. "The Official Mind and the Problem of Agrarian Indebtedness in India, 1870–1910." Ph.D. diss, University of Cambridge, 1972.

———. "The Rehabilitation of the Peasant Proprietor in Nineteenth-Century Economic Thought." *History of Political Economy* 6 (1974): 17–47.

Dirks, Nicholas. *Castes of Mind: Colonialism and the Making of Modern India*. Princeton: Princeton University Press, 2001.

Drayton, Richard. *Nature's Government: Science, Imperial Britain, and the "Improvement" of the World*. New Delhi: Orient Blackswan, 2005.

Dreyfus, Hubert L., and Paul Rabinow. *Michel Foucault: Beyond Structuralism and Hermeneutics*. Chicago: University of Chicago Press, 1983.

D'Souza, Rohan. *Drowned and Dammed: Colonial Capitalism and Flood Control in Eastern India*. Delhi: Oxford University Press, 2006.

Dumont, Louis. "The 'Village Community' from Munro to Maine." *Contributions to Indian Sociology* 9 (December 1966): 67–89.

Edney, Mathew. *Mapping an Empire: The Geographical Construction of British India (1765–1843)*. Chicago: University of Chicago Press, 1997.

Fenn, Robert Anthony. *James Mill's Political Thought*. New York: Garland, 1987.

Fitzmaurice, Andrew. *Sovereignty, Property and Empire, 1500–2000*. Cambridge: Cambridge University Press, 2014.

Fontana, Bianca. "Whigs and Liberals: The *Edinburgh Review* and the 'Liberal Movement' in Nineteenth-Century Britain." In *Victorian Liberalism: Nineteenth-Century Political Thought and Practice*, edited by Richard Bellamy, 42–57. London: Routledge, 1990,

Foucault, Michel. *The Birth of Biopolitics: Lectures at the College de France, 1978–79*. New York: Palgrave Macmillan, 2008.

———. *The Order of Things: An Archaeology of the Human Sciences*. New York: Vintage Books, 1994 (1970).

———. *Security, Territory, Population: Lectures at the Collège de France, 1977–1978*. London: Palgrave Macmillan, 2007.

Frykenberg, R. E. "Village Strength in South India." In *Land Control and Social Structure in Indian History*, edited by R. E. Frykenberg, 227–48. Madison: University of Wisconsin Press, 1969.

Golinski, Jan. *Making Natural Knowledge: Constructivism and the History of Science*. Chicago: University of Chicago Press, 1998.

Govind, Rahul. "Revenue, Rent . . . Profit? Early British Imperialism, Political Economy and the Search for a *differentia specifica* (*inter se*)." *Indian Economic and Social History Review* 48 (2011): 177–213.

Guha, Ranajit. *A Rule of Property for Bengal: An Essay on the Idea of Permanent Settlement*. Durham, N.C.: Duke University Press, 1996 (1963).

Hilton, Boyd. *The Age of Atonement: The Influence of Evangelicalism on Social and Economic Thought, 1785–1865*. Oxford: Oxford University Press, 1988.

Hollander, Samuel. "William Whewell and John Stuart Mill on the Methodology of Political Economy." *Studies in the History and Philosophy of Science* 14 (1983): 127–68.

Howe, Stephen, ed. *The New Imperial Histories Reader*. New York: Routledge, 2010.

Husain, Imtiaz. *Land Revenue Policy in North India: The Ceded and Conquered Provinces, 1801–33*. Calcutta: New Age, 1967.

Irschick, Eugene F. *Dialogue and History: Constructing South India, 1795–1895*. Berkeley: University of California Press, 1994.

Islam, Sirajul. *Bengal Land Tenure: The Origin and Growth of Intermediate Interests in the 19th Century*. Calcutta: K. P. Bagchi, 1988.

Kinzer, Bruce L. "J. S. Mill and Irish Land: A Reassessment." *Historical Journal* 27 (1984): 111–27.

Ludden, David. "Introduction: Agricultural Production and Indian History." In *Agricultural Production and Indian History*, edited by David Ludden, 1–35. Delhi: Oxford University Press, 1994

———. *Peasant History in South India*. Delhi: Oxford University Press, 1989.

Maas, Harro. "'A Hard Battle to Fight': Natural Theology and the Dismal Science, 1820–50." *History of Political Economy* 40 (2008): 143–67.

——. *William Stanley Jevons and the Making of Modern Economics*. Cambridge: Cambridge University Press, 2005.

Mantena, Karuna. *Alibis of Empire: Henry Maine and the Ends of Liberal Imperialism*. New Delhi: Permanent Black, 2010.

Martin, David E. "The Rehabilitation of the Peasant Proprietor in Nineteenth-Century Economic Thought: A Comment." *History of Political Economy* 8 (1976): 297–302.

Mclaren, Martha. *British India and British Scotland, 1780–1830: Career Building, Empire Building and a Scottish School of Thought on Indian Governance*. Akron: University of Akron Press, 2001.

Mehta, Uday Singh. *Liberalism and Empire: A Study in Nineteenth-Century British Liberal Thought*. Chicago: University of Chicago Press, 1999.

Metcalf, Thomas R. *Land, Landlords, and the British Raj: Northern India in the Nineteenth Century*. Berkeley: University of California Press, 1979.

Michael, Bérnardo A. "Making Territory Visible: The Revenue Surveys of Colonial South Asia." *Imago Mundi* 59 (2007): 78–95.

Miller, William L. "Richard Jones's Contribution to the Theory of Rent." *History of Political Economy* 9 (1977): 346–65.

Misra, B. B. *The Central Administration of the East India Company, 1773–1834*. Manchester: Manchester University Press, 1959.

Mubayi, Yaaminey. "The Paik Rebellion of 1817: Status and Conflict in Early Colonial Orissa." *Studies in History* 15 (1999): 43–74.

Mukherjee, Nilmani, and R. E. Frykenberg. "The Ryotwari System and Social Organization in the Madras Presidency." In *Land Control and Social Structure in Indian History*, edited by R. E. Frykenberg, 217–26. Madison: University of Wisconsin Press, 1969.

Mukhopadhyay, T. K. *The Agrarian Society of Orissa: Nineteenth Century*. Kolkata: Progressive, 2008.

Neale, Walter C. "Land Is to Rule." In *Land Control and Social Structure in Indian History*, edited by R. E. Frykenberg, 3–16. Madison: University of Wisconsin Press, 1969.

Padhi, Sakti. *Land Relations and Agrarian Development in India: A Comparative Historical Study of Regional Variations*. Thiruvananthapuram: Centre for Development Studies, 1999.

Patnaik, Gorachand. *The Famine and Some Aspects of the British Economic Policy in Orissa, 1866–1905*. Cuttack: Vidyapuri, 1980.

Patnaik, N. R., ed. *Economic History of Orissa*. New Delhi: Indus, 1997.

Patra, K. M. *Orissa Under the East India Company*. New Delhi: Munshiram Manoharlal, 1971.

Peabody, Norbert. "Tod's Rajasthan and the Boundaries of Imperial Rule in Nineteenth-Century India." *Modern Asian Studies*30 (1996): 185–220.

Phillimore, Colonel R. H., comp. *Historical Records of the Survey of India, Volume I*, 18th Century. Dehradun: Surveyor General of India, 1945.

——. *Historical Records of the Survey of India, Volume II*, 1800–1815. Dehradun: Surveyor General of India, 1950.

——. *Historical Records of the Survey of India, Volume III*, 1815–1830. Dehradun: Surveyor General of India, 1954.

——. *Historical Records of the Survey of India, Volume IV*, 1830–1845. Dehradun: Surveyor General of India, 1958.

Pitts, Jennifer. "Political Theory of Empire and Imperialism." *Annual Review of Political Science* 13 (2010): 211–35.

———. *A Turn to Empire: The Rise of Imperial Liberalism in Britain and France.* Princeton: Princeton University Press, 2005.

Poovey, Mary. *A History of the Modern Fact: Problems of Knowledge in the Sciences of Wealth and Society.* Chicago: University of Chicago Press, 1998.

Rabitoy, Neil. "System v. Expediency: The Reality of Land Revenue Administration in the Bombay Presidency, 1812–1820." *Modern Asian Studies* 9 (1975): 529–46.

Rashid, Salim. "Richard Jones and Baconian Historicism at Cambridge." *Journal of Economic Issues* 13 (1979): 159–73.

Ray, Ratnalekha. *Change in Bengal Agrarian Society: 1760–1850.* New Delhi: Manohar, 1979.

Robb, Peter. *Ancient Rights and Future Comfort: Bihar, the Bengal Tenancy Act of 1885 and British Rule in India.* London: Routledge, 1997.

———. "Law and Agrarian Society in India: The Case of Bihar and the Nineteenth-Century Tenancy Debate." *Modern Asian Studies* 22 (1988): 319–54.

Rosselli, J. "Theory and Practice in North India." *Indian Economic and Social History Review* 8 (1971): 134–63.

Samal, J. K. *History of Modern Orissa.* Calcutta: Firma KLM, 1989.

Sartori, Andrew. "Custom and Political Economy in Bengal's 'Great Rent Case,' 1859–1865." Unpublished paper, 2008.

———. "A Liberal Discourse of Custom in Colonial Bengal." *Past and Present* 212 (August 2011): 163–97.

———. *Liberalism in Empire: An Alternative History.* Berkeley: University of California Press, 2012.

Scott, David. "Colonial Governmentality." *Social Text* 43 (1995): 191–220.

Snyder, Laura J. "It's *All* Necessarily So: William Whewell on Scientific Truth." *Studies in History and Philosophy of Science* 25, no. 5 (1994): 785–807.

———. "The Mill-Whewell Debate: Much Ado About Induction." *Perspectives on Science* 5, no. 2 (1997): 159–98.

———. *The Philosophical Breakfast Club: Four Remarkable Friends Who Transformed Science and Changed the World.* New York: Broadway Books, 2011.

———. *Reforming Philosophy: A Victorian Debate on Science and Society.* Chicago: University of Chicago Press, 2006.

Srinivas, M. N. *The Dominant Caste and Other Essays.* Delhi: Oxford University Press, 1987.

Steele, E. D. "J. S. Mill and the Irish Question: The Principles of Political Economy, 1848–1865." *Historical Journal* 13 (June 1970): 216–36.

———. "J. S. Mill and the Irish Question: Reform, and the Integrity of the Empire, 1865–70." *Historical Journal* 13 (September 1970): 419–50.

Stein, Burton. "Idiom and Ideology in Early Nineteenth-Century South India." In *Rural India: Land, Power and Society Under British Rule,* edited by Peter Robb, 27–41. New Delhi: Oxford University Press, 1992.

———. "State Formation and Economy Reconsidered: Part One." *Modern Asian Studies* 19 (1985): 387–413.

———. *Thomas Munro: The Origins of the Colonial State and His Vision of Empire.* Delhi: Oxford University Press, 1989.

Stokes, Eric. *The English Utilitarians and India.* Delhi: Oxford University Press, 1989.

———. *The Peasant and the Raj: Studies in Agrarian Society and Peasant Rebellion in Colonial India.* Cambridge: Cambridge University Press, 1978.

Sturman, Rachel. *Government of Social Life in Colonial India: Liberalism, Religious Law, and Women's Rights*. Cambridge: Cambridge University Press, 2012.

Travers, Robert. "British India as a Problem in Political Economy: Comparing James Steuart and Adam Smith." In *Lineages of Empire*, edited by Duncan Kelly, 137–60. London: Oxford University Press, 2009.

———. *Ideology and Empire in Eighteenth-Century India: The British Bengal*. Cambridge: Cambridge University Press, 2007.

Tribe, Keith. "Ground Rent and the Formation of Classical Political Economy: A Theoretical History." Ph.D. thesis, University of Cambridge, 1976.

———. *Land, Labour and Economic Discourse*. London: Routledge and Kegan Paul, 1978.

———. "Professors Malthus and Jones: Political Economy at the East India College, 1806–58." *European Journal of the History of Economic Thought* 2 (1995): 327–54.

Washbrook, D. A. "Law, State and Agrarian Society in Colonial India." *Modern Asian Studies* 15 (1981): 649–721.

———. "Ricketts, Henry." *Oxford Dictionary of National Biography* https://www.oxforddnb.com/view/10.1093/ref:odnb/9780198614128.001.0001/odnb-9780198614128-e-23602.

Wilson, Jon E. *The Domination of Strangers: Modern Governance in Eastern India, 1780–1835*. Basingstoke: Palgrave Macmillan, 2008.

Winch, Donald. *Malthus*. Oxford & New York: Oxford University Press, 1987.

Yeo, Richard. *Defining Science: William Whewell, Natural Knowledge and Public Debate in Early Victorian Britain*. Cambridge: Cambridge University Press, 1993.

INDEX

ACKNOWLEDGMENTS

It has been a long journey from doctoral dissertation to published book. Most of this journey was spent in being involved with the challenging process of the establishment of a new university. It was, and continues to be, a difficult, rare, and rewarding experience.

I was introduced to the fundamentals of reading, thinking, writing, and arguing by Presidency College and Jawaharlal Nehru University. I remain especially thankful to Dipankar Gupta, Radhika Singha, Soumyabrata Chowdhury, Susan Visvanathan, Tanika Sarkar, and V. Sujatha for this unforgettable experience. While at JNU, and later, Avijit Pathak's teachings have always evoked respect.

In my brief conversations with Neeladri Bhattacharya, I learned to think through agrarian categories. I learnt about modes of critique and pedagogy. I feel lucky to have spent good times with him.

In engaging with Peter Robb, I felt the joys of the labor of thinking. I understood, while writing my doctoral dissertation under his supervision, that Peter's knowledge of the agrarian archives of British India knows no limit, and his interrogations are penetrating. His constant demand for debate made me argue carefully. His critical comments on the details made me rethink time and again. Even today, he continues to be one of my most rewarding interlocutors.

Over these years, a number of people have read, discussed, and commented on parts of the dissertation, book chapters, and papers presented at conferences. I am grateful for their insights. I sincerely thank Agnibho Gangopadhyay, Anandaroop Sen, Anil Persaud, Anirban Das, Anish Vanaik, Aryama, Atig Ghosh, Bodhisattva Kar, Brian Hatcher, Christopher Alan Bayly, David Washbrook, Daud Ali, Eleanor Newbegin, Faisal Chaudhry, Gayatri Chakrabarty Spivak, Harro Maas, Iman Mitra, Jon Wilson, Lakshmi Subramaniam, Manish Thakur, Maitrayee Chaudhuri, Norbert Peabody, Partha Chatterjee, Peter D'Souza, Prathama Banerjee, Projit B. Mukharji, Raghav Kishore,

Rahul Govind, Rajarshi Ghose, Ravi Ahuja, Robert Travers, Rohan Deb Roy, Rosinka Chaudhuri, Sasheej Hegde, Satish Deshpande, Sayam Ghosh, Shabnum Tejani, Shinjini Das, Shrimoy Roychoudhury, Sibaji Bandopadhyay, Sukanya Sarbadhikary, Surinder Singh Jodhka, Tanika Sarkar, and Tapati Guha Thakurta for their valuable contributions to this work.

Parts of this book appeared in earlier versions as "Agrarian Localities: Political Economy as Local Power in Early-Nineteenth Century British India," *Modern Asian Studies* 50, no. 3 (2016): 898–933, and "The Problem of Property: Local Histories and Political-Economic Categories in British India," *Journal of the Economic and Social History of the Orient* 61, nos. 5–6 (2018): 1005–1035). I am grateful to the editors and reviewers of the journals for their comments and criticism.

Without Simon Schaffer's assurances, my forays into the history of science and political economy would have remained hesitant and uncertain. I have greatly benefited from his breadth of knowledge and analytically incisive observations.

I am a great admirer of the work of Faisal Chaudhry. Exchanging with him ideas on the overlapping histories of law, political economy, empire, and agrarian South Asia has been most helpful for this project.

Andrew Sartori has nurtured this work with exceptional care. My book can only hope to come close to Andrew's depth of learning in history and social theory. It is also remarkably unusual to find someone so invested in the works of younger scholars, without being necessarily professionally involved with them. I remain deeply indebted to Andrew for his support and commitment.

Karuna Mantena was an incredible source of support for this book. All along, from the stage of book proposal onward, she was one of the most engaging readers of the manuscript. Her detailed and insightful comments made me reflect on some of the most central issues of this work in a way I never did before. I feel fortunate to have worked on this book under her kind and rigorous mentoring.

The two anonymous reviews at the University of Pennsylvania Press were elaborate, sharp, and empathetic—ideal for any manuscript. My gratitude to the press and Peter Agree, the editor who looked after the entire review process.

Damon Linker, who took charge of the manuscript after Peter at Penn Press, was unstintingly supportive—intellectually and logistically—in taking the manuscript to production. I am thankful for his attention. I am grateful to the entire team at Penn Press, especially Noreen O'Connor-Abel,

Zoe Kovacs, and Tracy Kellmer for their efficient assistance even amid the global crisis.

The book would have been inconceivable without the numerous documents studied at different libraries and archives in India and the United Kingdom. I thank the staff of the British Library, London, National Archives of India, New Delhi, National Library, Kolkata, Orissa State Archives, Bhubaneswar, West Bengal State Archives, Kolkata, and Wren Library, Trinity College, Cambridge, for their assistance.

The book grew out of my work at School of Oriental and African Studies, London which was made possible by the generous funding of the Felix Trust. I thank them for having faith in me.

Without the care and support of Professor Jatin Nayak, Supriya, and Ashish, I would not have survived in Bhubaneswar. I thank them for making my trips productive.

My gratitude to Suhrita Saha, a dear friend, and head of the Department of Sociology at Presidency University, who always went out of her way to support all my academic endeavors.

My students at Presidency have been a source of happy companionship and serious intellectual learning. I have grown, in thinking, through their varied academic practices. I am especially thankful to Sandipan Mitra for helping with all kinds of work related to this book—regular reminders, the formatting of files, bibliographic editing, and much more.

I am grateful for the financial assistance provided by the Faculty Research and Professional Development Funds at Presidency University, which enabled me to discuss different parts of this book in conferences and workshops.

My dearest friends, Anandaroop, Leo, and Rohan, are part of the entire field of ideas and experiences shaping this book. Their contributions must not be specified for this project. I have cherished the company of Zaid, Romit, Debaditya, Himadri, Garima, Kaustubhmani and Anwesha since I returned to Kolkata. Their presence enlivened my work.

I am indebted to my in-laws, Debasish and Reshma, for showering me with boundless love, care, and blessings. I am grateful for the conditions that brought me close to such wonderful people.

I do not know where to put my parents, Ashis and Bhaswati, in this list. They have been parents, friends, and teachers at every point in my life. In their own very different ways, they have taught me how to live. My aunt, Saswati, in her affectionate way, has been very concerned about the publication of this book. I am happy that she will finally see it in print.

Young Darshan is blissfully unaware of this book. And his presence in my life made me free of all the worries that often accompany acts of academic publishing. I sincerely hope that the two of us can grow together in such bliss.

It has been almost two decades now that I have known Sukanya. Her way of being brings together rigorous thought and ethical living in a way that is singular and inspiring. I believe these realizations must have animated this book, and its practices of writing and thinking, somehow, somewhere.

www.ingramcontent.com/pod-product-compliance
Lightning Source LLC
LaVergne TN
LVHW091529200926
848483LV00002B/342